THE CUSTOM LOOK

THE ART OF SEWING

THE
CUSTOM
LOOK

BY THE EDITORS OF TIME-LIFE BOOKS

TIME-LIFE BOOKS, NEW YORK

TIME-LIFE BOOKS

FOUNDER: Henry R. Luce 1898-1967

Editor-in-Chief: Hedley Donovan
Chairman of the Board: Andrew Heiskell
President: James R. Shepley
Chairman, Executive Committee:
James A. Linen
Group Vice President: Rhett Austell

Vice Chairman: Roy E. Larsen

MANAGING EDITOR: Jerry Korn
Assistant Managing Editors: David Maness,
Martin Mann, A. B. C. Whipple
Planning Director: Oliver E. Allen
Art Director: Sheldon Cotler
Chief of Research: Beatrice T. Dobie
Director of Photography: Melvin L. Scott
Senior Text Editors: Diana Hirsh, Ogden Tanner
Assistant Art Director: Arnold C. Holeywell

PUBLISHER: Joan D. Manley
General Manager: John D. McSweeney
Business Manager: John Steven Maxwell
Sales Director: Carl G. Jaeger
Promotion Director: Paul R. Stewart
Public Relations Director: Nicholas Benton

THE ART OF SEWING
SERIES EDITOR: Carlotta Kerwin
EDITORIAL STAFF FOR
THE CUSTOM LOOK:
Assistant Editor: David Lawton
Assistant to the Editor: David L. Harrison
Designer: Virginia Gianakos
Associate Designer: Herbert H. Quarmby
Text Editors: Helen Barer, Frank K. Kappler,
Gerry Schremp
Staff Writers: Sondra Albert, Angela Dews,
Marian G. Goldman, Suzanne Seixas,
Sandra Streepey
Picture Staff: Carole Kismaric,
Kathleen Shortall, Gabrielle Smith
Research Staff: Jane Edwin, Nancy Miller,
Cinda Siler
Art Staff: Patricia Byrne, Sanae Colton,
Robert McKee
Editorial Assistant: Kathleen Beakley

EDITORIAL PRODUCTION
Production Editor: Douglas B. Graham
Assistant: Gennaro C. Esposito
Quality Director: Robert L. Young
Assistant: James J. Cox
Copy Staff: Rosalind Stubenberg (chief),
Susan B. Galloway, Mary Orlando,
Florence Keith
Picture Department: Dolores A. Littles,
Jessy S. Faubert

Portions of this book were written by Michael
Durham, Margaret Elliott and Eileen L. Hughes.
Valuable assistance was provided by these
departments and individuals of Time Inc.: Editorial
Production, Norman Airey, Nicholas Costino Jr.;
Library, Benjamin Lightman; Picture Collection,
Doris O'Neil; Photographic Laboratory, George
Karas; TIME-LIFE News Service, Murray J. Gart,
Correspondents Margot Hapgood (London), Maria
Vincenza Aloisi and Josephine du Brusle (Paris),
Ann Natanson (Rome).

THE CONSULTANTS:
Gretel Courtney is a member of the staff of the
French Fashion Academy in New York. She has
studied pattern making and design at the Fashion Institute of Technology and haute couture at
the French Fashion Academy in New York.

Jo Springer has been a writer and consultant on
home sewing for numerous publications including the *1,001 Decorating Ideas Home Library* and
Woman's Day, where she spent five years on the
editorial staff. She is the author of *Creative Needlework* and *The Pleasures of Crewel.*

Julian Tomchin is a textile designer who has been
awarded the Vogue Fabric Award and a Coty
Award of the American Fashion Critics. A graduate of Syracuse University's Fine Arts College,
he has been chairman of the Textile Design Department at the Shenkar College of Fashion and
Textile Technology in Tel Aviv and now teaches
at the Parsons School of Design in New York.

Erica Wilson, a graduate of the Royal School of
Needlework in England, is a designer, teacher
and writer on all aspects of needlecraft. She is the
author of *Crewel Embroidery, Fun with Crewel*
and *Erica Wilson's Embroidery Book,* and has
had her own instructional television series.

CONTENTS

1
SEWING AT ITS FINEST

very field of creative endeavor has a peak, a pinnacle toward which the best artists or performers constantly strive. There, they are sure, is the big money, the name in lights, the lasting fame. In women's fashions, that pinnacle is haute couture, the custom designing and sewing of elegant clothes in the great fashion houses of Paris, Rome and New York. The showing of a couturier's latest collection is an artistic event akin to an opening

THE COUTURIER: MASTER OF DRESSMAKING

night on Broadway or an operatic debut at La Scala; there is the same anxious excitement, the same popping flashbulbs and famous faces, the same shredded nerves and clammy palms as the designer's first models hit the runway. And always there is the same telling moment of truth, the verdict of failure or success.

The world of haute couture is a glamorous one, and a spectacularly artificial one in many ways. Grown men soberly ponder and dispute a few millimeters' difference in the length of a skirt. Fortunes hang on the set of a shoulder, the shape of an armhole, the width of a pleat. Designers portentously declare that this is the year of the bust, or the waist, or the shoulders. At times there seems to be an aura of insanity about the whole intense, expensive business. Nevertheless, there is a center, an eye in the midst of fashion's tempests, a hub that holds couture's furiously spinning wheel. This center is occupied by the creative talent of the great custom couturiers—such legendary figures as Chanel, Schiaparelli, Balenciaga, Dior, Balmain, Norell, Givenchy, Saint Laurent. It is they and their predecessors who have established unchanging standards in the face of ever-changing styles. It is their tradition of excellence in design and in craftsmanship that bestows upon custom couture its stability and its significance in a world of otherwise declining standards, cut corners and shoddy goods.

What makes a custom garment so special? Not cost, though there are no more expensive clothes in the world. And not the name of its designer, though designers' names have a powerful cachet among the wealthy women who can afford to buy their clothes. To most of these women it is rather the personal satisfaction of owning and wearing something that has been made for them in perfect fit and flawless detail.

Couture begins with a design—an image that a woman, once she sees it created by a designer, finds congenial and somehow expressive of her own personality. The design may be simple and understated, unruffled by passing fads and fancies, or it may be extravagant, even extreme in color, cut or fabric, a trend-setter perhaps, a harbinger of things to come. No matter; there is room for all kinds in the world of haute couture. What is indispensable, the one characteristic that any custom-look design worth its name must have, is true elegance. This means taste and refinement, a purity of line and finish, a sense of completeness and appropriateness in every detail—in simplest terms, the best of everything.

Just as vital as the design is the fabric in which it is executed. Couture fabrics, whether for a simple day dress or for a sumptuous ball gown, for a country suit or for slinky evening pants, are always of the best quality. Traditionally, designers have preferred to work with pure natural fibers—silks such as crepe de Chine or Indian raw silk, English and Scottish tweeds, French woolens, Irish linen, Sea Island cottons. But they do not ignore the best of the new synthetics and blends of natural and synthetic fibers.

The crucial matter to a designer when he considers any fabric is not so much what it is made of as how well it will work for him. Someone once noted that a new collection begins with a single thread; the statement is not far off the mark. Often a material with a new weave, an unusual design, even a subtle new dye, sets a designer's imagination on an entirely new tack. But first he must see how it looks and feels, how it acts when it is cut and stitched, how it moves and clings when it is fitted on a woman's body. Often a couturier works directly with one or more custom weavers to obtain precisely the right design, color, texture and weight of fabric in order to create a single dress out of an entire collection. It is this unremitting insistence on perfection, almost regardless of cost, that makes the fabric of a couture garment such an important factor in its success.

No less important a consideration is fit, the precise measuring, sizing and shaping of a custom dress to the unique form of its intended wearer. There is simply no better fit available than in custom design because each garment is made to order for one particular woman. To begin with, her measurements are taken in every conceivable way—around the upper torso as many as 17 different ways, up and down the back and arms, up and down and around the waist and the hips. With all these measurements in hand, a muslin prototype, which is called a *toile de corps,* is then cut to fit her and her alone.

As the toile is basted together, repeated fittings are made to be sure these measurements are correct, that the seam lines of the design move about her body in the most flattering and comfortable way. Minor adjustments are made at every step: a fraction of an inch at the shoulder or bust seam, a tiny lowering of the waistline. A buttonhole may be moved (it has only been marked, not cut, during early fittings) or the width changed a millimeter in each of the narrow knife pleats that go around a skirt. Seemingly insignificant changes in themselves, all are vital when added up. It is this attention to every minute dimension that produces the perfect fit of haute couture.

Attention to detail continues through the sewing itself. Stitching in custom clothesmaking, even the simplest kind, is at its best a marvel of expertise and love. The skilled fingers of professional seamstresses do more than sew; they mold and manipulate the fabric as they work. There is no machine, no matter how sophisticated, that can replace such experienced hands, gently easing the material as they stitch to join a sleeve to a difficult curved seam, taking an extra stitch here to ensure a sharp collar-point, registering at every moment the elasticity of the fabric and the tension of the thread as they build a set-in waistband. It is painstaking, time-consuming work; no shortcuts are taken, or allowed. Every detail in a dress —from the binding of an inside buttonhole that will never show to the bold, raised outline of a welt pocket—is treated with equal respect, and receives equal attention. When the last stitch has been sewn and the final steaming or pressing has been completed, not a wrinkle or pucker mars the garment's lines. It has the "custom look"—it is made to order in every sense—and it is, quite simply, a work of art.

Unlikely as it may seem, it took an Englishman who had moved to Paris, a man named Charles Worth, to turn this art of fine needlework in clothes—the basic meaning of haute couture—into a business that not only prospered but also brought him international fame. A century ago, while Worth was an assistant in one of Paris' fashionable fabric stores, Maison Gagelin, he began designing dresses for his wife, Marie, who wore them as she worked by his side in the shop. Marie, who had been a Gagelin *ven-*

deuse when he met her, was a Frenchwoman with an innate sense of style. She might have been content to cling to the conventional dress that had been her fashion before Charles came along. He prevailed, however, and Marie became couture's first mannequin. Wealthy customers began asking who her dressmaker was, and Worth persuaded his employers to allow him to set up a small, separate dressmaking business right on the premises.

In time, Worth tired of this arrangement and with the aid of a Swedish businessman launched a tiny business of his own. It was not he, however, but Marie, who set the new firm on the road to fame. Carrying an album of her husband's prettiest designs, she presented herself at the door of the Princess Pauline de Metternich, the recently arrived wife of the Austrian ambassador. Her selling job was a two-way success: Worth's designs did wonders for the Princess, who by Parisian standards lacked chic, and the Princess's custom led Worth straight to the royal court. She wore a Worth ball gown to the Palace of the Tuileries and the fashion-conscious Empress Eugénie, immediately impressed, arranged that its creator call at Court the following morning. Worth established himself as the first true grand couturier of Paris, and indeed of the world; his days as a fashion designer, in the

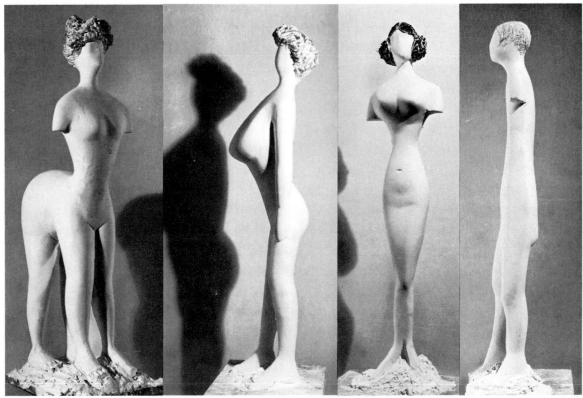

How couturiers try to shape the female form to their ideas is caricatured in these sculptures at New York's Museum of Modern Art. If a woman's body conformed to the fashion extremes of her time, she would have been shaped like *(left to right)* a centaur in the bustle-laden 1870s; a pillar with a shelflike bosom about 1904; a mermaid in the hobble-skirt days before the outbreak of World War I; and a totally flat-chested slab in the 1920s.

waning years of the 19th Century, are known still as the Age of Worth.

The establishment Charles Worth began was what would be known today as a couture house. Like later couturiers, he assembled under one roof a staff of experienced and skilled seamstresses who, beginning with his original designs and under his direction, created out of the materials of high fashion—beautiful fabrics and linings, ribbons and laces, belts and buckles, buttons and braid—custom clothes for individual clients. Until he opened his doors, rich and titled women often depended on little dressmakers who copied existing designs from the clients' own wardrobes, from engravings or from miniature models called fashion dolls; the clients themselves supplied the fabrics and decorative trim. The lack of real guidance in matters of taste and form, or any real authority as to what was fashionable and what was passé, was perhaps the true reason for Worth's rapid success. He had very definite ideas on fashion, running to lavish, fanciful decoration and fine detailing, and was eager to impress his thinking on the court ladies whom he dressed.

Fashion design when Worth came along was dominated by a devotion to elaborate corsetry and hoops. As his influence increased he was able to banish one of its most prevalent excesses, the crinoline skirt. But in other respects the time was too strait-laced morally, as the women were literally, and Worth was too conventional a thinker to do anything truly revolutionary about the shape of women's clothes. That was left to future designers like Paul Poiret, and later Madeleine Vionnet and Coco Chanel.

These three Parisian couturiers were wildly different in personal style and professional technique, but they were bent on the same mission: the freeing of women from confining corsets and the ever-present high-boned collar. Poiret came on the scene first, in 1905. An exuberantly theatrical man, he was much caught up with Oriental motifs, the avant-garde successes of the Diaghilev ballet and the brilliantly colored Fauvist paintings that were then in vogue. He put his clients in a variety of styles, from soft, flowing Empire-waisted dresses to tunics of colorful chiffon and charmeuse. There was always a sense of "dressing up" with Poiret's clothes.

Madame Vionnet, on the other hand, strove for simplicity. In the 1920s and '30s she based her clothes on a whole new way of cutting and handling fabric. She laid out dress segments on the bias (pages 38-39). Her artfully sewn seams shaped the fabric so it moved fluidly over the natural lines of the body. One of her most original contributions was to take the soft silk crepe de Chine out of the inside of garments, where it had been used exclusively for linings, and make it the new luxury fabric for garments themselves. She then persuaded French silk manufacturers to produce it in more generous widths of 48 and 54 inches to accommodate her bias-cut designs. Deeply influenced by Vionnet's genius with the bias cut, Alix Grès, a current-day French designer, still works in this manner, producing some of the most handsomely draped garments in contemporary couture.

Coco Chanel, who had come on the fashion scene in 1915, felt as Vionnet did that what women really wanted in clothes was a sense of freedom, a sense of complete ease and naturalness. She gave them sportier looks than Vionnet: little jersey skirts topped by loose overblouses, "humble" tweed suits that suggested a walk in the country and simple tube dresses that hung like men's sweaters. (At the Côte d'Azur, Chanel once startled and delighted the stylish crowd by appearing in a man's pullover, belted at the waist to transform it into a dress.) Though widely touted as the "poor" look, her dresses and suits were in fact, as she created them, true high fashion. Chanel is one of the legendary figures of haute couture; her genius lay in her strong sense of cut and proportion, in the relation of every detail—the width of a cuff, the curve of a yoke, the high cut of an armhole, the swing of a skirt—to the garment as a whole. Always understated and uncluttered, her soft collarless necklines filled with ropes of frankly fake pearls, Chanel's essential look is part of haute couture's permanent history.

For different reasons, with dash and extravagance, Elsa Schiaparelli, an Italian working in Paris at about the same time, also carved a special niche for herself. "Schiap," as she was nicknamed, loved color (she popularized the celebrated "shocking pink"). She also favored boldly patterned fabrics and fanciful decoration, particularly exotic buttons. Much in tune with the overheated frivolity and decadence of Europe in the 1930s, Schiaparelli was the first couturier to put women in long evening suits and exaggerated padded shoulders.

It took another foreigner, the brooding Spaniard Cristobal Balenciaga, to perfect elaborately constructed form in female apparel, as well as to shape clothes in architectural curves. With his very first collection, shown in Paris in 1937 to great acclaim, Balenciaga displayed his talent for molding clothes so they had a sculptural quality to them. Cecil Beaton has called Balenciaga the "Picasso of fashion" and indeed, like his fellow countryman, Balenciaga displayed in his stark, compelling designs an innate, instinctive respect for tradition and form. Certainly in his all-consuming passion for his vocation he earned his title as "a couturier's couturier." There is, quite literally, no other designer, living or dead, who has had quite the same all-pervading influence upon his peers as Balenciaga.

In the United States this influence has been readily acknowledged by such eminent designers as Norman Norell, who until his death in 1972 was considered the dean of American couturiers. A sculptural quality can be seen immediately in Norell's simple but beautifully crafted clothes; in his long, sequin-studded sheaths, in handsome culottes, in perfectly molded, set-in waistbands, shape is everything. Norell was firm in his conviction that fit must be the ultimate aim of the couturier; he once said, "The longer I work the more I am interested in the Perfect Pattern."

There is a kind of stateliness to both Balenciaga's and Norell's view of fashion. Many of the younger couturiers working today—in Paris, Rome, Madrid, London, New York—respect this stateliness, this tradition of quality, but they work in a livelier spirit. Fascinated by technological changes in fabrics, more responsive to the active pulse of modern women's lives, designers like Emilio Pucci, Yves Saint Laurent, André Courrèges, Valentino and Pierre Cardin reflect new attitudes toward materials and design. Out of fabrics like vinyl and Qiana, metallics and fake fur, double-faced wools and featherweight silk jerseys, they create clothes that appeal to the quickening tempo of the young. These designers even take the techniques of haute couture—the "nuts and bolts" as Courrèges puts it—and lay them daringly on the line, making design elements out of buttons, zippers and boldly stitched welt seams.

Almost before the models get off the runway at a showing of the collections of these younger couturiers, the designs find their way into the mainstream of contemporary fashion. Whether through the couturiers' own fashion boutiques, through the sale of designs to ready-to-wear manufacturers for copying in less expensive fabrics or through the adaptations in patterns for the home sewer, the looks generated in today's haute couture are now readily available to ordinary mortals.

The couturier patterns, also called designer patterns by some manufacturers, are a boon to women who wish to take the time and effort to create their own custom clothes. The patterns vary from the original models of the designer but generally in only modest respects, so that the basic look remains. Very difficult seaming is occasionally simplified for ease of fitting or to avoid complicated technical sewing feats. Intricate detailing may be toned down or eliminated. Certain inner constructions that require special knowledge or materials may also go.

The instructions accompanying these patterns tend to be slightly more complex than pattern instructions for everyday clothes, often requiring greater sewing knowledge and dexterity on the part of the user. But with patience and concentration, these elegant designs will amply repay the extra effort they require.

Such patterns deserve the best of fabrics —fabrics that belong in a custom garment. Often frankly luxurious, with bold patterns or imaginative border designs in brilliant colors, sometimes woven with metallic thread to light up an evening look, these materials are not for the timid. Nor are they cheap. The important thing is to understand how to handle them. Many of the most handsome and most used of these materials need some special attention as you work with them. It may be a matter of how you cut a pattern to take best advantage of a large, repeated print design. Or it may be a question of matching oversize plaids or extra-wide stripes. Take heart, however; a fashion designer is constantly up against the same problems every time he uses a fabric that is unfamiliar to him. To make it easier for you, the practical characteristics of custom fabrics are analyzed in the section beginning on page 28, including the charts on pages 32-33 and 36.

One of the surest ways of making your custom garment look more professional is to make a prototype of it in muslin. For the amateur dressmaker, such a muslin serves as a trial run for fitting purposes so as to avoid fatal cutting errors in expensive fabric. Choose a weight of muslin that is as close to that of your final material as possible, a lightweight for delicate fabrics, the heaviest weight if you plan to work in gabardine or a sturdy, tightly woven tweed. Any major fitting problems can be dealt with in the muslin and pieces recut to fit if necessary; adjustments can then be transferred to the paper pattern before it is laid out for cutting on the final fabric. Making a first-run muslin is time-consuming, to be sure, but it takes a good deal of the risk out of making custom garments.

The actual making of a finished couture garment is an exciting, if sometimes demanding, business requiring special techniques to assure the best results: the addition of a piece of reinforcing fabric to a corner seam or the point of a godet, a length of binding tape added to control a stretchy strip along a curved seam, the insertion of stiffening fabric into a standing collar or a hem. In both welt seams and slot seams, careful basting as well as hand smoothing of the fabric is necessary to avoid puckering at the time of the final machine stitching. Special basting stitches such as the diagonal stitch are sometimes used, as in a rolled collar, to hold the fabric firmly in place until the entire garment is finished. Meticulous measuring is called for to make certain a row of narrow knife pleats are all the same width; they must then be carefully basted up and down their length as well as around the waistline. What all this attention to detail means is that you spend a good deal more time working with your hands than you do working with your machine.

In this hand work, it is the flow, the natural bent, of the fabric that your hands are searching for. You first begin to sense this when you finish the hand basting required for fitting. Then after the fitting adjustments have been made, you will baste again, this time adding any small extra supporting fabric or tapes that are to be sewn permanently into the garment. Shape is beginning to become apparent in the fabric and often this is the time, before you start the machine stitching, when you work the fabric more smoothly together at the stitching lines. It may be that a few extra basting stitches at a tricky turn of a seam will do it, or still another patch of underlining may be needed to round a curve more gracefully and remove a wrinkle. This is what is meant by getting a feel for the fabric and actually molding it by hand into perfect shape; it is, in fact, the heart of custom sewing.

Custom techniques are the best there are in sewing; there is nothing hit-or-miss about them. And they are, when you master them, splendidly useful. Once you understand their logic and what they are meant to accomplish in terms of look and fit, you can apply them to other more workaday clothes in your wardrobe. Or you can use them to make attractive, handsome tablecloths, bed covers, pillows and valances. Similarly, both the difficulties and the rewards of custom sewing apply to the elegant craft of needlepoint. The whole idea of turning custom looks and techniques to new uses is, of course, part and parcel of a couturier's raison d'être, and it is an idea you too can put to use. With practice, you will find that you can produce clothes that express your taste uncompromisingly. That day you will have reached for, and perhaps found, your own pinnacle of haute couture.

The craft behind the custom look

The pace-setting chic of the couture fashions sketched on these and the following pages is solidly based on craftsmanship. The essentials of such craft are construction, or how the garment is cut out and then put together, and detailing—both visible, such as pleats or cuffs, and invisible, such as underlinings that ensure proper fit. Sometimes couturiers stress one element over the other. For instance, the designers represented on these two pages emphasized construction. André Courrèges underscored the cut of his breezy little daytime dress (left) by using externalized seams to define the armholes, neckline, bustline and button-down front. The components of Pierre Cardin's jumpsuit (right) are as plain in his starkly simple ensemble as they would be lying cut out on a sewing table waiting to be stitched together. And the austere lines of Emanuel Ungaro's winter dress (far right) gain interest from such details as the rounded side panels carved from the fabric and then sewn in with contrasting trim.

André Courrèges

16

Pierre Cardin

Emanuel Ungaro

17

Details for high fashion

These dresses succeed because of fine fabrics and fine detailing. For his two-piece dress *(right),* James Galanos used scores of hand-sewn knife pleats to enhance the effect of linked brown diamond shapes cascading down white crepe de Chine. The chevron pattern of the skirt and cardigan in Ottavio and Rosita Missoni's rayon-knit ensemble *(center)* is repeated in the hat, and all are set off by the tie-neck scarf. The romantic lines of the House of Antonelli's dress of fuchsia and spring green *(far right)* are made even more fluid by knife pleats that run from the yoke clear down the skirt.

James Galanos

Missoni

Antonelli

19

A blending of techniques

Haute couture designers know how to superimpose meticulous detailing upon high-quality construction. To shape his satin evening pajamas *(left)*, Norman Norell underlined and lined the pants with silk and covered the buttons with the pajama satin. Yves Saint Laurent accentuated the shape of his unlined pants suit *(right)*, then added jaunty details: tie neck, shirt-front opening and belt of matching fabric. Valentino cut a flowing evening dress to show off the Art Nouveau design by swirling it across the bodice and skirt; anchoring it from floating away is a shape-keeping lining of georgette.

Yves Saint Laurent

Norman Norell

Valentino

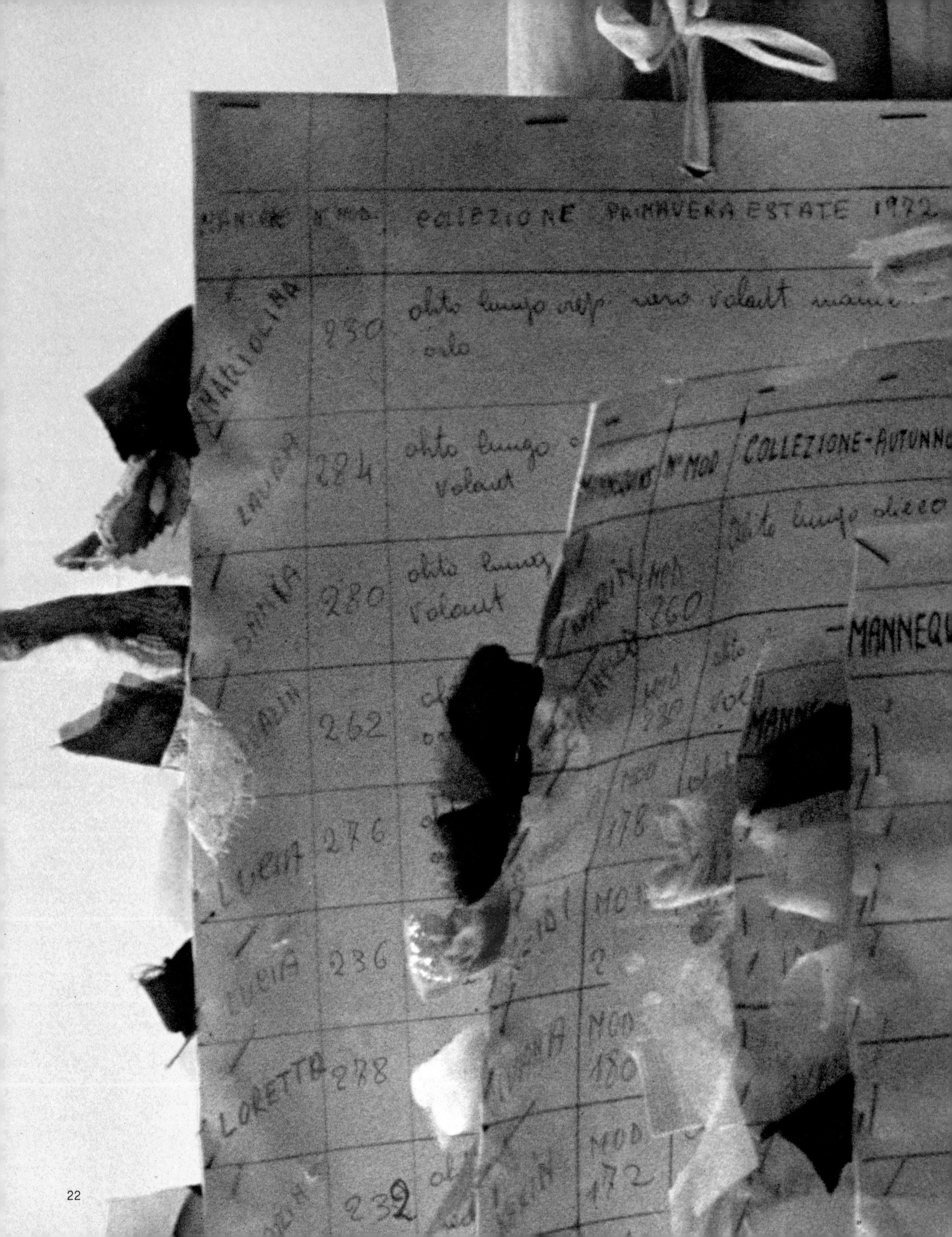
COLLEZIONE PRIMAVERA ESTATE 1972
COLLEZIONE-AUTUNNO
MANNEQU

CAPO GRUPPO

CATERINA

VERNO-1972-73

GRUPPO

4°Mod COLLEZIONE-AUTUNNO-INVERNO 1973-74 CAPO GRUPPO

1
Abito giorgette nero con volant
ony. nero
Giovanni

2
Abito lungo rosa con bolze profilate
in chamuse rosa
Caterina

3
Abito giorgette rosa a pieghe con volant.
ony. vitium ricamoto
Giuliana

4
abito crep verde doppeggiato d'arpuno
giaca ricamata
Amalia

5
Abito lungo crep. rosa a bolze con
volant.
Giuliana

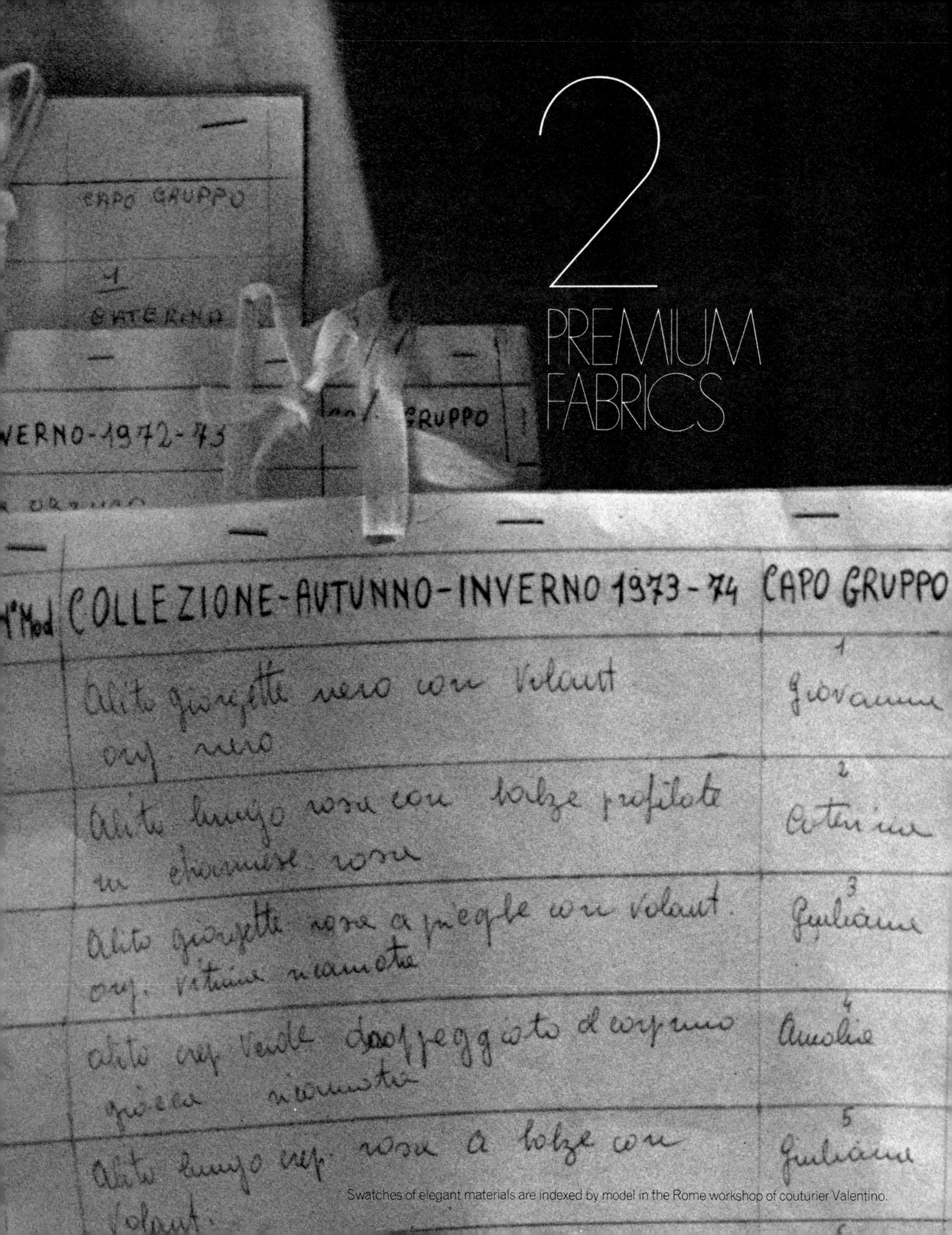

Swatches of elegant materials are indexed by model in the Rome workshop of couturier Valentino.

Before there were rayons and nylons, or polymer chemists to dream them up, there were miracle fibers, and their names were linen, wool, cotton and silk. And after thousands of years they, and the synthetics that most closely resemble them, are still the fibers that dressmakers turn to when they want fabrics for a fine dress. For these four natural fibers offer characteristics that lend unusual beauty and comfort to clothing.

QUALITES OF QUALITY MATERIALS

Of the four major natural fibers, linen may well be the oldest. It was worn by Egyptians at least 5,000 years before Christ, and it continues to be used for everything from the heaviest canvases to sheer handkerchiefs; but above all it remains the classic material for summer dresses, blouses, skirts and suits. Made from the fibers of the flax plant, which in the finest linens are as long as 40 inches, it is a strong, smooth, long-lasting fabric whose natural finish gains its famous creamy luster from the wax content of the fibers themselves. Linen's association with summer is soundly based: it is a good conductor of heat, allowing warmth to pass quickly from the body, and it absorbs and releases moisture rapidly to create a cool, crisp, dry feeling.

Wool, more naturally resilient and even more versatile than linen, is nearly as old. It was first spun and woven from the fleece of sheep raised in the Middle East as long ago as 4000 B.C.

Among the reasons for wool's popularity are its warmth, softness and resiliency, which stem from the peculiar structure of its fibers. From one to 14 inches long, each is made up of millions of molecules linked in a wavy ladder that in turn imparts springiness to the fibers themselves. Therefore, wrinkles quickly "hang out." The space between the rungs of the wavy ladder of each fiber traps air and thus provides excellent insulation against cold. In addition, a good wool will absorb up to 30 per cent of its weight in moisture without feeling damp—a fact long appreciated by outdoorsmen. The same quality of absorbency also makes wool a good summer fabric in its lighter weights and allows it to accept and hold a wide range of dye colors.

Wool fibers can be spun to make yarns called woolens, which have a soft, fuzzy feel, or the longest fibers can be combed and tightly twisted to produce worsteds—harder, smoother, stronger fabrics. Both woolen and worsted yarns lend themselves especially well to knit fabrics too, which add the elasticity of a fishnet structure to the natural elasticity of the fibers, making jerseys and double-knits not only extraordinarily supple and form-fitting but also virtually wrinkleproof.

Coolness and shape-retention, rather than warmth and elasticity, are the best-known qualities of cotton, which has been made from the seed fibers of the cotton plant since its origin in India about 5,000 years ago. The finest cottons, like the finest wools and linens, start with the longest fibers, which in the case of cotton are relatively short; even the longest staples —Egyptian and Sea Island cottons—are only 2 1/2 inches long, but produce soft, easily spun fabrics that are admirably light, absorbent, comfortable and cool.

Cotton appeals to couture designers in exalted forms that approach the qualities of silk, the queen of fabrics. Around 2600 B.C., a legendary Chinese princess accidentally dropped a silkworm's cocoon in water and watched its magic filament unwind. Ever since, silk has been the symbol of luxury, romance and intrigue.

Of all the natural fibers, silk is the most astonishing: a smooth, translucent substance that the silkworm extrudes in a filament and wraps about itself in an almost endless coil. Just one of these cocoons, when soaked in hot water to loosen the gum that binds the coils together, can yield a continuous filament nearly a mile long. Silk fiber is lighter than linen, cotton and wool but also stronger; it has greater tensile strength than a like filament of steel. Its great strength permits the weaving of very thin fabrics, but even they are not as cool to wear as cotton in hot weather. Of all its qualities, however, silk is treasured most for the deep natural luster of its fibers. They are twisted or "thrown" into fine yarn that can be woven and dyed or printed in brilliant colors of great clarity, producing rich, durable fabrics that range from crisp, watermarked moirés, to glossy, ribbed failles, "raw" shantungs, fine honans, shining satins and lustrous crepes.

Matching the cloth to the dress

When a couturier or professional designer is conceiving a new dress, he goes through a process of elimination to select the fabric. He begins by considering the function of the dress: where and when it is to be worn. Then he decides what particular qualities his design will require in the fabric—pleat-retention or stretchiness, crispness or clinginess, firm body suitable for tailoring or fragile gauziness.

These two considerations are usually enough to narrow the range of possible fabric selections to one or two of the major fiber groups. But within each group there is still such an array of possibilities, so many fabrics that are related and yet different from one another, in the way they are woven or knitted and in the way they are finished.

To narrow the range still further, the designer flips through swatches seeking materials that will best express his ideas for the dress. The designer weighs a number of essential characteristics of each of the cloths from which he is making his selection.

The contribution made by these four basic characteristics may be subtle, but they all weigh significantly in the appearance and wearability of the finished garment. Within each major fiber group, fine quality can be distinguished from average by these characteristics.

First, the designer asks, what is the material's "hand"? He means the character of a particular fabric as communicated through the sense of touch. A good summer worsted, for example, feels as smooth and cool as it should when worn, warming only slowly to the touch. When squeezed, it feels substantial, yielding under pressure, yet springing back when it is released. With the same testing a good linen feels crisp and cool, a good cotton broadcloth feels smoother, thinner and just as cool, and a good silk crepe feels fluid, slinky and soft. If the designer has narrowed his range of choice to silks, he will now be using the criterion of "hand" to discriminate among them, distinguishing the slinky from the merely shiny.

Next, the professional looks for "drape" —the way a fabric falls naturally when it is hung. A medium-weight linen, when held up in the hands, may have just the right stiffness desired for a formal, tailored dress for daytime wear. A wool crepe may have the hugging ability to move with changing contours of the body in a cocktail dress. A silk satin may produce the perfect, rounded folds that can be gathered opulently for an evening gown. By contrast, a lesser material might hang in relatively rigid, wrinkled sheets, with all the distinction of a hospital orderly's smock.

The third quality is texture. A country woolen, for example, looks richer and warmer if it has the soft, fuzzy nap of an unfinished worsted; this might be quite out of character on lounging pajamas—but they, on the other hand, would gain allure from the smoothness and luster of silk satin or spun rayon with a similar finish.

And finally there is what the eye may see first: color. The fibers of some fabrics—notably silk, wool and certain rayons—accept dyes exceptionally well. Silks and rayons can blaze with brilliant hues; woolens take dyes less flamboyantly, producing prized subtleties in depth and richness of shading. Other materials, in addition to displaying the colors dyed into them, may provide glitter from metallic threads in their weaves.

To get exactly the combination of qualities that they desire, many couturiers order fabrics that have been specially woven to suit their designs. Rarely can nonprofessionals afford to go to such lengths. But the choice among commercial fabrics nowadays has become so extensive that no matter how elegant a custom dress you plan to sew, a material to match it can be bought off the bolt—if you know fabric and have learned how to gauge quality.

The French silk taffeta in this dress was so prized it had three incarnations. Experts at New York's Costume Institute removed the 19th Century neck ruffle and found a 1785 *robe à l'anglaise,* shown restored at right.

Under the diagonal bodice "pleats" of the 1785 dress, the investigators discovered there was the armhole of a still earlier *robe à la française,* that dated from the 1760s.

Lasting virtues of wool and linen

Woven and knitted into weights and textures most popular with couturiers, linen and wool—the oldest fabrics—and some modern substitutes drape opulently across the page. The red and black wool gabardines pictured are relatively heavy and have a firm, flat surface that designers favor for tailored garments. The brown crepe and dark green double knit, though differing in texture, are lightweight woolens equally adapted to suits or dresses. Tailored lines suit the crisp gold linen and its less crushable lookalike, the light blue spun rayon. The light green single knit, a downy blend of angora, lamb's wool and nylon, suggests body-clinging clothes; the dark blue Qiana nylon jersey, which drapes similarly, makes an elegant evening gown or even a simple shirt. For guidance on sewing and caring for these fabrics and for those shown on the following two pages, see the chart on pages 32-33.

The silks and their artful mimics

From the time of its legendary origin —around 2500 B.C.—silk has been virtually synonymous with luxury. Cotton, rayon and nylon make their way into couture by aping silk.

The slinky siren of the silks is crepe de Chine, shown here in orange in a luxurious charmeuse version that does more than drape—it pours. The green double-textured crepe at left, heavier, less supple and more crinkly, needs simple lines; the lightweight blue honan is ideal for fine detailing. The pink shantung, light in weight as the honan but more slubbed in texture, is imitated by the medium blue cotton shantung. These natural-fiber shantungs are best in soft lines; the stiffer, bright pink spun-rayon shantung requires more tailoring, as does the yellow silk faille. Elegant for evening gowns are the violet silk taffeta faille, with its rippled optical pattern, and the green Qiana nylon satin.

Special tips for handling fine fabrics

In the chart at right are procedures recommended for handling a variety of custom fabrics. Most of those that tend to shrink have been preshrunk by the manufacturer; for any that have not, follow the preshrinking instructions given here.

Before working with knit fabrics, let them lie flat on the floor or a bed overnight to allow the yarns to assume their natural shape; place them, as well as crepes, on a working surface large enough so that none of the fabric hangs over the edge. To hold silks and other slippery fabrics, cover the work surface with a sheet or a piece of felt.

When machine stitching knits, test a folded swatch first, adjusting the needle and bobbin thread tensions until a balanced stitch is obtained; when stitching the garment, stretch the knit fabric slightly by applying firm tension with your fingers behind and in front of the needle. Fabrics like crepes ought to be handled the same way but should be held taut rather than stretched.

FABRIC	PREPARING THE FABRIC
COTTON shantung	If not preshrunk, soak the fabric in lukewarm water, squeeze and hang to drip dry. Press out wrinkles (last column).
LINEN dress weight	If not preshrunk, dry clean, or soak in lukewarm water, squeeze and hang to dry (soak colored linens to set the dye). Before cutting, press out wrinkles (last column).
NYLON Qiana nylon knit	Preshrinking is not required. Before cutting, press out any wrinkles (last column).
NYLON Qiana nylon satin	Preshrinking is not required. Before cutting, press out any wrinkles (last column).
RAYON spun (linen type)	If not preshrunk, dry clean the fabric, or soak in lukewarm water, squeeze gently and hang up to drip dry. Before cutting, press out any wrinkles (last column).
RAYON spun (shantung type)	If not preshrunk, dry clean the fabric. Before cutting, press out any wrinkles (last column).
SILK crepe	Preshrinking is not required. Before cutting, press out any wrinkles (last column).
SILK faille	Preshrinking is not required. Before cutting, press out any wrinkles (last column).
SILK honan	Preshrinking is not required. Press out wrinkles (last column).
SILK moiré	Preshrinking is not required. Before cutting, press out any wrinkles (last column).
SILK shantung	Preshrinking is not required. Before cutting, press out any wrinkles (last column).
WOOL crepe	If not preshrunk, dry clean the fabric. Before cutting, press out any wrinkles (last column).
WOOL double knit	If not preshrunk, dry clean the fabric. Before cutting, press out any wrinkles (last column).
WOOL gabardine	If not preshrunk, dry clean the fabric, or soak in cold water, squeeze gently and hang up to drip dry. Before cutting, press out any wrinkles (last column).
WOOL single knit	Preshrinking is not required. Before cutting, press out any wrinkles (last column).

MARKING, CUTTING AND BASTING	MACHINE SEWING	FINISHING	CLEANING AND PRESSING
Attach the pattern with silk pins; mark with a tooth-edged tracing wheel. Baste with a Size 7 needle and mercerized cotton thread (No. 50) or polyester thread.	Use a Size 14 needle and mercerized cotton thread (No. 50) or polyester thread, setting the machine at 10 to 12 stitches per inch.	Line or underline, depending on the style of the garment (pages 113-117).	Dry clean, or hand wash in lukewarm water and mild soap. Squeeze, hang to drip dry. Press on the wrong side while damp, with the iron set for "cotton" and "steam."
Attach the pattern with silk pins, mark with a tooth-edged tracing wheel. Baste with a Size 7 needle and mercerized cotton (No. 50) or polyester thread.	Use a Size 14 needle and mercerized cotton thread (No. 50) or polyester thread, setting the machine at 10 to 12 stitches per inch.	To prevent fraying, finish seams with machine zigzag stitching or hand overcasting (page 204). Line or underline, depending on the style of the garment (pages 113-117).	Dry clean, or hand wash in lukewarm water and mild soap. Squeeze, hang to drip dry. Press on the wrong side while damp, with iron set for "linen" and "steam."
Attach the pattern with ballpoint pins, using a "nap layout." Transfer markings with a smooth tracing wheel. Baste with a Size 9 ballpoint needle, polyester thread.	Use a Size 11 ballpoint needle and polyester thread, setting the machine at 14 to 18 stitches per inch. Adjust machine tensions and stretch the fabric as you stitch.	Avoid underlining, which constricts the fabric flexibility; use a separate lining if desired. Knits stretch, so hang the garment overnight before hemming.	Dry clean, or machine wash in warm water (100° F.) with detergent; tumble dry at the "warm" setting. Press on the wrong side, setting the iron for "nylon" and "steam."
Attach the pattern following a "nap layout," using silk pins. Transfer markings with a tooth-edged tracing wheel. Baste with a Size 7 needle, polyester thread.	Use a Size 11 needle and polyester thread, setting the machine at 10 to 12 stitches per inch. Adjust machine tensions and stretch the fabric slightly as you stitch.	To prevent fraying, finish seams with machine zigzag stitching or hand overcasting (page 204). To prevent puckering avoid underlining; use a separate lining if desired.	Dry clean, or machine wash in warm water (100° F.). Press on the wrong side, with iron set for "nylon" and "steam," and brown paper under the seams.
Attach the pattern with silk pins, transfer markings with a tooth-edged tracing wheel. Baste with a Size 7 needle and mercerized cotton (No. 50) or polyester thread.	Use a Size 14 needle and mercerized cotton thread (No. 50) or polyester thread, setting the machine at 10 to 12 stitches per inch.	To prevent fraying, finish seams with machine zigzag stitching or hand overcasting (page 204). Line or underline, depending on the style of the garment (pages 113-117).	Dry clean, or hand wash in lukewarm water and mild soap. Squeeze, hang to drip dry. Press on the wrong side while damp with iron set for "rayon" and "steam."
Attach the pattern with silk pins, mark with a tooth-edged tracing wheel. Baste with a Size 7 needle and mercerized cotton (No. 50) or polyester thread.	Use a Size 14 needle and polyester thread; set the machine at 10 to 12 stitches per inch. Test a swatch, adjust machine tensions and keep the fabric taut as you stitch.	To prevent fraying, finish seams with machine zigzag stitching or hand overcasting (page 204). Line or underline, depending on the style of the garment (pages 113-117).	Dry clean only. Press the fabric on the wrong side, setting the iron for "rayon" and "steam."
Attach pattern pieces with silk pins at 2-inch intervals to prevent slipping; transfer markings with tailor tacks. Baste with a Size 8 needle and silk ("A") or polyester thread.	Use a Size 11 needle and silk ("A") or polyester thread; set the machine at 10 to 12 stitches per inch (12 to 15 for light crepe). Adjust tensions and keep fabric taut.	To prevent fraying, finish seams with machine zigzag stitching or hand overcasting (page 204). Use a separate lining. Hang the garment overnight before hemming	Dry clean. Press on the wrong side, using a press cloth covered by damp cheesecloth; set the iron for "silk" and "dry." Place brown paper under seams to avoid marks.
Attach pattern pieces with silk pins and transfer markings with tailor tacks. Baste with a Size 8 needle and silk ("A") or polyester thread.	Use a Size 11 needle and silk thread or polyester thread, setting the machine at 10 to 12 stitches per inch. Test a swatch, adjust tensions and keep the fabric taut.	To prevent fraying, finish seams with machine zigzag stitching or hand overcasting (page 204). Line or underline, depending on the style of the garment (pages 113-117).	Dry clean. Press on the wrong side using a press cloth covered by damp cheesecloth; set the iron for "silk" and "dry." Place brown paper under seams to avoid marks.
Attach pattern pieces with silk pins and transfer markings with tailor tacks. Baste with a Size 8 needle and silk ("A") or polyester thread.	Use a Size 11 needle and silk ("A") or polyester thread, setting the machine at 10 to 12 stitches per inch.	To prevent fraying, finish the seams with machine zigzag stitching or hand overcasting (page 204). Line or underline the garment (pages 113-117).	Dry clean, or if silk is washable, hand wash with cold-water soap. Squeeze and hang to drip dry. Press on the wrong side while damp, setting the iron for "silk" and "dry."
Attach pattern pieces with silk pins, following the guide for "nap layout." Transfer markings with tailor tacks. Baste with a Size 8 needle and silk ("A") or polyester thread.	Use a Size 11 needle and silk ("A") or polyester thread, setting the machine at 10 to 12 stitches per inch. Adjust tensions and keep the fabric taut as you stitch.	To prevent fraying, finish seams with machine zigzag stitching or hand overcasting (page 204). Line or underline, depending on the style of the garment (pages 113-117).	Dry clean only. Press the fabric on the wrong side, setting the iron for "silk" and "dry."
Attach pattern pieces with silk pins and transfer markings with tailor tacks. Baste with a Size 8 needle, silk ("A") or polyester thread.	Use a Size 11 needle and silk ("A") or polyester thread, setting the machine at 12 to 15 stitches per inch.	To prevent fraying, finish seams with machine zigzag stitching or hand overcasting (page 204). Line or underline, depending on the style of the garment (pages 113-117).	Dry clean only. Press on the wrong side, using a press cloth covered by a damp cheesecloth and setting the iron for "silk" and "dry."
Attach pattern pieces with silk pins and transfer markings with tailor tacks. Baste with a Size 7 needle and mercerized cotton thread (No. 50) or polyester thread.	Use a Size 14 needle and mercerized cotton (No. 50) or polyester thread; set the machine at 10 to 12 stitches per inch. Adjust tensions and keep fabric taut.	Line or underline, depending on the style of the garment (pages 113-117). Because crepe tends to stretch, hang up the garment overnight before hemming.	Dry clean only. Press gently on the wrong side, setting the iron for "wool" and "steam."
Attach the pattern with ballpoint pins, following the "nap layout." Mark with a smooth tracing wheel. Baste with Size 7 ballpoint needle, polyester thread.	Use a Size 14 ballpoint needle and polyester thread, setting the machine at 10 to 12 stitches per inch. Adjust tensions and stretch the fabric slightly as you stitch.	Avoid underlining, which constricts fabric flexibility; use a separate lining if desired. Knits tend to stretch, so hang the garment up overnight before hemming.	Dry clean only. Press the fabric on the wrong side, setting the iron for "wool" and "steam."
Attach the pattern with silk pins, following a "nap layout." Transfer markings with a tooth-edged tracing wheel. Baste with Size 7 needle, polyester thread.	Use a Size 14 needle and mercerized cotton thread (No. 50) or polyester thread, setting the machine at 10 to 12 stitches per inch.	Use an underlining suitable to the weight of the fabric (pages 113-117).	Dry clean only. Press on the wrong side; set the iron for "wool" and "steam." Place brown paper under seams to avoid press marks.
Attach the pattern with ballpoint pins, following the "nap layout." Mark with a smooth tracing wheel. Baste with Size 7 ballpoint needle, polyester thread.	Use a Size 14 ballpoint needle and polyester thread, setting the machine at 10 to 12 stitches per inch. Adjust tensions and stretch the fabric slightly as you stitch.	Avoid underlining, which constricts fabric flexibility; use a separate lining if desired. Knits tend to stretch, so hang the garment up overnight before hemming.	Hand wash and rinse in cool water, squeeze and lay on toweling to dry. Press lightly on the right side with a press cloth with iron set for "wool" and "steam."

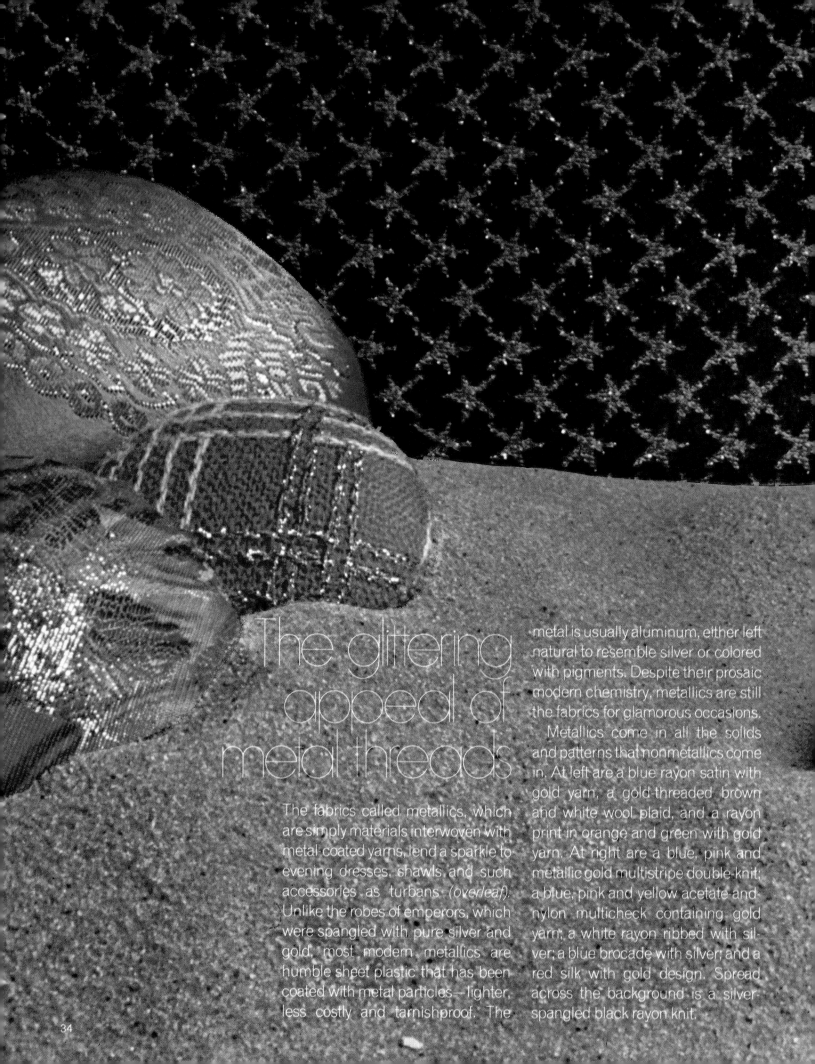

The glittering appeal of metal threads

The fabrics called metallics, which are simply materials interwoven with metal-coated yarns, lend a sparkle to evening dresses, shawls and such accessories as turbans (overleaf). Unlike the robes of emperors, which were spangled with pure silver and gold, most modern metallics are humble sheet plastic that has been coated with metal particles—lighter, less costly and tarnishproof. The metal is usually aluminum, either left natural to resemble silver or colored with pigments. Despite their prosaic modern chemistry, metallics are still the fabrics for glamorous occasions.

Metallics come in all the solids and patterns that nonmetallics come in. At left are a blue rayon satin with gold yarn, a gold-threaded brown and white wool plaid, and a rayon print in orange and green with gold yarn. At right are a blue, pink and metallic gold multistripe double-knit; a blue, pink and yellow acetate and nylon multicheck containing gold yarn; a white rayon ribbed with silver; a blue brocade with silver; and a red silk with gold design. Spread across the background is a silver-spangled black rayon knit.

Working with metallics

PREPARING THE FABRIC	Most modern fabrics containing metallic yarns have been treated to prevent tarnishing, so if the fabric has not been preshrunk, you can dry clean or soak it as recommended for the type of fabric with which the metallic strands have been combined *(chart, pages 32-33)*. Before working with the material, press out any wrinkles, following the instructions given below under "Cleaning and Pressing."
MARKING, CUTTING AND BASTING	Attach the pattern pieces to the fabric with ballpoint pins, according to the cutting guide, placing them well within the seam allowances; transfer pattern markings to the fabric with tailor tacks. Baste with a ballpoint needle, from Size 5 for heavy fabrics up to Size 10 for light ones. Use a thread appropriate to the fabric (silk for silk fabrics, cotton for cotton ones) or an all-purpose polyester thread; a thimble will help prevent snagging the threads on your finger.
MACHINE SEWING	Use a Size 11 ballpoint needle for lightweight fabrics, setting the machine at 10 to 12 stitches per inch; for medium-weight fabrics, use a Size 14 ballpoint needle and a setting of 12 to 15 stitches per inch. Use a thread appropriate to the fabric (silk for silk, cotton for cotton) or an all-purpose polyester thread. If sewing with a zigzag machine, always use the straight-stitch throat plate and presser foot to prevent snagging the metallic threads.
FINISHING	Because most metallic fabrics tend to fray, finish seams with machine zigzag stitching or hand overcasting *(page 204)*. To prevent the metallic threads from scratching the wearer, line or underline the garment depending on its fabric and style *(pages 112-117)*; use satin cording to finish off rough edges at neckline, armholes and hems.
CLEANING AND PRESSING	Dry clean or hand wash according to the method recommended for the fiber or fibers with which the metallic yarn has been combined *(chart, pages 32-33)*. Press the fabric on the wrong side, using a press cloth on top and setting the iron for "metallics" (or "warm") and "steam." For raised metallics like brocade, pad the ironing board with a bath towel to help keep the fabric surface from flattening, and be careful not to press heavily with the iron.

Basic steps in layout and cutting

To make a garment hang properly, the pattern pieces are marked with arrows indicating alignment on the "grain," or weave, of woven fabrics. Whether this alignment is to be straight, on the "true grain" (parallel to the lengthwise threads) or on the bias (diagonal), you must first make sure that the grain has not been twisted by handling of the cloth; if it has, straighten it.

To check grain alignment, first find the true crosswise grain *(right)*. Then fold the fabric in half lengthwise, align the lengthwise edges against one edge of a table and the raw crosswise edge against the other. If the raw edges do not match each other and the corners do not form right angles, the grain is off. To straighten, fold the material in half lengthwise, wrong side out. Pin the open sides together and straighten with a steam iron.

Arrange pattern pieces on the straightened fabric following your cutting guide. For both straight and bias cuts, the grain-line arrows on the pattern pieces must be parallel to the selvages. If you make a pattern piece, mark the grain-line arrows as shown at right.

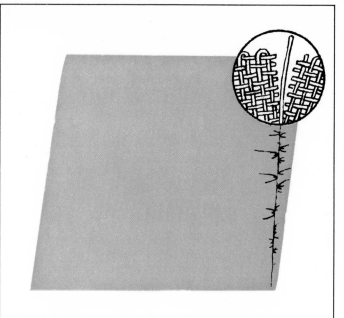

1. Make a small cut into one finished, or selvage, edge of the fabric and snag a crosswise thread with a pin. Gently pull on the thread so that it shows up as a puckered line along the width of the fabric.

2. Cut along the puckered line from one selvage to the other; this is the true crosswise grain.

3. Repeat at the opposite end of the fabric so that the ends can be matched for straightening the grain as explained at left.

FINDING THE TRUE BIAS

1. After straightening the fabric *(left),* place it on a flat surface and fold it diagonally so that one selvage is parallel to the crosswise edge and perpendicular to the other selvage. The diagonally folded edge is the true bias.

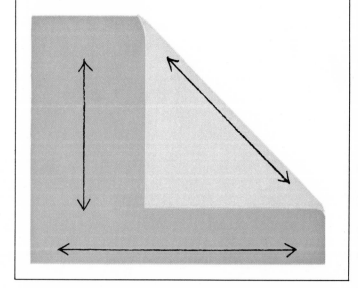

LAYING OUT ON-GRAIN PATTERNS

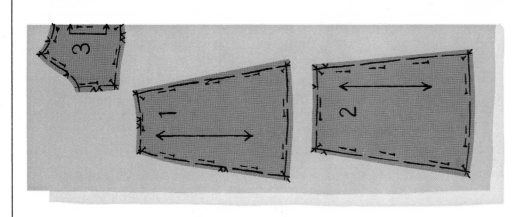

1. Pin all pattern pieces having a line that is marked "place on fold" to the fabric so that the line marking aligns with the fold.

2. Arrange the other pieces according to the pattern cutting guide, placing the printed grain-line arrows parallel to the fold and to the selvage edges.

3. Pin each pattern piece diagonally at the corners; then pin parallel to, and just inside, the cutting line.

LAYING OUT BIAS-CUT PATTERNS

1. Make a duplicate pattern (page 46) for each pattern piece from which more than one garment section will be cut, such as a left skirt back that must be flopped to cut a right skirt back. Trace the grain-line arrow on each duplicate piece.

2. Spread open the straightened fabric and loosely arrange the pattern pieces according to the accompanying pattern cutting guide, making certain the grain-line arrows are parallel to the selvage edges.

3. Pin each pattern piece diagonally at the corners; then pin parallel to, and just inside, the cutting line. Arrange and pin all pattern pieces before cutting any.

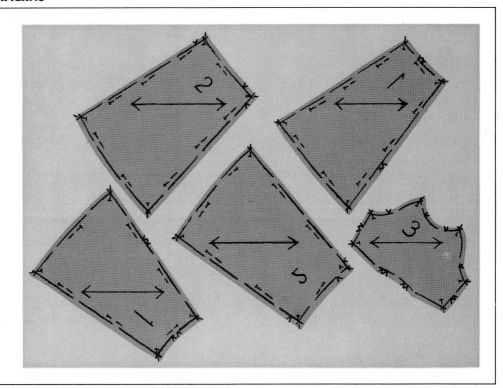

MARKING GRAIN LINES ON HOMEMADE PATTERNS

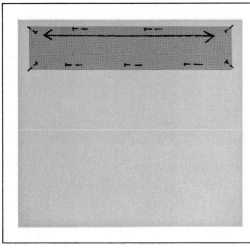

1. If the fabric section is to be cut on the grain, mark an arrow parallel to the lengthwise edges of the homemade pattern.

2. If the fabric section is to be cut on the bias, make a mark about midway along one lengthwise edge of the homemade pattern. Using a protractor, rule the grain line at a 45-degree angle from this point.

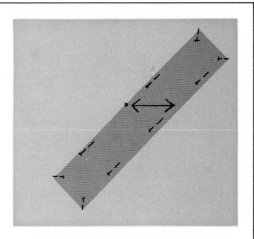

Verve from stripes, plaids and flowers

Back in the 17th and 18th centuries, when the craze for elaborately patterned silks reached its peak, styles of clothing changed very slowly and it was the pattern of the silk, not the cut of the garment, that had to be different every year. A silk fabric popular one season lost a third of its value by the next. The practice of pirating the sophisticated silk patterns of the master textile designers of Lyons, the center of France's silk industry, became so prevalent that stiff penalties were imposed on those who sold or smuggled patterns to foreign competitors.

And as late as the 19th Century, when Charles Worth dominated French fashion, he could dictate exactly which patterns and colors he wanted and could even order special patterns woven to suit the design of a single ball gown (right).

The appeal of unique patterns continues, and modern designers create fabrics to be made up just for their dresses. But now the patterns are less likely to be delicate butterflies than vibrant prints and plaids. The pattern of the fabric itself is often the garment's most eye-catching element. The bold patterns restrict the choice of style, calling for a simple design with a minimum of darts and seams. Even so, the fabric patterns demand special care in cutting and stitching, and a garment that in a plain material could be made by elementary methods calls for the special techniques of the couturier when the material is boldly patterned.

What makes a pattern bold? It may be the size of the design element—a huge rose, for example—or the size of the "repeat," the self-contained unit of related design elements and spaces that is duplicated along the lengthwise direction (called the warp) of the material.

Both the design elements themselves and the repeats affect sewing. The way a bold plaid is cut—and even the kind of garment that can be made from it—depends on whether it is regular, with its lengthwise and crosswise lines equally spaced in each direction from the most dominant lines, or irregular, with lines unequally spaced from the dominant lines lengthwise, crosswise or both. Instructions for matching irregular lengthwise plaids, irregular crosswise plaids and totally irregular plaids are on pages 49-51. Matching techniques for diagonally striped fabrics are on page 47.

A special problem is raised by another favorite of the couturiers, the border print (page 47)—fabric bearing a pattern only along one selvage edge. The design is meant to appear at the hemline, jacket edge or cuff, requiring that pattern pieces be placed vertically on the crosswise dimension of the fabric—usually 45 inches. This arrangement is possible only if there is a separate bodice or a seamed waistline; a border print will not work with a floor-length A-line or shift dress.

In order to match irregular plaids and to position bold patterned fabrics whose designs run in one direction, it is necessary to use a nap layout—that is, all the pattern pieces must face in one direction. All nap layouts require some extra fabric; that fact is usually marked on the pattern envelope. In the case of irregular plaids, one-way bold repeats or prints, if the pattern envelope does not advise otherwise, allow 1/2 yard more fabric than normally required.

But positioning demands more than mechanical alignment. The motif of a large floral or repeat print *(pages 46 and 48)* must be placed over the body in a balanced and attractive arrangement so that the eye sees the fabric as a whole and is not distracted by one large, dominating point.

Always match the sections of the garment at important seams—sides, center front, back—and on the seam lines, not on the cutting lines. On plaids and bold repeat prints, always match horizontal lines and make sure the design runs continuously from the bodice front into the sleeve.

The techniques of cutting and positioning fabrics with bold designs may seem more formidable than they actually are. Some care and attention to detail will enable you to handle patterns that at first glance raise difficulties. If you choose a plaid or print that is in scale with your figure, you can have a striking garment—one that is eye-catching and uniquely your own.

The pattern that embellishes this ice-blue satin gown was planned to permit butterflies to cascade down the panels of the umbrella-shaped skirt onto the train.

Each of the butterflies on the 19th Century gown at left, seen in close-up above, is strategically placed. The material was woven to order to ensure that each butterfly would appear on the finished gown only where the designers of the House of Worth intended it to appear.

Large floral prints are generally most successful on long, loose or A-line gowns, jumpsuits or flaring pants.

Suiting prints to figure and dress

The bold prints and plaids dancing in the silhouettes at right and on the next two pages are striking fabrics that delight designers. The few special problems they pose are easily handled. Besides requiring careful matching and cutting *(pages 46-51)*, large-scale prints must be positioned on the body so that no focal point jars the eye, such as a big rose right on the bust, hips or buttocks. Border prints used on a hemline, particularly those with prominent repeated motifs, look best with the designs centered at the front and back.

The heaviest horizontal lines of plaids and repeat prints *(overleaf)* are more attractive at or near hemlines. Similarly, a plaid's widest vertical stripes are best centered in front and back or balanced on either side, and diagonal stripes should be slanted in one direction only.

Border prints are decorative on full or
pleated skirts with straight hems, at
the edges of sleeves, pants and coats,
or as accents on cuffs and necklines.

Diagonal stripes lend themselves to simple tunics and swirling capes or caftans, but not to pants or fitted garments that require many darts.

Irregular plaids work best on classic jumpers or slacks, on long wraparound skirts or on coats and suits that have boxy, rather than fitted, jackets.

44

Bold repeat prints go well on pleated
or gathered skirts and long, unfitted
garments. They are unsuited to pants
or close-fitting blouses or jackets.

47

Laying out and matching bold designs

The key to handling boldly patterned fabrics is to make duplicates *(right, top)* of all pattern pieces in which matching or positioning is crucial. Then lay out all the pattern pieces on the spread-out fabric and cut nothing until everything is matched and attractively positioned.

On these pages, model layouts are shown for a variety of stylized patterns. Each pattern represents a style appropriate to the particular fabric illustrated.

Flowers in large-scale floral prints *(below, right)* should be matched whenever they fall on seams. Diagonal stripes can be matched only at the back *(opposite, top)*.

The border of a border print may be used at a straight-edged hem. The pattern pieces must be placed vertically on the crosswise grain of the fabric *(opposite, bottom)*. Bold repeat prints, too, need straight-hem patterns; irregular plaids can have straight or curved hems. Align all hemlines of the pattern on the same horizontal stripe of a plaid, or on lines of a bold repeat *(pages 48-51)*.

Plaids that are irregular lengthwise can be matched only when the pattern has a center seam in front and back. Cut with the duplicate piece upside down *(page 50)*.

MAKING A DUPLICATE PATTERN PIECE

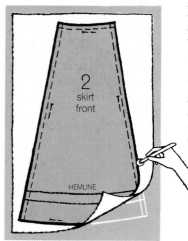

1. Place a light-colored transparent sheet of tracing paper, the size of the pattern piece to be copied, on a firm, flat surface. Tape two pieces together if necessary to accommodate the pattern piece.

2. Place a sheet of carbon paper of the same size, carbon side down, over the tracing paper.

3. Place the pattern piece, marked side up, over the carbon paper and pin the three pieces together.

4. With a smooth-edged tracing wheel, outline the entire pattern piece and trace over all notches, seam lines and other markings.

5. Remove the original pattern piece and the tracing paper, cut out the duplicate pattern piece and mark it with the same number as the original.

LAYING OUT A LARGE FLORAL PRINT

1. Lay the fabric wrong side down and pin the original dress front pattern piece to the fabric with markings up. Align it so that the designs fall off-center vertically, above or below the bustline, and are balanced by designs near the bottom.

2. Pin the duplicate dress front piece to the fabric, markings down, aligning its center fold line with that of the original piece and following the other instructions in Step 1. Adjust both pieces to make the designs symmetrical.

3. Pin the original pattern piece for the dress back to the fabric with pattern markings facing up, making sure that any large designs are placed off-center vertically and are above or below the buttocks.

4. Pin the duplicate pattern piece for the dress back to the fabric with pattern markings facing down, following the placement instructions in Step 3.

5. Cut out first those pieces for which the original pattern piece was marked with a fold line. The original and duplicates of such pieces must be cut together so that the fabric for both parts of each section form a single unit.

6. Cut out the other pinned pieces separately.

7. Pin and cut out any remaining pattern pieces that are not part of the basic body section—such as collars and facings —following your pattern guide, without any further attempt at positioning the design.

LAYING OUT A DIAGONAL STRIPE

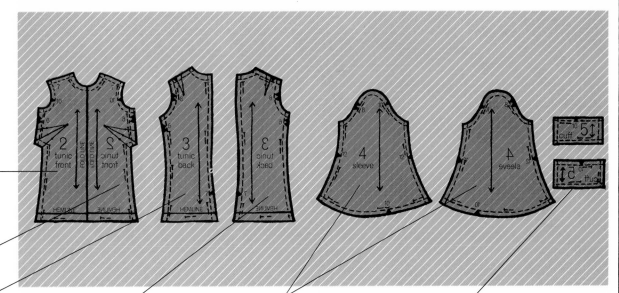

1. Lay out the fabric wrong side down, and pin the original pattern piece for the tunic front to the fabric with pattern markings facing up.

2. Pin the duplicate pattern piece for the tunic front to the fabric with pattern markings facing down, aligning the center front fold line with that of the original pattern piece.

3. Pin the original pattern piece for the tunic back to the fabric with pattern markings facing up, aligning the hemline with that of the front and making sure that the notches on the side seam (No. 6 in this example) fall in the same position on the stripe as their numbered counterparts on the tunic front.

4. Pin the duplicate pattern piece for the tunic back to the fabric with pattern markings facing down, following the placement instructions in Step 3 and making sure that the notch on the back seam (No. 7 in this example) falls in the same position on the stripe as its numbered counterpart on the original pattern piece.

5. Pin the original pattern piece for the sleeve to the fabric with pattern markings facing up, aligning the pattern piece in the same lengthwise direction as the pattern pieces for the tunic front and back. However, make no attempt to match the stripes to the armholes of the body sections. Then pin the duplicate pattern piece for the sleeve to the fabric with pattern markings facing down in the same way.

6. Pin the original pattern piece for the cuff to the fabric with pattern markings facing up, aligning it so that the diagonal lines run in the same direction as those on the sleeve. Then pin the duplicate pattern piece for the cuff to the fabric with pattern markings facing down and aligned with the original.

7. Cut out, following the instructions for laying out a large floral print, Steps 5 and 6.

8. Pin and cut out any remaining pattern pieces according to the instructions for laying out a large floral print, Step 7.

LAYING OUT A BORDER PRINT

1. Lay the fabric wrong side down, and pin the original pattern piece for the skirt front to the fabric with pattern markings facing up. Align the pattern so that the hemline marking is 1/2 inch above the selvage edge of the fabric and the center fold line falls in the middle of one main element in the design (the center of a flower in this example).

2. Pin the duplicate pattern piece for the skirt front to the fabric with pattern markings facing down, aligning its center fold line with that of the original pattern piece and following the other placement instructions in Step 1.

3. Pin the original piece for the skirt back to the fabric with pattern markings up, the hemline marking 1/2 inch above the selvage edge and the center seam line —not the cutting edge—in the middle of a main element in the design.

4. Pin the duplicate pattern piece for the skirt back to the fabric with pattern markings facing down, following the placement instructions in Step 3.

5. Cut out the pattern pieces following the instructions for laying out a large floral print, Steps 5 and 6.

6. Pin and cut out remaining pattern pieces following the instructions for laying out a large floral print, Step 7.

1. Lay out the fabric wrong side down on a firm, flat surface. Pin the original pattern piece for the skirt front to the fabric with pattern markings facing up, aligning it so that the hemline marking of the pattern falls on a heavier line of the print and the waistline falls on a lighter section.

2. Pin the duplicate pattern piece for the skirt front to the fabric with the pattern markings facing down, aligning its center fold line with that of the original pattern piece and following the other placement instructions in Step 1.

3. Pin the original pattern piece for the skirt back to the fabric with pattern markings facing up, aligning it so that the hemline marking falls along the same heavy line as the two front pieces and the notch on the side seam (No. 6 in this example) falls in the same position on the design as its numbered counterpart on the skirt front.

4. Pin the duplicate pattern piece for the skirt back to the fabric with pattern markings facing down, following the placement instructions in Step 3, making sure the notch on the center back seam (No. 5 in this drawing) falls in the same position on the design as its numbered counterpart on the original pattern piece.

5. Pin the original pattern piece for the bodice front to the fabric with pattern markings facing up, aligning it so that the heavier lines of the design fall above and below the bustline, which is at the apex of the dart.

6. Pin the duplicate pattern piece for the bodice front to the fabric with pattern markings facing down, aligning its center fold line with that of the original pattern piece, following the other placement instructions in Step 5.

7. Pin the original pattern piece for the bodice back to the fabric with pattern markings facing up, aligning it so that the numbered notch on the side seam (No. 2 in this example) falls in the same position on the design as its numbered counterpart on the bodice front.

8. Pin the duplicate pattern piece for the bodice back to the fabric with pattern markings facing down, following the placement instructions in Step 7.

9. Pin the original pattern piece for the sleeve to the fabric with pattern markings facing up, aligning it so that the notch on the sleeve cap (No. 16 in this example) falls in the same position on the design as its numbered counterpart on the armhole of the bodice front.

10. Pin the duplicate pattern piece for the sleeve to the fabric with pattern markings facing down, following the placement instructions in Step 9.

11. Cut out the pattern following the instructions for laying out a large floral print, Steps 5 and 6 (page 46).

12. Pin and cut out remaining pattern pieces following the instructions for laying out a large floral print, Step 7 (page 46).

1. Lay out the entire piece of fabric wrong side down on a firm flat surface. Pin the original pattern piece for the skirt front to the fabric with the pattern markings facing up. Align it so that the center fold line of the pattern falls along the center of a narrow vertical stripe. If the hemline of the garment is curved, as in this example, align its center front edge with that of a narrow horizontal stripe. If the hemline is straight, follow instructions for laying out an irregular plaid, Step 1 (page 51).

2. Pin the duplicate pattern piece for the skirt front to the fabric with pattern markings facing down aligning its center fold line with that of the original pattern piece and following the other placement instructions in Step 1.

3. Pin the original pattern piece for the skirt back to the fabric with pattern markings facing up, aligning it so that the center back seam line—not the cutting edge—falls along the center of a narrow vertical stripe and the hemline falls along the edge of a similar narrow horizontal stripe as that of the skirt front. Make sure that the notch on the side seam (No. 4 in this example) falls in the same position on the plaid as its numbered counterpart on the skirt front.

4. Pin the duplicate pattern piece for the skirt back to the fabric with pattern markings facing down, following the placement instructions in Step 3.

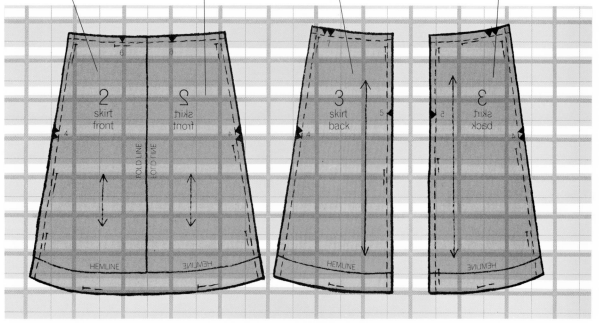

5. Pin the original pattern piece for the bodice front to the fabric with the pattern markings facing up, aligning it so that the center fold line falls along the center of a narrow vertical stripe and the wide horizontal stripe falls above or below the bustline, which is at the apex of the dart.

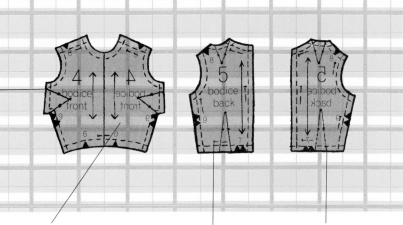

6. Pin the duplicate pattern piece for the bodice front to the fabric with pattern markings facing down, aligning its center fold line with that of the original pattern piece, and following the other placement instructions in Step 5.

7. Pin the original bodice back piece to the fabric, pattern markings up, so the center back seam line—not the cutting edge—falls along the center of a narrow vertical stripe and the notch on the side seam (No. 9 here) falls in the same position on the plaid as its numbered counterpart on the bodice front.

8. Pin the duplicate pattern piece for the bodice back to the fabric with pattern markings facing down, following the placement instructions in Step 7.

9. Cut out the pattern pieces following the instructions for laying out a large floral print, Steps 5 and 6 (page 46).

10. Pin and cut out any remaining pattern pieces according to the instructions for laying out a large floral print, Step 7 (page 46), without attempting any further matching.

1. Lay the fabric wrong side down and pin the original pattern piece for the front of the dress to the fabric with the pattern markings facing up. Align the pattern piece so that any wide vertical stripe in the fabric falls at least 3 inches in from the center front seam line or the armhole seam line on the pattern. If the hemline is curved, align its center front edge with that of a narrow horizontal stripe. If the hemline is straight, follow the instructions for laying out an irregular plaid, Step 1 *(page 51)*.

2. Turn the duplicate pattern piece for the dress front upside down and pin it to the fabric with pattern markings facing down, following the placement instructions in Step 1. Make sure that the center front notches (No. 1 and No. 2 in this example) fall in the same positions on the plaid as their numbered counterparts on the original dress front.

3. Pin the original pattern piece for the dress back to the fabric with pattern markings facing up, aligning it so that the center back seam line, the hemline and the notch on the side seam (No. 5 in this example) all fall in the same position on the plaid as their counterparts on the dress front.

4. Turn the duplicate pattern piece for the dress back upside down and pin it to the fabric with pattern markings facing down, following the placement instructions in Step 3.

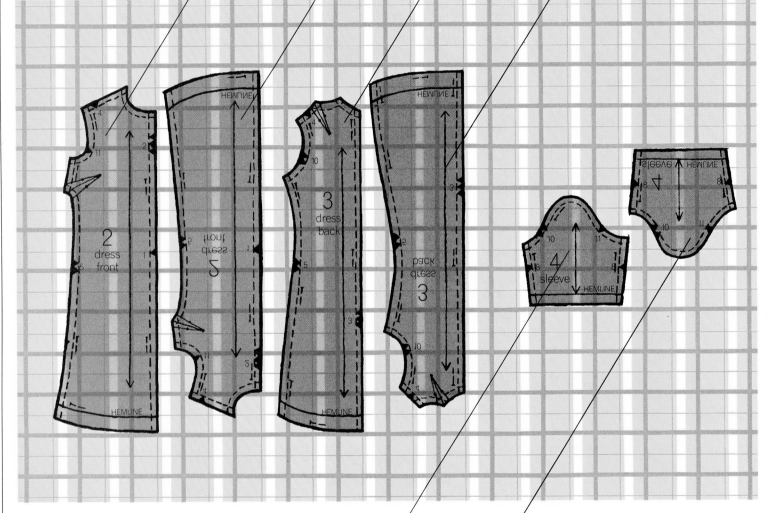

5. Pin the original pattern piece for the sleeve to the fabric with pattern markings facing up. Align it so that the wide vertical stripe falls down the center of the sleeve and make sure that the notch on the sleeve cap (No. 11 in this example) falls in the same position on the plaid as its numbered counterpart on the armhole of the dress front.

6. Turn the duplicate pattern piece for the sleeve upside down and pin it with the pattern markings facing down, following the placement instructions in Step 5.

7. Cut out the pattern pieces.

8. Pin and cut any remaining pattern pieces following the instructions for laying out a large floral print, Step 7 *(page 46),* without attempting any further matching.

LAYING OUT AN IRREGULAR LENGTHWISE AND CROSSWISE PLAID

1. Lay the fabric wrong side down, and pin the original pattern piece for the pants front to the fabric with pattern markings facing up, aligning it so that the center of the pattern piece—the point equidistant from the inner leg seam and the outer leg seam—falls on a wide vertical stripe. If the hemline of the garment is straight, as in the example, align its edge with that of a wide horizontal stripe. If the hemline is curved, follow instructions for laying out an irregular lengthwise plaid, Step 1 *(page 50)*.

2. Pin the duplicate pattern piece for the pants front to the fabric with pattern markings facing down, following the placement instructions in Step 1. Make sure that the notch at the crotch seam (No. 11 in this example) falls in the same position on the plaid as its numbered counterpart on the original pattern piece.

3. Pin the original pattern piece for the pants back to the fabric with pattern markings facing up. Align it so that the center of the pattern piece, as explained in Step 1, and its hemline edge fall on similar vertical and horizontal stripes as those on the pants front. Make sure that the notches on the side seam (No. 8 in this example) fall in the same position on the plaid as their numbered counterparts on the pants front.

4. Pin the duplicate pattern piece for the pants back to the fabric with pattern markings facing down, following the placement instructions in Step 3. Make sure that the notch on the crotch seam (No. 12 in this example) falls in the same position on the plaid as its numbered counterpart on the original pattern piece.

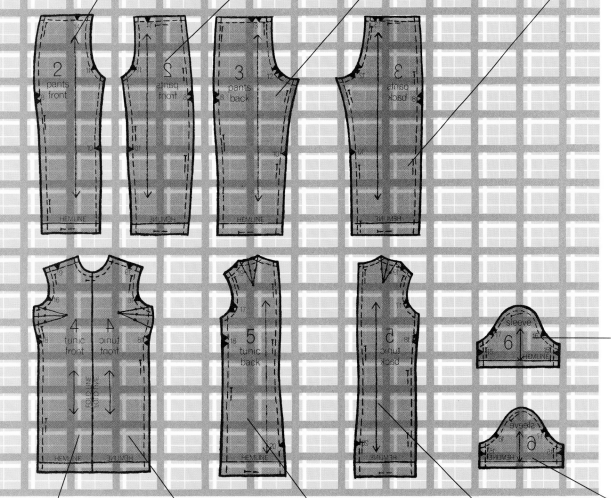

9. Pin the original pattern piece for the sleeve to the fabric with pattern markings up. Align it so that the wide vertical stripe falls down the center of the sleeve and make sure that the sleeve cap notch (No. 16 in this example) falls in the same position on the plaid as its numbered counterpart on the armhole of the tunic front.

10. Pin the duplicate pattern piece for the sleeve with pattern markings facing down following the placement instructions in Step 9.

11. Cut out the pieces following the instructions for laying out a large floral print, Steps 5 and 6 *(page 46)*.

12. Pin and cut out any remaining pattern pieces following the instructions for laying out a large floral print, Step 7 *(page 46)*, without attempting any further matching.

5. Pin the original pattern piece for the tunic front to the fabric with pattern markings facing up, aligning it so that any wide vertical stripe falls about 3 inches in from the center front fold line or the armhole seam line. Because its hemline is straight, follow the instructions in Step 1, making sure that the hemline edge falls on a similar wide horizontal stripe as that of the pants pieces.

6. Pin the duplicate pattern piece for the tunic front to the fabric with pattern markings facing down, aligning its center fold line with that of the original pattern piece and following the other placement instructions in Step 5.

7. Pin the original piece for the tunic back to the fabric with markings up, so that any wide vertical stripe falls about 3 inches from the center back seam line or the armhole seam line and the hemline edge falls on a similar wide horizontal stripe as the tunic front. Make sure that the notch on the side seam line (No. 18 in this example) falls in the same position on the plaid as its numbered counterpart on the tunic front.

8. Pin the duplicate pattern piece for the tunic back to the fabric with pattern markings facing down, following the placement instructions in Step 7.

3

MEASUREMENTS
PATTERN
ADJUSTMENTS
THE MUSLIN

Studying a mirrored mannequin, couturier Valentino orders an adjustment of a muslin prototype for a new design.

Situated on a fashionable street—perhaps in Paris, perhaps in Rome—a quietly imposing town house rises behind a row of shade trees. In a spacious, high-ceilinged room on an upper floor, daylight floods in through balconied French windows and reflects from mirrored walls. The few furnishings are a pristine white, the floor a gleaming black tile. No area rugs spill hues upon it; no brilliant prints adorn the walls. There are

A PROFESSIONAL TOOL FOR A PERFECT FIT

no other colors that might clash with the fabrics to be displayed in these chaste surroundings.

At an elaborately carved mantelpiece, one of the staff talks with a client about a new gown for a charity ball. Two or three other staff members hover attentively in the wings, managing to convey a mixture of deference and authority—in a manner not unlike that of Swiss bankers or Monte Carlo croupiers, professionals whose craft also involves separating the rich from their money, and doing it in style.

They work for one of the great houses of fashion. Its name is known from Seventh Avenue to Singapore, but its precincts are visited only by a few, the women who wear the world's most nearly perfect clothes.

There are other rooms in this house of fashion. No other one is so spacious and elegant as this one; indeed, some of them are locked and dark. But they are nonetheless important.

In one such room, if a visitor could gain admission, he would see shelf upon shelf of plain-looking manila envelopes stuffed with pieces of coarse beige material; they are the carefully guarded treasure of the house. The labels on the envelopes are inked with instantly recognizable names: along one wall, the motion-picture star who married a prince, the present baroness of the banking family that once financed Napoleon, the wife of the President of the Republic; on another wall, the woman who directs a major Madison Avenue advertising agency, the wife of an Asian vice president who has been linked to the opium trade.

Each of these envelopes contains an object that is as much the stock of haute couture as are imagination and taste. It is a *toile de corps* — literally, a cloth of the body — a prototype of a gown that has been sewn up in plain muslin, made and adjusted with such exquisite precision that only one woman in the world could wear it perfectly: the woman whose name is recorded on the envelope.

There are actually three types of toiles, or muslins, differentiated by the ways couturiers use them. The muslins in the envelopes are fitting shells, made for clients on the lines of a very close-to-the-body basic dress with straight skirt and used as a record of their measurements for the preliminary cutting and fitting of future gowns.

The second muslin is called the design muslin. This is the equivalent of the sculptor's clay model, made by the couturier in the process of designing the gown by wrapping and draping the muslin fabric around the figure of one of his house mannequins.

The third kind, the dress muslin, is a duplicate of an actual dress and is used to perfect the fit of the design to the measurements of its intended wearer.

Couturiers are insistent about the precision with which a fitting shell matches the figure of a client, but Madeleine Vionnet went to unusual lengths to duplicate her clients' figures. To provide herself with a model in the round — essential to the inimitable Vionnet cuts, clingingly draped and predominantly asymmetrical — she created figurine replicas of her clients and made her fitting toiles on them.

All of these muslins are stand-ins for the sumptuous fabric of which a gown is to be made. The experiments, adjustments and corrections that a couturier lavishes on a creation are worked out first in muslin. The reason is simple economy. The fabrics in which the great couturiers envision their patronesses can cost as much as $200 a yard, many times what muslin costs.

The dress muslin and the fitting shell are not only stand-ins for the design and its expensive material, but also for the woman herself. Once the client has selected the style of her gown and settled upon the fabric she wants, the staff can cut and begin to assemble the gown, using her fitting toile as a guide. This spares the client several tedious preliminary fittings, which is very practical and good business as well. Many of these women, after all, are the sort who must consult their little books to see what continent they will be on next week.

The design muslin is more the personal tool of a great couturier than are needle and thread. He conceives dresses in his mind's eye. He may transcribe the shapes and colors of his vision to a sketch pad, or he may not. But the moment of truth comes when he confronts the human form with a bolt of muslin. He swirls the material, gathers it, drapes it, pins it up, lets it down—and in the process a gown is born.

The process continues with the dress muslin until the vision is achieved. Swirling and draping give way to progressively finer modifications. The right arm may be a centimeter longer than the left, or the left shoulder a centimeter lower than the right. The hemline may have to be angled at a slight degree so that the client's natural posture will bring it to perfect horizontal.

When the process is complete, the muslin will be a masterpiece, as impressive in its way as a real gown. Stitching lines will be marked both along the grain and on the bias. The setting of sleeves, pockets, buttons and buttonholes, godets, collars, yokes and hems will all be meticulously indicated. To the seamstress's professional eye the dress muslin will convey as much as a blueprint does to the eye of an engineer.

Just as an architect turns his blueprints over to engineers for realization, so does the couturier rely upon a specialized staff to translate a muslin into the fabric he has specified for his creation. The sewing staff of a great couture house is as hierarchical as a Byzantine convent, and almost as immune to secular notions (like unions, bargaining and the eight-hour day). From *première* (first assistant) to *petite main* ("little hand," or junior seamstress), these artisans toil unremittingly at executing their master's design without a flaw.

It is precisely that flawlessness of execution that brings elegant women to a house of haute couture. From the slick fashion magazines and from the society pages an observer might receive the impression that elegant women demand, above all, uniqueness of design. How many times have columnists served up the familiar account of some exclusive social event at which two famous women appear wearing—shudder—the same dress?

The story tells more about society editors than it does about the real connection between haute couture or high fashion and the dressmaking business. In reality, just beyond the portals of the house of couture await the minions of other trades.

As soon as a couturier's creation makes an appearance in public it is subject to duplication—being "knocked off," in the argot of the ready-to-wear industry—in a loft or factory anywhere from New York City to Taipei. The couturiers can protest, as Canute protested the incoming of the tide. Or they can acquiesce, and lend their names for a fee. Most of them take the fee.

For their part, the couturiers' regular clients know full well that their "exclusive" designs will eventually appear not just on a friend at a charity ball but on shopgirls and stenotypists as well. They are not really lured by prospects of owning a dress that no other woman will ever possess. What brings these wealthy and elegant women to the celebrated couturiers is not design alone, but meticulous attention to detail and perfection of fit. Indeed, the source of the design, far from being exclusive, may not matter at all: the house of Balmain recently executed a pair of blue jeans for a valued client—they are surely the best-fitting dungarees in Europe.

The muslin that enables couturiers to offer their clients perfect fit can be adapted for use by an amateur dressmaker at home. A woman producing a gown for herself can skip some steps the professionals often employ. If she is using a pattern, she naturally has no need for a design muslin—the designer has already made it. The fitting muslin, too, is not always essential; its record of the figure is most useful to the woman who designs her own clothes or sews many different styles by couturier methods. When a single garment is to be made from a pattern, the dress muslin alone is sufficient, and it can be produced directly by using body measurements *(pages 60-61)* to adapt the

All great couturiers have shared an obsession for perfect line and fit, but they have pursued these objectives in widely different ways. In the 1920s and '30s Madeleine Vionnet *(left)* worked with miniature design muslins on dolls. In the 1930s and '40s, Coco Chanel *(center)* put a tentative dress on a model, then redesigned it with pins. In the 1950s Jacques Fath *(right)* summoned up inspiration by swathing models in bolts of raw cloth.

purchased pattern *(pages 62-63).* The preparation of the dress muslin is well worth the effort required, partly because it prevents expensive waste of fine fabric, but mainly because it provides the superb fit demanded of the couturier dress.

The birth of a gown in rough cloth

Moving down the runway in a casually autocratic saunter, the couturier's mannequin shows off the house's latest evening gown. Its fit is perfection—which is not surprising, for the dress was constructed first in a muslin prototype that was faultlessly shaped to the model's figure.

In couture houses, the adjusting of a dress muslin is usually supervised by the chief fitter and two assistants. They painstakingly pin and baste the muslin for perfect fit *(right).* After a final inspection by the designer, the dress muslin goes to the sewing room; there, under the head cutter's vigilant eye, it is translated into the final gown. It usually takes two or three fittings before a couturier's dress muslin is finished.

Even after a dress is completed, the muslin may continue to see service: it may be sold to exclusive shops or to ready-to-wear manufacturers, who will duplicate the design in a variety of fabrics for different purposes and tastes.

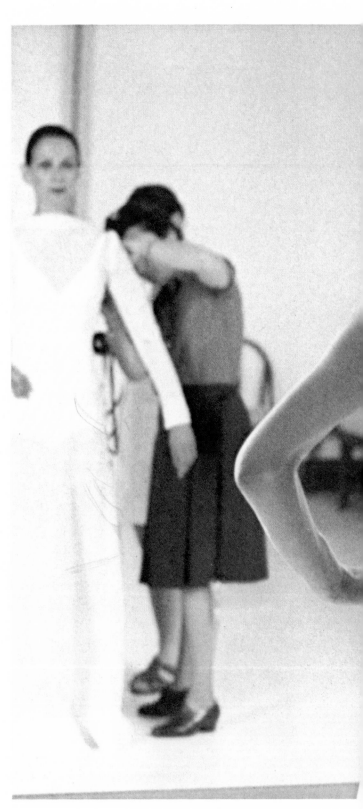

In Valentino's Rome workroom, the chief fitter pins a sleeve on a muslin for a new gown *(left)* and for its bolero jacket *(right),* which is made of darker muslin than the gown. At center, black tape on the fabric grain ensures that the bias skirt will hang properly.

Measurement: first step to precision fit

Getting a dress that you make from a commercial pattern to fit you as well as custom-made dresses fit the patrons of the great haute couture houses starts with the basic process of measuring your body.

The red and blue bands on the figures at right show the measurements that you will need for buying the pattern and for altering its pieces to get a muslin version of the garment from which the final pattern adjustments will be made. Most of these measurements are the same as those made for simple, classic garments, but some extra ones—the shoulder width and the front-waist length—are required to achieve the finer fit that is a distinguishing characteristic of couturier clothes.

The bustline is the hardest part of a dress to alter, and where several bust sizes appear likely candidates, make your choice on the basis of the other horizontal measurements listed on the pattern envelope—the waist and the hips—rather than on the vertical ones, because the vertical ones are the easiest to adjust.

When measuring, wear the same kind of undergarments that you will wear with the finished dress, and stand in a normal posture. You can take your body front and circumference measurements by yourself—checking the tape in a full-length mirror—but you will need help to measure the back of your body and your arm length.

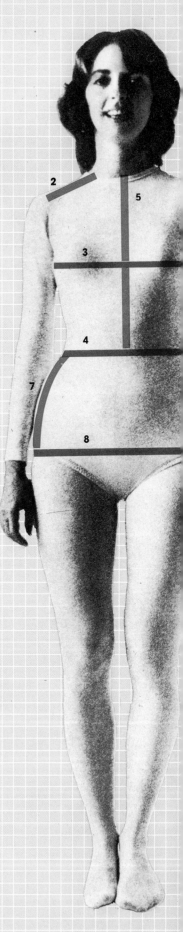

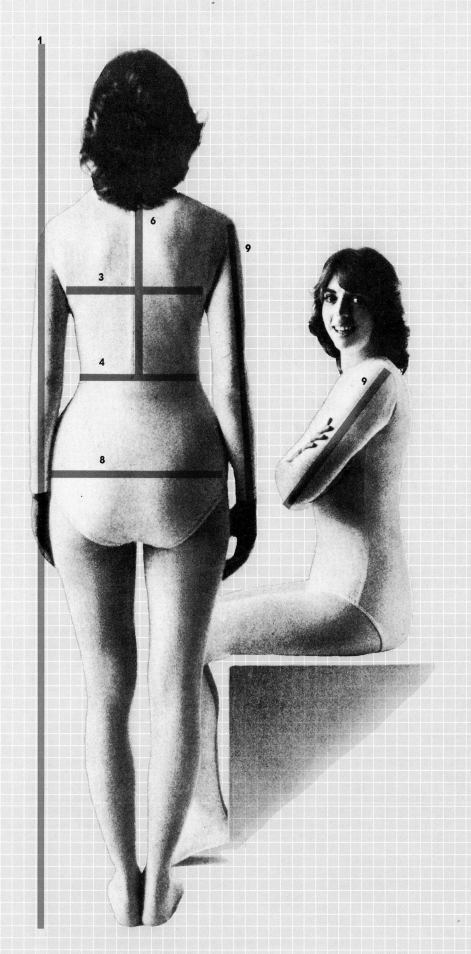

HOW TO MEASURE

Measure with the tape held snugly but not tightly against the body, following the instructions below and the guide lines on the figures at left. The red lines indicate measurements that generally appear on pattern envelopes; blue lines are the additional measurements you will need to achieve a perfect fit.

1. HEIGHT: Stand erect, without shoes, flat against a wall. Place a 12-inch ruler flat on your head and touching the wall; lightly mark the point where the ruler touches the wall. Measure from the mark to the floor.

2. SHOULDER WIDTH: Measure at the side from the base of your neck to the shoulder-bone point.

3. BUST: Measure around the fullest part of the bust with the tape horizontal in back.

4. WAIST: Tie a cord around the narrowest part of the waist and measure the circumference along the cord. Leave the cord at the waist as a guide line for other measurements.

5. FRONT-WAIST LENGTH: Measure from the center of the base of the neck above the collarbone to the center of the waistline cord.

6. BACK-WAIST LENGTH: Measure from the top of the spine to the center of the waistline cord.

7. WAIST TO HIP LENGTH: Measure at the side from the waistline cord to the fullest part of the hips; this is usually 7 to 9 inches down from the waistline.

8. FULL HIP: Measure around the fullest part of the hips, with the tape horizontal in back.

9. ARM LENGTH: Measure from the shoulder-bone point to the elbow. Then, with the elbow slightly bent, measure from the shoulder-bone point to the wristbone.

Matching the pattern to measurements

After you have taken your measurements and selected your pattern, the next step is to correct the pattern pieces so that you can make a dress muslin conforming to your measurements. Resist the temptation to hold the pieces up and fit them to your body, adding a bit here and taking a snippet there. For a custom fit, you need precise measures made as shown on the preceding pages.

The steps used to alter a custom pattern are identical to those used to alter the simplest garments. They are shown here in condensed form to indicate basic processes that can be adapted to a variety of styles; the final adjustments to achieve superlative fit are made with the help of a muslin garment sewn from the pattern *(following pages).*

Begin by trimming the pattern pieces on the cutting lines and pressing each piece. Then simply compare your body measurements with those on the pattern envelope and add or subtract the difference on the pattern piece or pieces. Depending on the style of the garment, other adjustments can be made by comparing your measurements to the pattern itself. Adjustments for horizontal measurements are made on the side seam lines of the pattern pieces; for vertical measurements, on the printed adjustment lines.

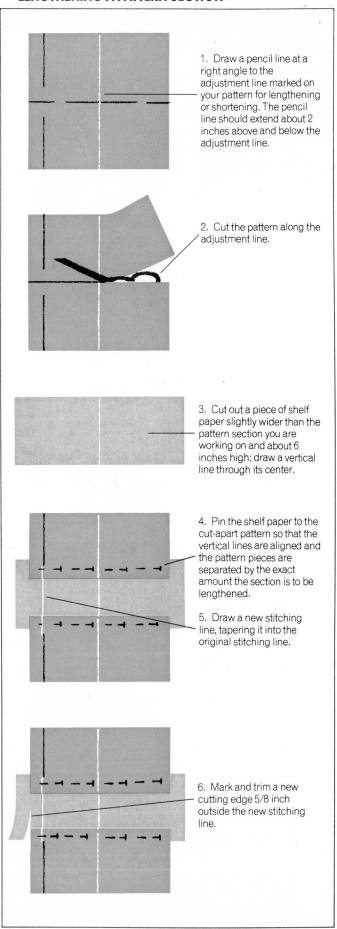

LENGTHENING A PATTERN SECTION

1. Draw a pencil line at a right angle to the adjustment line marked on your pattern for lengthening or shortening. The pencil line should extend about 2 inches above and below the adjustment line.

2. Cut the pattern along the adjustment line.

3. Cut out a piece of shelf paper slightly wider than the pattern section you are working on and about 6 inches high; draw a vertical line through its center.

4. Pin the shelf paper to the cut-apart pattern so that the vertical lines are aligned and the pattern pieces are separated by the exact amount the section is to be lengthened.

5. Draw a new stitching line, tapering it into the original stitching line.

6. Mark and trim a new cutting edge 5/8 inch outside the new stitching line.

SHORTENING A PATTERN SECTION

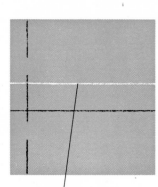

1. Draw a line above the adjustment line marked on your pattern for lengthening or shortening. The distance should be exactly equal to the amount the pattern section is to be shortened.

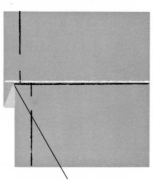

2. Fold the pattern so that the adjustment line meets the new line.

3. Press the fold flat with a warm iron.

4. Pin a paper extension to your pattern.

5. Draw a new stitching line, tapering it into the original stitching line.

6. Mark and trim a new cutting edge 5/8 inch outside the new stitching line

REDUCING A PATTERN SECTION

1. At the point where you need to reduce your pattern piece, measure in from the stitching line and mark 1/4 of the total amount to be reduced on each side seam.

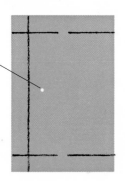

2. Draw a new stitching line, making a graduated curve from the point of reduction to the original stitching line.

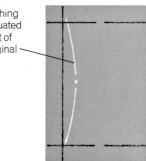

3. Mark and trim a new cutting edge 5/8 inch outside the new stitching line.

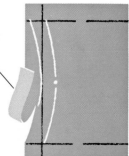

ENLARGING A PATTERN SECTION

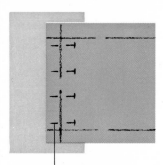

1. Lay your pattern piece on a strip of shelf paper cut to extend about 2 inches underneath the pattern and about 2 inches beyond the edge. Pin the pattern to the shelf paper.

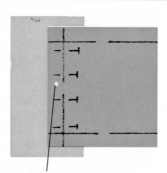

2. At the point where you need to enlarge your pattern piece, measure out from the stitching line and mark 1/4 of the total amount to be enlarged on each seam. Measure onto the seam allowance—or beyond it onto the shelf paper, if necessary.

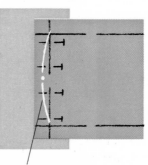

3. Draw a new tapered stitching line from the point of enlargement into the original stitching line.

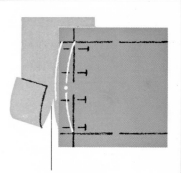

4. Mark and trim a new cutting edge 5/8 inch outside the new stitching line.

Matching the pattern to the muslin

Measuring yourself and altering the paper pieces to match are the first two steps in personalizing a pattern. The next step is to make up the garment in inexpensive muslin—using machine basting that is easy to change—so that you can try on the muslin version of the pattern and see how well it follows the contours of your body. Working from muslin to paper and then back, you can adjust the pattern seam by seam, eliminating imperfections with the techniques shown on the following pages, until it fits you as if it were couturier-made.

Since a dress hangs from its shoulder seams, start the fitting there and work down; adjusting one seam at a time with pins, re-baste, then try on again. After completing each alteration in a seam of the muslin, transfer the revision onto the paper pattern with pins and a pencil; later alterations may make it necessary to readjust alterations made earlier. When the muslin fits impeccably and the grain lines fall straight, you can safely ink in and tape down the revisions on the paper pattern.

The dress fabric, of course, may drape differently from the muslin and require further changes at the basting stage, but making the major fitting adjustments on the muslin makes certain that these final corrections will be minor ones.

IF THE INSET-SLEEVE SHOULDER IS LOOSE...

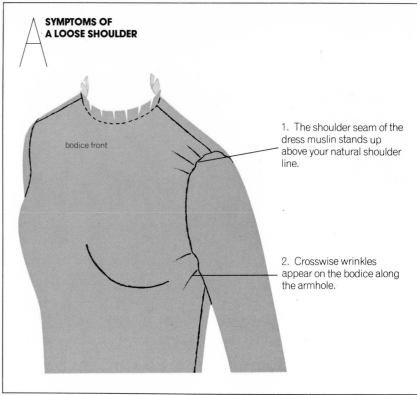

A SYMPTOMS OF A LOOSE SHOULDER

bodice front

1. The shoulder seam of the dress muslin stands up above your natural shoulder line.

2. Crosswise wrinkles appear on the bodice along the armhole.

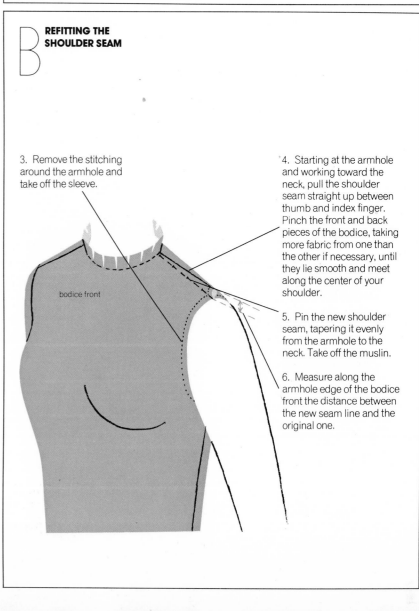

B REFITTING THE SHOULDER SEAM

3. Remove the stitching around the armhole and take off the sleeve.

bodice front

4. Starting at the armhole and working toward the neck, pull the shoulder seam straight up between thumb and index finger. Pinch the front and back pieces of the bodice, taking more fabric from one than the other if necessary, until they lie smooth and meet along the center of your shoulder.

5. Pin the new shoulder seam, tapering it evenly from the armhole to the neck. Take off the muslin.

6. Measure along the armhole edge of the bodice front the distance between the new seam line and the original one.

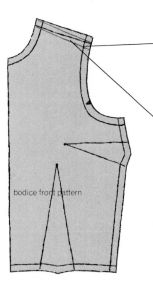

bodice front pattern

7. Measure the distance found in Step 6 down from the original shoulder seam line on the bodice front pattern and pencil a dot.

8. Draw a new seam line from the dot to the point where the old seam line meets the neck seam line. Draw a new cutting line 5/8 inch outside the new seam line and parallel to it.

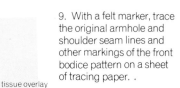

tissue overlay

9. With a felt marker, trace the original armhole and shoulder seam lines and other markings of the front bodice pattern on a sheet of tracing paper. .

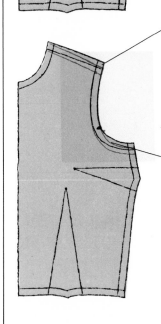

10. Slide the tracing of the armhole under the pattern and align the shoulder seam line of the tracing with the new shoulder seam line on the pattern, matching the side seam edge of the tracing to the side seam of the pattern.

11. Following the line on the tracing paper, draw a new armhole seam line, complete with pattern markings, lower than the original one—on the bodice front pattern. Then draw a new cutting line 5/8 inch outside the new seam line and parallel to it.

12. Repeat Steps 6-11 on the bodice back pattern.

13. Using the revised armhole seam and cutting lines, re-cut the armhole of the dress muslin and baste the sleeve into the revised armhole.

IF THE RAGLAN-SLEEVE SHOULDER IS LOOSE...

A SYMPTOMS OF A LOOSE SHOULDER

1. The shoulder dart of the dress muslin stands up above your natural shoulder line.

2. Crosswise wrinkles appear below the shoulder dart near the arm.

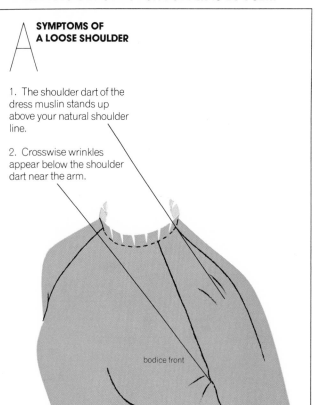

bodice front

B REFITTING THE SHOULDER DART

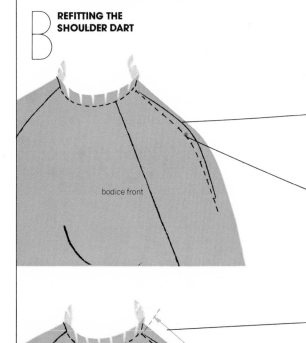

bodice front

3. Starting at the point of the shoulder and working toward the neck, pull the shoulder dart straight up between thumb and index finger. Pinch the front and back of the sleeve together, taking more fabric from one than the other if necessary, until they lie smooth and meet along the center of your shoulder.

4. Pin the new shoulder dart seam, tapering it first from the shoulder point to the neck and then from the shoulder point down the arm, lengthening the dart until the curve at the shoulder is smooth. Pencil a dot at the shoulder point. Take off the muslin.

5. Measure along the pin markings made in Step 4 from the neck seam line to the shoulder point.

6. At the shoulder point, measure from the pin marking to the original seam line on both the front and the back of the sleeve.

7. Measure from the point of the original dart to the new dart point.

continued

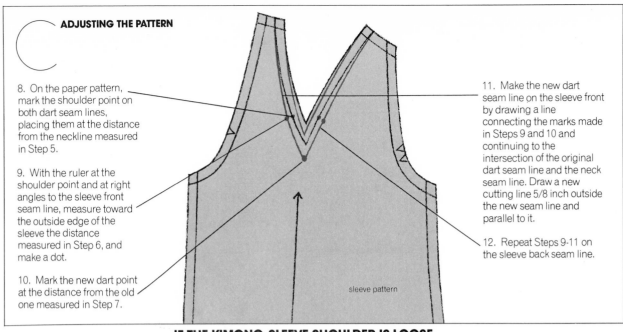

C ADJUSTING THE PATTERN

8. On the paper pattern, mark the shoulder point on both dart seam lines, placing them at the distance from the neckline measured in Step 5.

9. With the ruler at the shoulder point and at right angles to the sleeve front seam line, measure toward the outside edge of the sleeve the distance measured in Step 6, and make a dot.

10. Mark the new dart point at the distance from the old one measured in Step 7.

11. Make the new dart seam line on the sleeve front by drawing a line connecting the marks made in Steps 9 and 10 and continuing to the intersection of the original dart seam line and the neck seam line. Draw a new cutting line 5/8 inch outside the new seam line and parallel to it.

12. Repeat Steps 9-11 on the sleeve back seam line.

sleeve pattern

IF THE KIMONO-SLEEVE SHOULDER IS LOOSE...

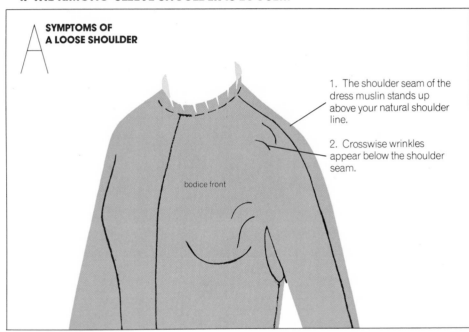

A SYMPTOMS OF A LOOSE SHOULDER

1. The shoulder seam of the dress muslin stands up above your natural shoulder line.

2. Crosswise wrinkles appear below the shoulder seam.

bodice front

B REFITTING THE SHOULDER SEAM

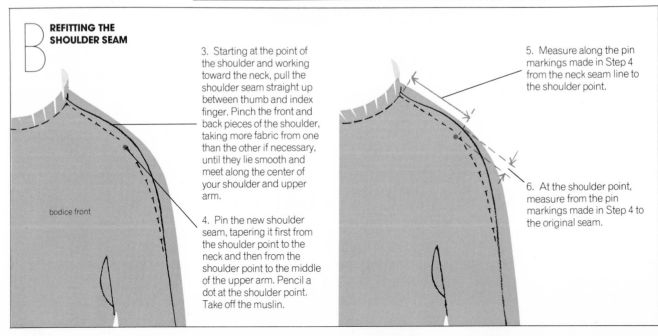

3. Starting at the point of the shoulder and working toward the neck, pull the shoulder seam straight up between thumb and index finger. Pinch the front and back pieces of the shoulder, taking more fabric from one than the other if necessary, until they lie smooth and meet along the center of your shoulder and upper arm.

4. Pin the new shoulder seam, tapering it first from the shoulder point to the neck and then from the shoulder point to the middle of the upper arm. Pencil a dot at the shoulder point. Take off the muslin.

5. Measure along the pin markings made in Step 4 from the neck seam line to the shoulder point.

6. At the shoulder point, measure from the pin markings made in Step 4 to the original seam.

bodice front

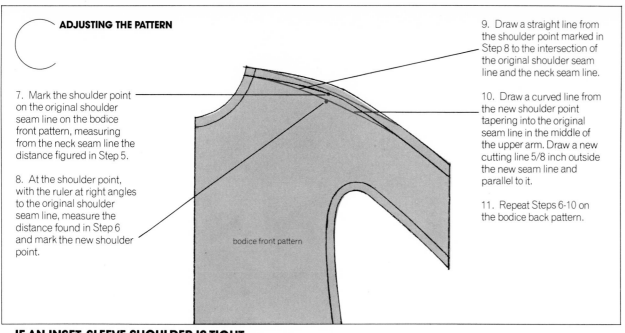

C ADJUSTING THE PATTERN

7. Mark the shoulder point on the original shoulder seam line on the bodice front pattern, measuring from the neck seam line the distance figured in Step 5.

8. At the shoulder point, with the ruler at right angles to the original shoulder seam line, measure the distance found in Step 6 and mark the new shoulder point.

bodice front pattern

9. Draw a straight line from the shoulder point marked in Step 8 to the intersection of the original shoulder seam line and the neck seam line.

10. Draw a curved line from the new shoulder point tapering into the original seam line in the middle of the upper arm. Draw a new cutting line 5/8 inch outside the new seam line and parallel to it.

11. Repeat Steps 6-10 on the bodice back pattern.

IF AN INSET-SLEEVE SHOULDER IS TIGHT...

A SYMPTOMS OF A TIGHT SHOULDER

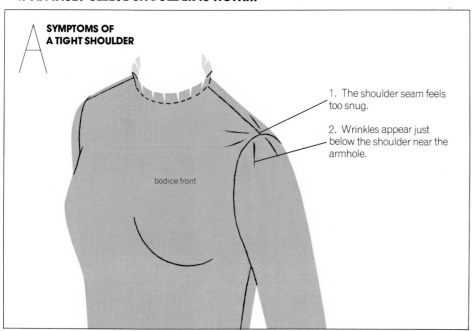

bodice front

1. The shoulder seam feels too snug.

2. Wrinkles appear just below the shoulder near the armhole.

B REFITTING THE SHOULDER SEAM

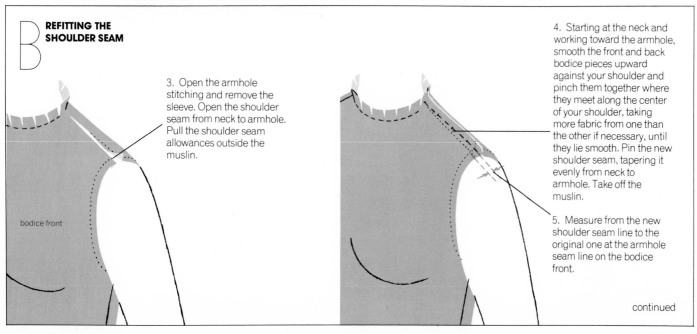

bodice front

3. Open the armhole stitching and remove the sleeve. Open the shoulder seam from neck to armhole. Pull the shoulder seam allowances outside the muslin.

4. Starting at the neck and working toward the armhole, smooth the front and back bodice pieces upward against your shoulder and pinch them together where they meet along the center of your shoulder, taking more fabric from one than the other if necessary, until they lie smooth. Pin the new shoulder seam, tapering it evenly from neck to armhole. Take off the muslin.

5. Measure from the new shoulder seam line to the original one at the armhole seam line on the bodice front.

continued

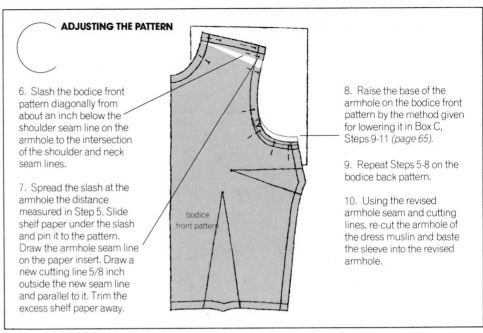

C ADJUSTING THE PATTERN

6. Slash the bodice front pattern diagonally from about an inch below the shoulder seam line on the armhole to the intersection of the shoulder and neck seam lines.

7. Spread the slash at the armhole the distance measured in Step 5. Slide shelf paper under the slash and pin it to the pattern. Draw the armhole seam line on the paper insert. Draw a new cutting line 5/8 inch outside the new seam line and parallel to it. Trim the excess shelf paper away.

8. Raise the base of the armhole on the bodice front pattern by the method given for lowering it in Box C, Steps 9-11 (page 65).

9. Repeat Steps 5-8 on the bodice back pattern.

10. Using the revised armhole seam and cutting lines, re-cut the armhole of the dress muslin and baste the sleeve into the revised armhole.

IF THE RAGLAN-SLEEVE SHOULDER IS TIGHT...

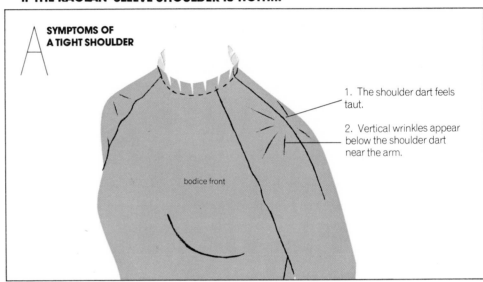

A SYMPTOMS OF A TIGHT SHOULDER

1. The shoulder dart feels taut.

2. Vertical wrinkles appear below the shoulder dart near the arm.

B REFITTING THE SHOULDER DART

3. Open the shoulder dart and pull the seam allowances outside the muslin.

4. Starting at the neck and working toward the arm, smooth the front and back of the sleeve upward against your shoulder and pinch them together, taking more fabric from one side than the other if necessary, until both lie smooth and meet along the center of your shoulder.

5. Pin the new shoulder dart seam, tapering it first from the neck to the shoulder point and then from the shoulder point down the arm, shortening the original dart until the curve at the shoulder is smooth. Pencil a dot at the shoulder point. Take off the muslin.

6. Measure along the new shoulder dart seam line from the neck seam line to the shoulder point.

7. Measure from the point of the original dart to the end of the new dart.

8. With the ruler at the shoulder point and at right angles to the new dart, measure from the new dart to the original one on both the front and back of the sleeve.

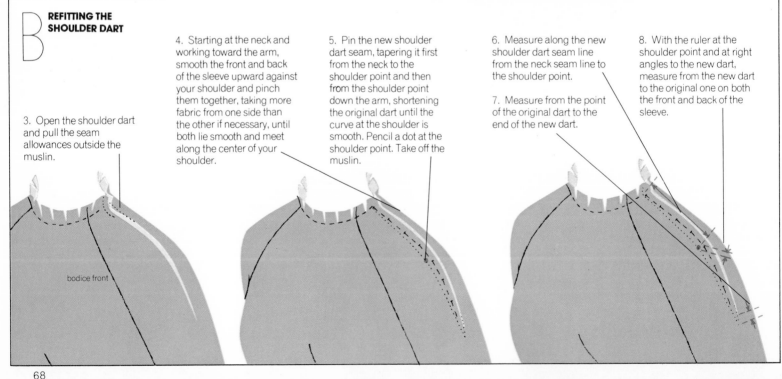

C ADJUSTING THE PATTERN

9. Measure on the pattern the distance measured in Step 6 on each original dart seam line to mark the shoulder points.

10. With the ruler at right angles to the dart seam line, measure outside the line from each shoulder point the distance measured in Step 8 and make new dots.

11. Measure from the original dart point the distance measured in Step 7 and mark the new dart point.

12. Slide shelf paper under the dart area and pin it to the pattern. Draw the new dart seam lines from the intersections of the original dart seam lines with the neck seam lines through the new shoulder points marked in Step 10, and then to the new dart point made in Step 11.

13. Draw new cutting lines 5/8 inch outside the new dart seam lines and parallel to them. Trim away excess shelf paper.

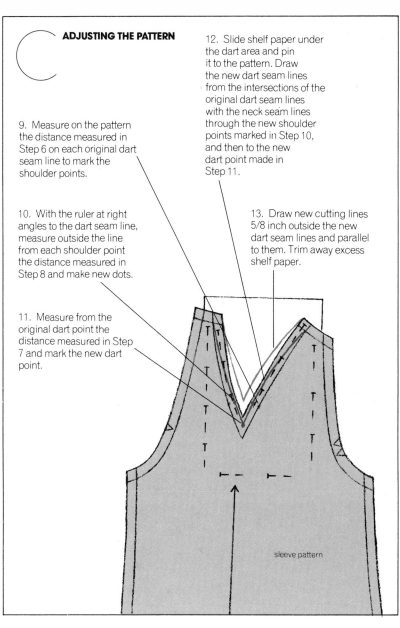

sleeve pattern

IF THE KIMONO-SLEEVE SHOULDER IS TIGHT...

A SYMPTOMS OF A TIGHT SHOULDER

1. The muslin binds the shoulder near the upper arm.

2. Vertical wrinkles appear below the shoulder point.

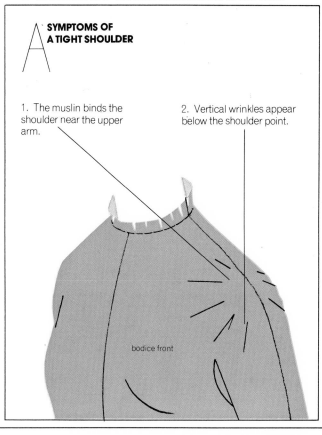

bodice front

B REFITTING THE SHOULDER SEAM

3. Open the shoulder seam from the neck to the bottom edge of the sleeve. Pull the shoulder seam allowances outside the muslin.

4. Starting at the neck and working over the shoulder to the upper arm, smooth the front and back bodice pieces upward and pinch the seam allowances together, taking more fabric from one side than the other if necessary, until both pieces lie smooth and meet along the center of your shoulder.

5. Pin the new shoulder seam, tapering it first from the neck to the shoulder point and then from the shoulder point into the original seam line in the middle of the upper arm. Pencil a dot at the shoulder point. Take off the muslin.

6. Measure along the new shoulder seam from the neck seam line to the shoulder point.

7. At the shoulder point measure the distance between the new shoulder seam line and the original seam line.

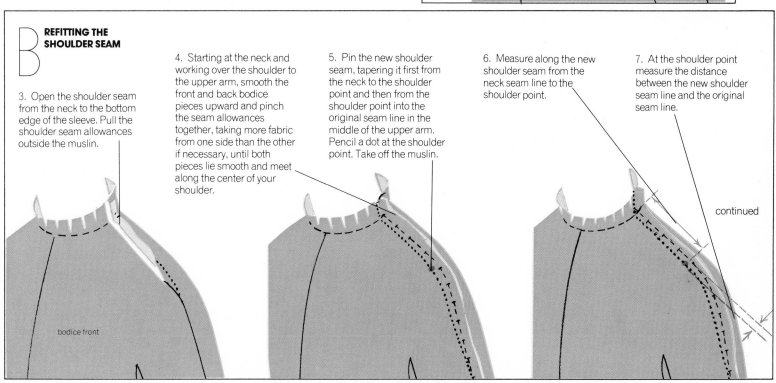

bodice front

continued

ADJUSTING THE PATTERN

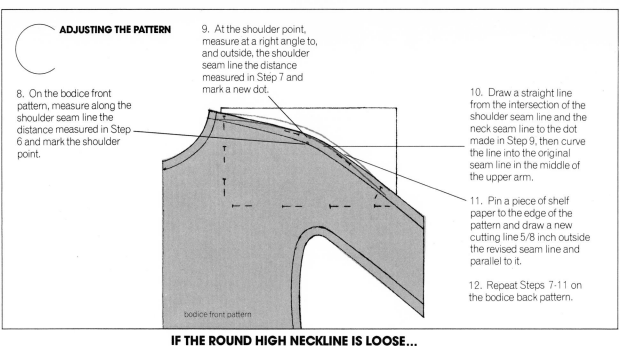

8. On the bodice front pattern, measure along the shoulder seam line the distance measured in Step 6 and mark the shoulder point.

9. At the shoulder point, measure at a right angle to, and outside, the shoulder seam line the distance measured in Step 7 and mark a new dot.

10. Draw a straight line from the intersection of the shoulder seam line and the neck seam line to the dot made in Step 9, then curve the line into the original seam line in the middle of the upper arm.

11. Pin a piece of shelf paper to the edge of the pattern and draw a new cutting line 5/8 inch outside the revised seam line and parallel to it.

12. Repeat Steps 7-11 on the bodice back pattern.

bodice front pattern

IF THE ROUND HIGH NECKLINE IS LOOSE...

SYMPTOMS OF A LOOSE NECKLINE

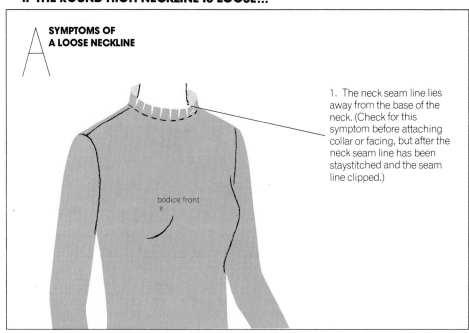

1. The neck seam line lies away from the base of the neck. (Check for this symptom before attaching collar or facing, but after the neck seam line has been staystitched and the seam line clipped.)

bodice front

REFITTING THE NECKLINE

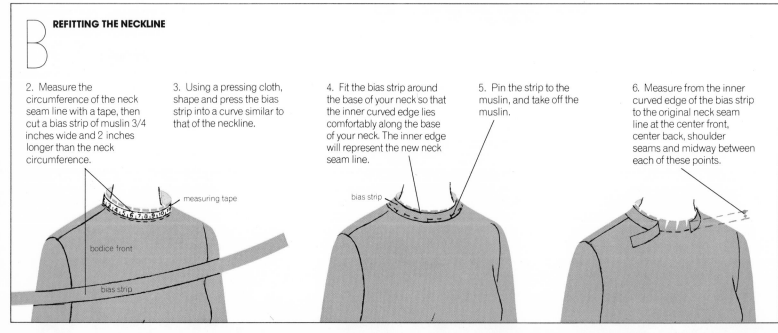

2. Measure the circumference of the neck seam line with a tape, then cut a bias strip of muslin 3/4 inches wide and 2 inches longer than the neck circumference.

3. Using a pressing cloth, shape and press the bias strip into a curve similar to that of the neckline.

4. Fit the bias strip around the base of your neck so that the inner curved edge lies comfortably along the base of your neck. The inner edge will represent the new neck seam line.

5. Pin the strip to the muslin, and take off the muslin.

6. Measure from the inner curved edge of the bias strip to the original neck seam line at the center front, center back, shoulder seams and midway between each of these points.

bodice front

bias strip

measuring tape

bias strip

ADJUSTING THE PATTERN

C

7. Pin a piece of shelf paper under the neckline of the bodice front pattern.

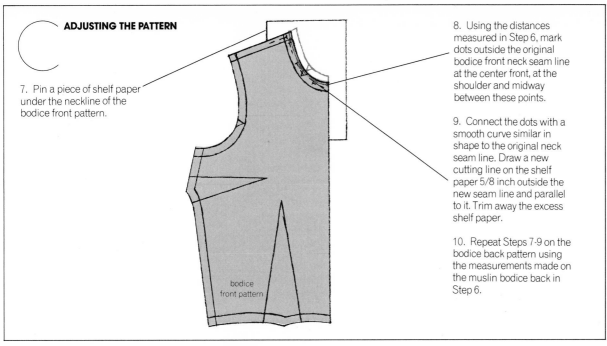

bodice
front pattern

8. Using the distances measured in Step 6, mark dots outside the original bodice front neck seam line at the center front, at the shoulder and midway between these points.

9. Connect the dots with a smooth curve similar in shape to the original neck seam line. Draw a new cutting line on the shelf paper 5/8 inch outside the new seam line and parallel to it. Trim away the excess shelf paper.

10. Repeat Steps 7-9 on the bodice back pattern using the measurements made on the muslin bodice back in Step 6.

IF THE ROUND HIGH NECKLINE IS TIGHT...

A **SYMPTOMS OF A TIGHT NECKLINE**

1. The neck is tight in the front, back, or both places. (Check for this symptom before attaching the collar or facing, but after the neck seam line has been staystitched and the seam allowance clipped.)

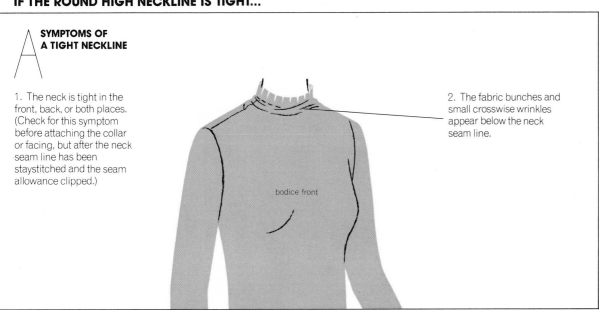

bodice front

2. The fabric bunches and small crosswise wrinkles appear below the neck seam line.

B **REFITTING THE NECKLINE**

3. Starting at the center front and working around the neckline, clip through the machine stitching on the neck seam line at 1/2-inch intervals.

4. Taking tiny cuts each time, gradually extend the depth of the clips around the neckline until the muslin lies comfortably along the base of your neck and the wrinkles disappear.

5. Draw a new neck seam line directly on the muslin around the bottom ends of the clips. Take off the muslin.

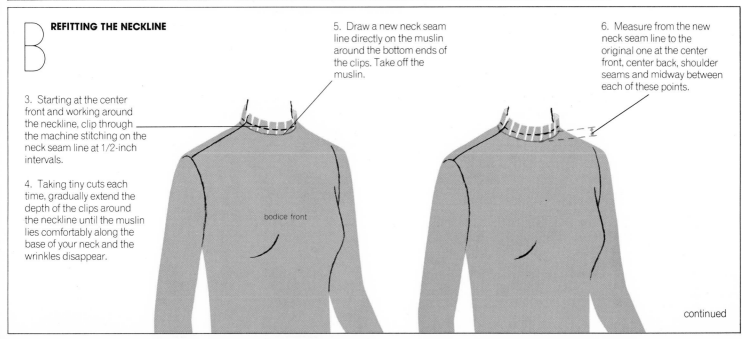

bodice front

6. Measure from the new neck seam line to the original one at the center front, center back, shoulder seams and midway between each of these points.

continued

ADJUSTING THE PATTERN

C

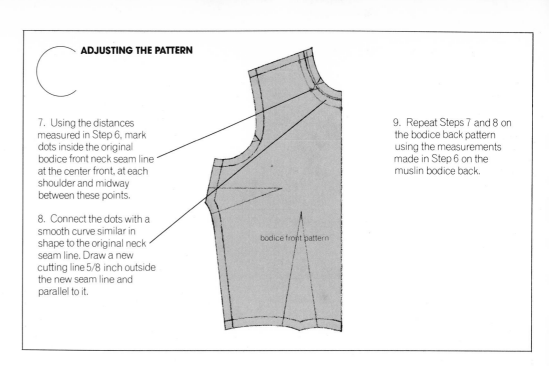

7. Using the distances measured in Step 6, mark dots inside the original bodice front neck seam line at the center front, at each shoulder and midway between these points.

8. Connect the dots with a smooth curve similar in shape to the original neck seam line. Draw a new cutting line 5/8 inch outside the new seam line and parallel to it.

9. Repeat Steps 7 and 8 on the bodice back pattern using the measurements made in Step 6 on the muslin bodice back.

bodice front pattern

IF THE UPPER BACK IS TIGHT...

A SYMPTOMS OF A TIGHT UPPER BACK

1. The back of the bodice feels snug over the shoulder.

2. The neckline stands away from the back of your neck.

3. Wrinkles radiate from the upper back toward the armholes.

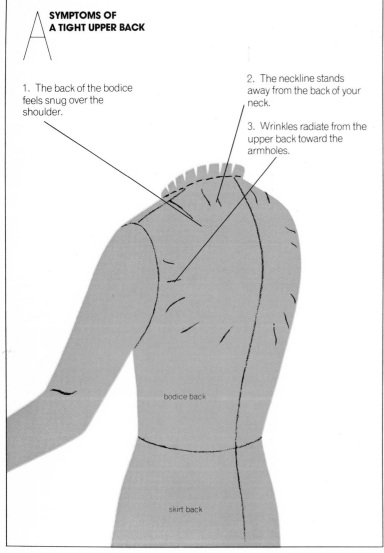

bodice back

skirt back

B REFITTING THE TIGHT UPPER BACK

4. Take off the muslin. Cut horizontally from the tip of one shoulder dart across the back to the tip of the other, then extend the slash from the darts horizontally to each armhole seam line. Put the muslin on again.

5. Slip an insert of muslin under the slash and spread the slashed edges of the bodice back apart until the dress feels comfortable.

6. Pin the cut edges of the slash to the muslin insert. Take off the muslin.

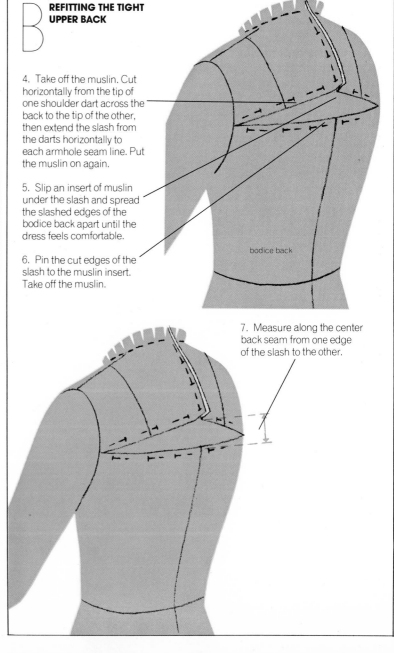

bodice back

7. Measure along the center back seam from one edge of the slash to the other.

8. With the ruler at the point of the back shoulder dart and at a right angle to the center back line, draw a line from the center back through the point of the dart to the armhole seam line. Cut along this line.

9. Cut the back shoulder dart down the center from the shoulder cutting line to within 1/8 inch of the point.

10. Cut a square insert of shelf paper, center it under the top of the bodice back pattern, and pin the pattern to the paper below the horizontal slash.

11. Lift the upper section of the pattern out of the way. Extend the center back line of the bottom section onto the shelf paper 6 inches above the horizontal slash.

12. Measure on the insert along the center back line from the horizontal slash the distance measured in Step 7; mark with a dot.

13. Place the upper pattern section over the insert, aligning the center back line with the line on the insert, and the slashed edge of the pattern section with the dot made in Step 12.

14. Pin the top of the pattern flat against the insert, first along the center back line, then along the edges of the back shoulder dart, which will have spread to form a dart wider than the original one. Finally, pin along the upper edge of the horizontal slash.

15. Draw a new shoulder cutting line by extending the original cutting lines until they intersect in an inverted V above the center of the widened dart. Trim away excess shelf paper.

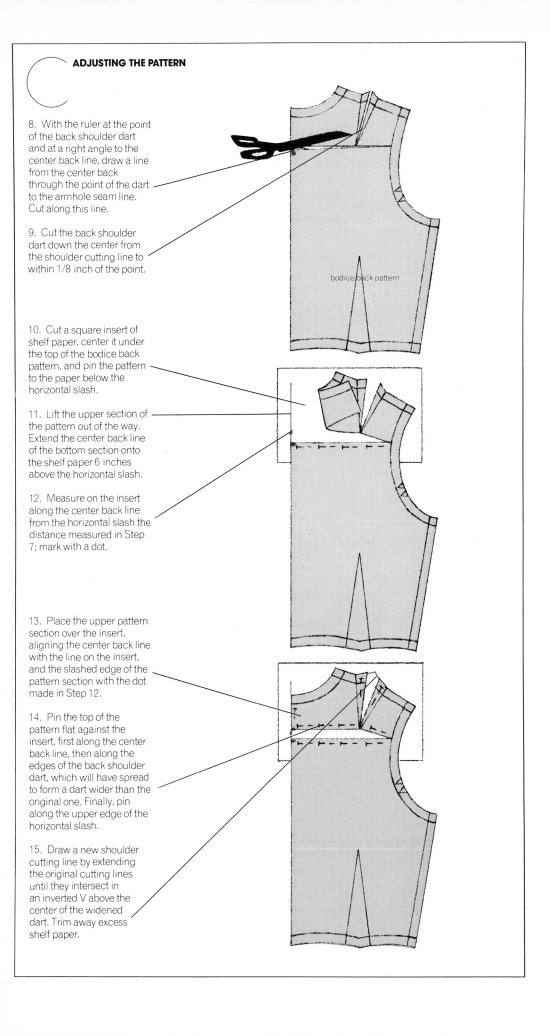

bodice back pattern

IF THE INSET-SLEEVE TOP IS LOOSE...

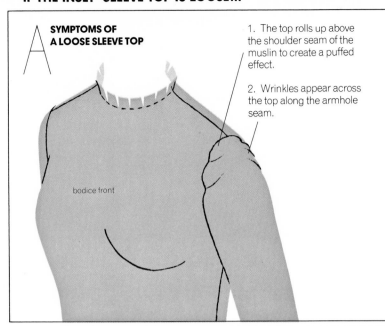

A SYMPTOMS OF A LOOSE SLEEVE TOP

1. The top rolls up above the shoulder seam of the muslin to create a puffed effect.

2. Wrinkles appear across the top along the armhole seam.

bodice front

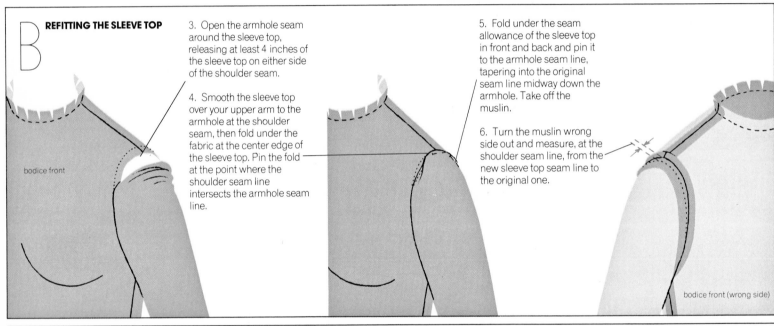

B REFITTING THE SLEEVE TOP

3. Open the armhole seam around the sleeve top, releasing at least 4 inches of the sleeve top on either side of the shoulder seam.

4. Smooth the sleeve top over your upper arm to the armhole at the shoulder seam, then fold under the fabric at the center edge of the sleeve top. Pin the fold at the point where the shoulder seam line intersects the armhole seam line.

5. Fold under the seam allowance of the sleeve top in front and back and pin it to the armhole seam line, tapering into the original seam line midway down the armhole. Take off the muslin.

6. Turn the muslin wrong side out and measure, at the shoulder seam line, from the new sleeve top seam line to the original one.

bodice front

bodice front (wrong side)

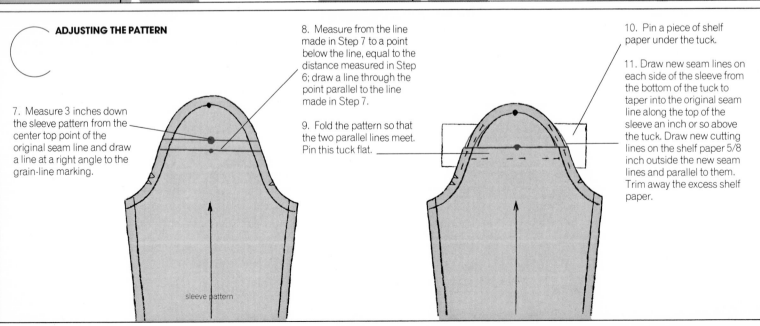

C ADJUSTING THE PATTERN

7. Measure 3 inches down the sleeve pattern from the center top point of the original seam line and draw a line at a right angle to the grain-line marking.

8. Measure from the line made in Step 7 to a point below the line, equal to the distance measured in Step 6; draw a line through the point parallel to the line made in Step 7.

9. Fold the pattern so that the two parallel lines meet. Pin this tuck flat.

10. Pin a piece of shelf paper under the tuck.

11. Draw new seam lines on each side of the sleeve from the bottom of the tuck to taper into the original seam line along the top of the sleeve an inch or so above the tuck. Draw new cutting lines on the shelf paper 5/8 inch outside the new seam lines and parallel to them. Trim away the excess shelf paper.

sleeve pattern

IF THE RAGLAN-SLEEVE TOP IS LOOSE...

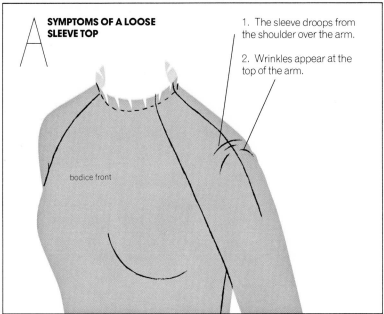

A **SYMPTOMS OF A LOOSE SLEEVE TOP**

1. The sleeve droops from the shoulder over the arm.

2. Wrinkles appear at the top of the arm.

bodice front

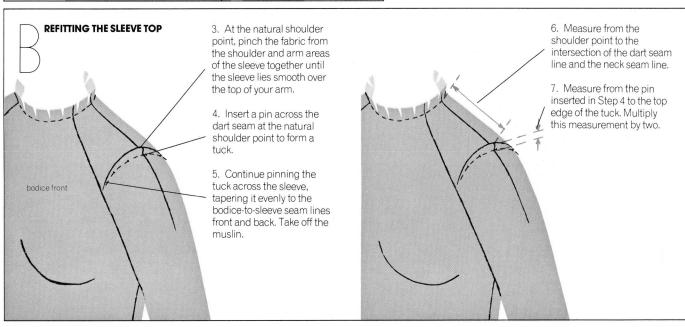

B **REFITTING THE SLEEVE TOP**

3. At the natural shoulder point, pinch the fabric from the shoulder and arm areas of the sleeve together until the sleeve lies smooth over the top of your arm.

4. Insert a pin across the dart seam at the natural shoulder point to form a tuck.

5. Continue pinning the tuck across the sleeve, tapering it evenly to the bodice-to-sleeve seam lines front and back. Take off the muslin.

bodice front

6. Measure from the shoulder point to the intersection of the dart seam line and the neck seam line.

7. Measure from the pin inserted in Step 4 to the top edge of the tuck. Multiply this measurement by two.

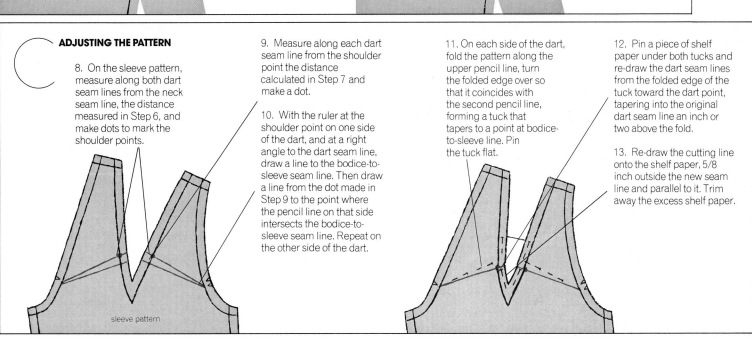

C **ADJUSTING THE PATTERN**

8. On the sleeve pattern, measure along both dart seam lines from the neck seam line, the distance measured in Step 6, and make dots to mark the shoulder points.

9. Measure along each dart seam line from the shoulder point the distance calculated in Step 7 and make a dot.

10. With the ruler at the shoulder point on one side of the dart, and at a right angle to the dart seam line, draw a line to the bodice-to-sleeve seam line. Then draw a line from the dot made in Step 9 to the point where the pencil line on that side intersects the bodice-to-sleeve seam line. Repeat on the other side of the dart.

11. On each side of the dart, fold the pattern along the upper pencil line, turn the folded edge over so that it coincides with the second pencil line, forming a tuck that tapers to a point at bodice-to-sleeve line. Pin the tuck flat.

12. Pin a piece of shelf paper under both tucks and re-draw the dart seam lines from the folded edge of the tuck toward the dart point, tapering into the original dart seam line an inch or two above the fold.

13. Re-draw the cutting line onto the shelf paper, 5/8 inch outside the new seam line and parallel to it. Trim away the excess shelf paper.

sleeve pattern

IF THE KIMONO-SLEEVE TOP IS LOOSE...

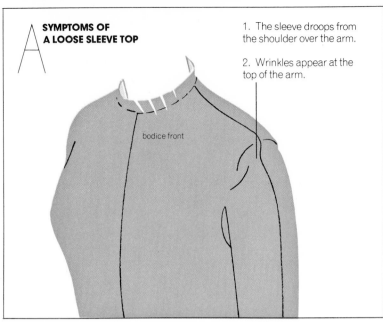

A **SYMPTOMS OF A LOOSE SLEEVE TOP**

1. The sleeve droops from the shoulder over the arm.

2. Wrinkles appear at the top of the arm.

bodice front

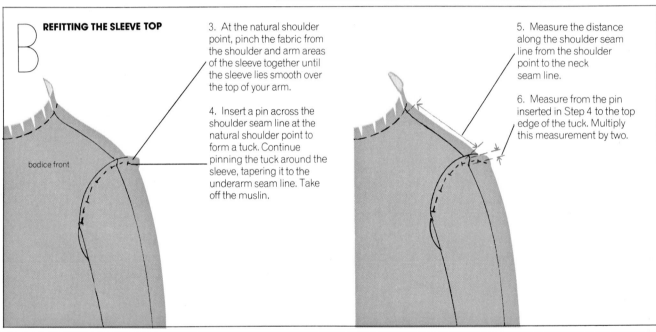

B **REFITTING THE SLEEVE TOP**

3. At the natural shoulder point, pinch the fabric from the shoulder and arm areas of the sleeve together until the sleeve lies smooth over the top of your arm.

4. Insert a pin across the shoulder seam line at the natural shoulder point to form a tuck. Continue pinning the tuck around the sleeve, tapering it to the underarm seam line. Take off the muslin.

5. Measure the distance along the shoulder seam line from the shoulder point to the neck seam line.

6. Measure from the pin inserted in Step 4 to the top edge of the tuck. Multiply this measurement by two.

bodice front

C **ADJUSTING THE PATTERN**

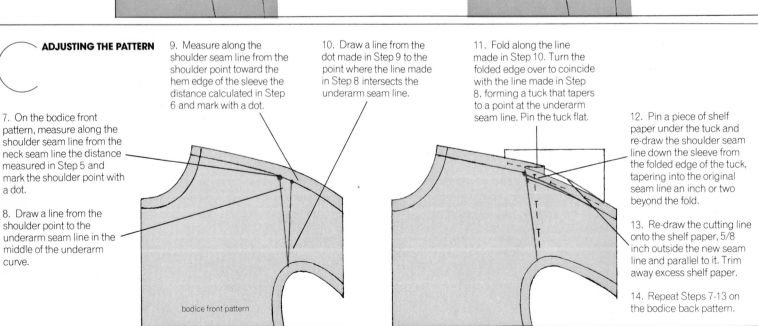

9. Measure along the shoulder seam line from the shoulder point toward the hem edge of the sleeve the distance calculated in Step 6 and mark with a dot.

10. Draw a line from the dot made in Step 9 to the point where the line made in Step 8 intersects the underarm seam line.

11. Fold along the line made in Step 10. Turn the folded edge over to coincide with the line made in Step 8, forming a tuck that tapers to a point at the underarm seam line. Pin the tuck flat.

7. On the bodice front pattern, measure along the shoulder seam line from the neck seam line the distance measured in Step 5 and mark the shoulder point with a dot.

8. Draw a line from the shoulder point to the underarm seam line in the middle of the underarm curve.

12. Pin a piece of shelf paper under the tuck and re-draw the shoulder seam line down the sleeve from the folded edge of the tuck, tapering into the original seam line an inch or two beyond the fold.

13. Re-draw the cutting line onto the shelf paper, 5/8 inch outside the new seam line and parallel to it. Trim away excess shelf paper.

14. Repeat Steps 7-13 on the bodice back pattern.

bodice front pattern

IF THE INSET-SLEEVE TOP IS TIGHT...

A SYMPTOMS OF A TIGHT SLEEVE TOP

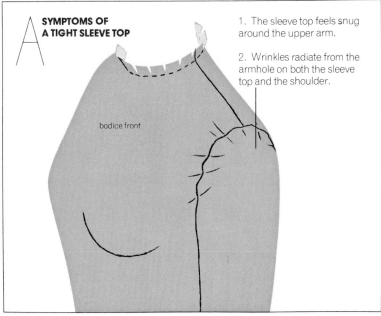

bodice front

1. The sleeve top feels snug around the upper arm.

2. Wrinkles radiate from the armhole on both the sleeve top and the shoulder.

B REFITTING THE SLEEVE TOP

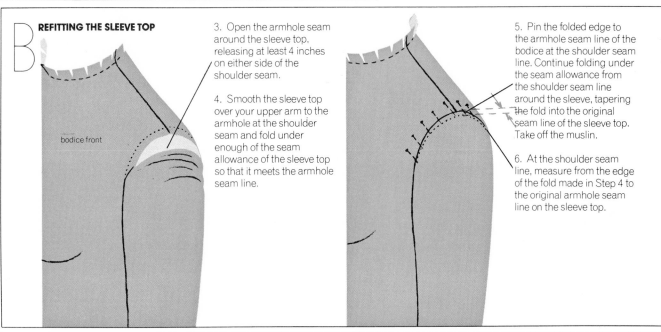

bodice front

3. Open the armhole seam around the sleeve top, releasing at least 4 inches on either side of the shoulder seam.

4. Smooth the sleeve top over your upper arm to the armhole at the shoulder seam and fold under enough of the seam allowance of the sleeve top so that it meets the armhole seam line.

5. Pin the folded edge to the armhole seam line of the bodice at the shoulder seam line. Continue folding under the seam allowance from the shoulder seam line around the sleeve, tapering the fold into the original seam line of the sleeve top. Take off the muslin.

6. At the shoulder seam line, measure from the edge of the fold made in Step 4 to the original armhole seam line on the sleeve top.

C ADJUSTING THE PATTERN

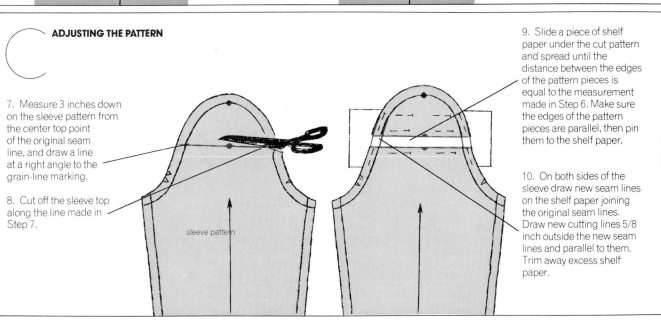

sleeve pattern

7. Measure 3 inches down on the sleeve pattern from the center top point of the original seam line, and draw a line at a right angle to the grain-line marking.

8. Cut off the sleeve top along the line made in Step 7.

9. Slide a piece of shelf paper under the cut pattern and spread until the distance between the edges of the pattern pieces is equal to the measurement made in Step 6. Make sure the edges of the pattern pieces are parallel, then pin them to the shelf paper.

10. On both sides of the sleeve draw new seam lines on the shelf paper joining the original seam lines. Draw new cutting lines 5/8 inch outside the new seam lines and parallel to them. Trim away excess shelf paper.

IF THE RAGLAN-SLEEVE TOP IS TIGHT...

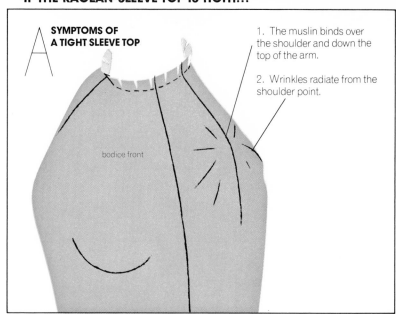

A SYMPTOMS OF A TIGHT SLEEVE TOP

1. The muslin binds over the shoulder and down the top of the arm.

2. Wrinkles radiate from the shoulder point.

bodice front

B REFITTING THE SHOULDER DART

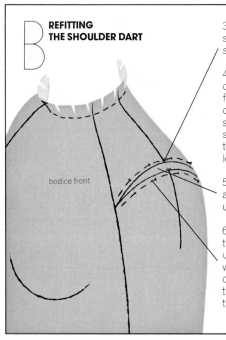

bodice front

3. Mark the natural shoulder point on the shoulder dart seam.

4. Take off the muslin and cut around the shoulder from the shoulder point down the front of the shoulder to the front sleeve seam, then down the back to the back sleeve seam, leaving the seams intact.

5. Put the muslin back on, and slip an insert of muslin under the slash.

6. Slide the arm section of the sleeve down your arm until it lies smooth and all wrinkles disappear. Pin the cut edges of the sleeve to the muslin insert. Take off the muslin.

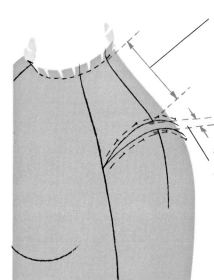

7. Measure along the shoulder dart seam line from the neck seam line to the upper edge of the slash.

8. Measure the distance between the cut edges of the slash in the sleeve at the shoulder dart seam line.

C ADJUSTING THE PATTERN

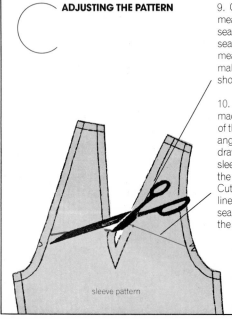

sleeve pattern

9. On the sleeve pattern, measure along both dart seam lines from the neck seam line, the distance measured in Step 7 and make dots to mark the shoulder point.

10. With the ruler at the dot made in Step 9 on one side of the dart, and at a right angle to the dart seam line, draw a line to the bodice-to-sleeve seam line. Repeat on the other side of the dart. Cut the pattern along these lines to the bodice-to-sleeve seam lines, but do not cut the pattern apart.

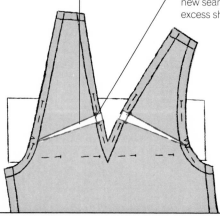

11. Slide an insert of shelf paper under both slashes and spread the cut edges apart until the distances between the edges of each slash match the measurement made in Step 8.

12. Pin the insert in place. Draw dart seam lines on both sides of the dart on the shelf paper, connecting the original dart seam lines on the pattern. Draw new cutting lines 5/8 inch outside and parallel to the new seam lines. Trim away excess shelf paper.

IF THE KIMONO-SLEEVE TOP IS TIGHT...

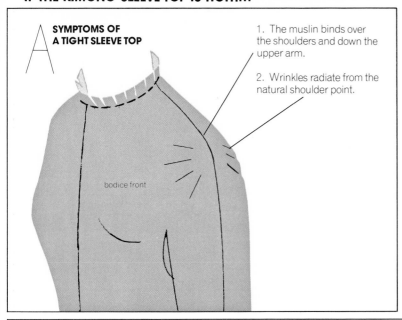

A SYMPTOMS OF A TIGHT SLEEVE TOP

1. The muslin binds over the shoulders and down the upper arm.

2. Wrinkles radiate from the natural shoulder point.

bodice front

B REFITTING THE SLEEVE TOP

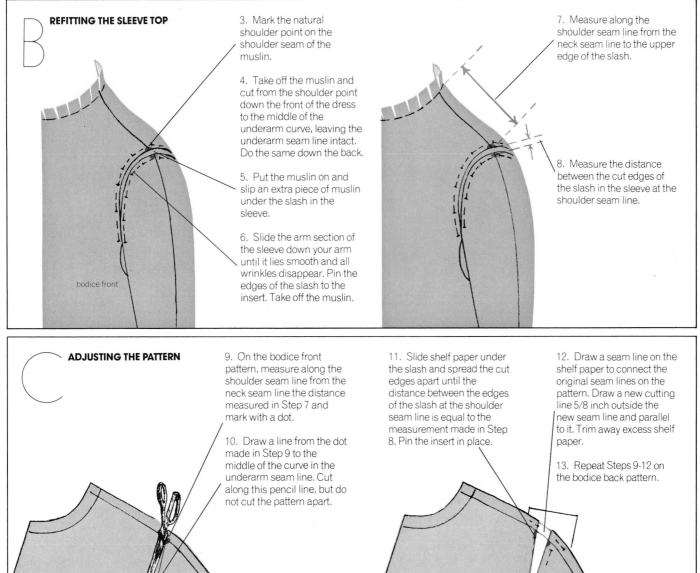

3. Mark the natural shoulder point on the shoulder seam of the muslin.

4. Take off the muslin and cut from the shoulder point down the front of the dress to the middle of the underarm curve, leaving the underarm seam line intact. Do the same down the back.

5. Put the muslin on and slip an extra piece of muslin under the slash in the sleeve.

6. Slide the arm section of the sleeve down your arm until it lies smooth and all wrinkles disappear. Pin the edges of the slash to the insert. Take off the muslin.

bodice front

7. Measure along the shoulder seam line from the neck seam line to the upper edge of the slash.

8. Measure the distance between the cut edges of the slash in the sleeve at the shoulder seam line.

C ADJUSTING THE PATTERN

9. On the bodice front pattern, measure along the shoulder seam line from the neck seam line the distance measured in Step 7 and mark with a dot.

10. Draw a line from the dot made in Step 9 to the middle of the curve in the underarm seam line. Cut along this pencil line, but do not cut the pattern apart.

11. Slide shelf paper under the slash and spread the cut edges apart until the distance between the edges of the slash at the shoulder seam line is equal to the measurement made in Step 8. Pin the insert in place.

12. Draw a seam line on the shelf paper to connect the original seam lines on the pattern. Draw a new cutting line 5/8 inch outside the new seam line and parallel to it. Trim away excess shelf paper.

13. Repeat Steps 9-12 on the bodice back pattern.

bodice front pattern

IF THE INSET-SLEEVE TOP IS IMPROPERLY PLACED...

A SYMPTOMS OF AN IMPROPERLY PLACED SLEEVE TOP

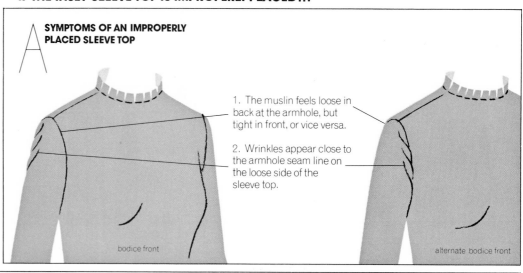

1. The muslin feels loose in back at the armhole, but tight in front, or vice versa.

2. Wrinkles appear close to the armhole seam line on the loose side of the sleeve top.

bodice front

alternate bodice front

B REFITTING THE SLEEVE TOP

3. Open the armhole seam at the top of the sleeve between the notches on either side of the sleeve top.

4. If the looseness is in the front of the sleeve top, move the center of the sleeve top back from the shoulder seam until the fullness of the sleeve top is evenly distributed. If the looseness is in the back of the sleeve top, move the center of the sleeve top forward.

5. Pin the seam line of the sleeve top to the armhole seam line of the bodice at the shoulder seam. Take off the muslin.

6. Turn the muslin wrong side out. Measure along the sleeve top seam line from the pin at the shoulder seam to the original pattern mark indicating the shoulder seam attachment point.

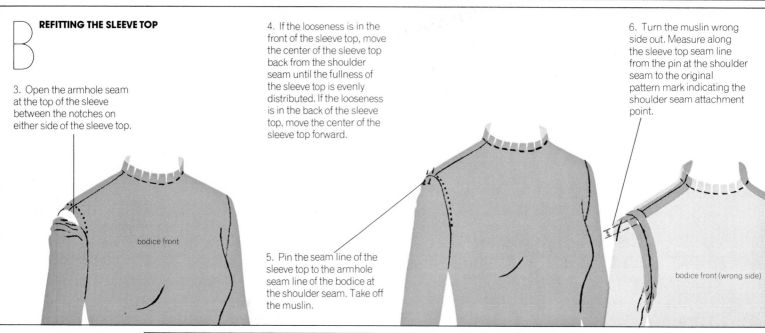

bodice front

bodice front (wrong side)

C ADJUSTING THE PATTERN

7. Measure along the sleeve top seam line of the pattern from the original top center marking the distance measured in Step 6 and mark with a dot. Check the notches identifying front and back to be sure that the measurement corresponds in direction to the one made in Step 6.

8. With the ruler at a right angle to the top end of the original grain line, measure the distance measured in Step 6 in the direction used in Step 7 and mark with a dot.

9. Draw a new grain line from this dot to the bottom end of the original grain line.

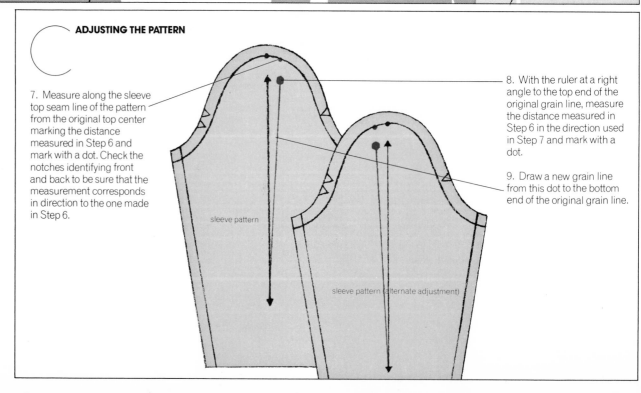

sleeve pattern

sleeve pattern (alternate adjustment)

IF THE DRESS BUSTLINE IS HIGH AND NARROW...

A SYMPTOMS OF A HIGH, NARROW BUSTLINE

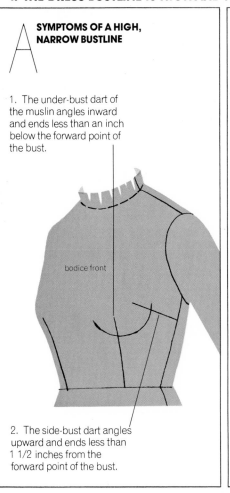

1. The under-bust dart of the muslin angles inward and ends less than an inch below the forward point of the bust.

2. The side-bust dart angles upward and ends less than 1 1/2 inches from the forward point of the bust.

B REFITTING THE BUSTLINE

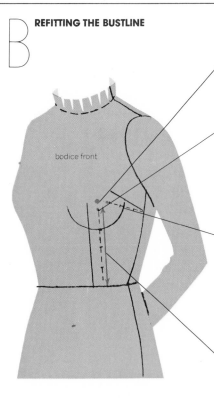

3. Mark the muslin at the forward point of the breast.

4. Measure 1 inch down toward the waist from the point marked in Step 3 and mark with a dot. Insert pins end to end from this dot to the waist seam line to mark the new under-bust dart.

5. To mark the new side-bust dart, measure 1 1/2 inches toward the side seam from the forward point of the bust and mark with a dot. Insert pins end to end from this dot to the base of the original side-bust dart. Take off the muslin.

6. Measure along the new under-bust dart seam line from the dot to the waist seam line.

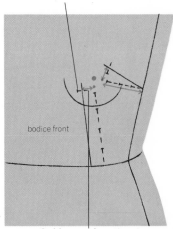

7. Insert a pin on the original under-bust seam line at the distance from the waist seam line measured in Step 6.

8. Measure from the pin inserted in Step 7 to the dot at the top of the new under-bust dart seam line.

9. Repeat Steps 6-8 on the side-bust dart, using corresponding dots and measurements from the base of the original dart at the side seam line.

C ADJUSTING THE PATTERN

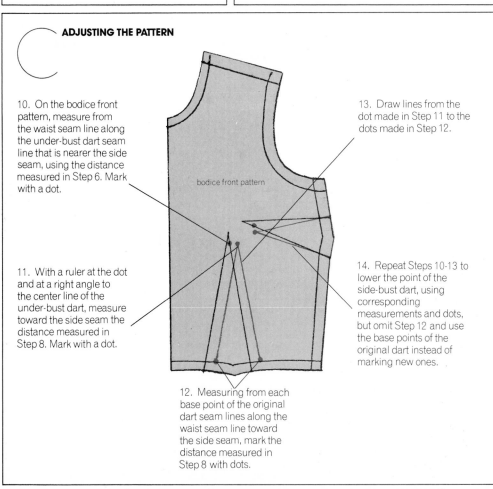

10. On the bodice front pattern, measure from the waist seam line along the under-bust dart seam line that is nearer the side seam, using the distance measured in Step 6. Mark with a dot.

11. With a ruler at the dot and at a right angle to the center line of the under-bust dart, measure toward the side seam the distance measured in Step 8. Mark with a dot.

12. Measuring from each base point of the original dart seam lines along the waist seam line toward the side seam, mark the distance measured in Step 8 with dots.

13. Draw lines from the dot made in Step 11 to the dots made in Step 12.

14. Repeat Steps 10-13 to lower the point of the side-bust dart, using corresponding measurements and dots, but omit Step 12 and use the base points of the original dart instead of marking new ones.

IF THE DRESS BUSTLINE IS LOW AND WIDE...

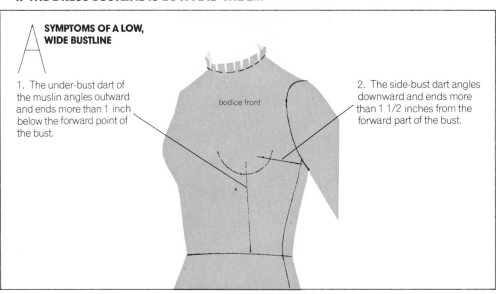

A SYMPTOMS OF A LOW, WIDE BUSTLINE

1. The under-bust dart of the muslin angles outward and ends more than 1 inch below the forward point of the bust.

2. The side-bust dart angles downward and ends more than 1 1/2 inches from the forward part of the bust.

B REFITTING THE BUSTLINE

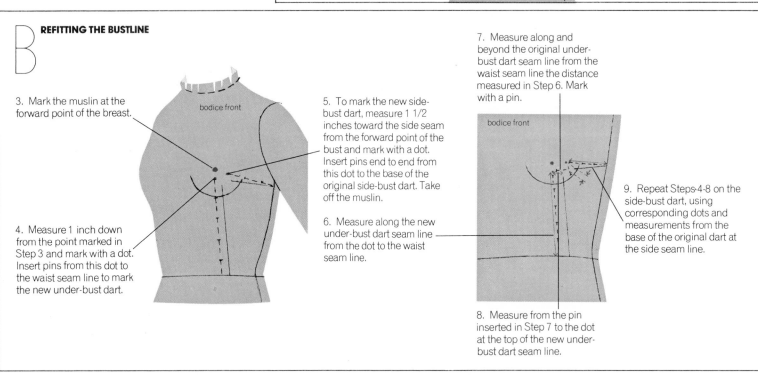

3. Mark the muslin at the forward point of the breast.

4. Measure 1 inch down from the point marked in Step 3 and mark with a dot. Insert pins from this dot to the waist seam line to mark the new under-bust dart.

5. To mark the new side-bust dart, measure 1 1/2 inches toward the side seam from the forward point of the bust and mark with a dot. Insert pins end to end from this dot to the base of the original side-bust dart. Take off the muslin.

6. Measure along the new under-bust dart seam line from the dot to the waist seam line.

7. Measure along and beyond the original under-bust dart seam line from the waist seam line the distance measured in Step 6. Mark with a pin.

8. Measure from the pin inserted in Step 7 to the dot at the top of the new under-bust dart seam line.

9. Repeat Steps 4-8 on the side-bust dart, using corresponding dots and measurements from the base of the original dart at the side seam line.

C ADJUSTING THE PATTERN

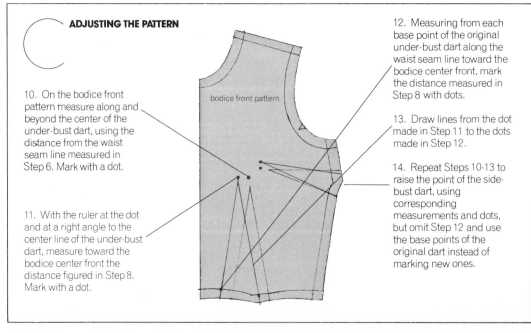

10. On the bodice front pattern measure along and beyond the center of the under-bust dart, using the distance from the waist seam line measured in Step 6. Mark with a dot.

11. With the ruler at the dot and at a right angle to the center line of the under-bust dart, measure toward the bodice center front the distance figured in Step 8. Mark with a dot.

12. Measuring from each base point of the original under-bust dart along the waist seam line toward the bodice center front, mark the distance measured in Step 8 with dots.

13. Draw lines from the dot made in Step 11 to the dots made in Step 12.

14. Repeat Steps 10-13 to raise the point of the side-bust dart, using corresponding measurements and dots, but omit Step 12 and use the base points of the original dart instead of marking new ones.

IF THE DRESS BUSTLINE IS TOO ROUNDED...

A SYMPTOMS OF A BUSTLINE THAT IS TOO ROUNDED

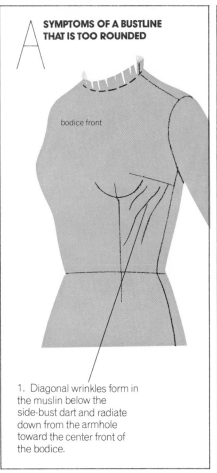

bodice front

1. Diagonal wrinkles form in the muslin below the side-bust dart and radiate down from the armhole toward the center front of the bodice.

B REFITTING THE BUSTLINE

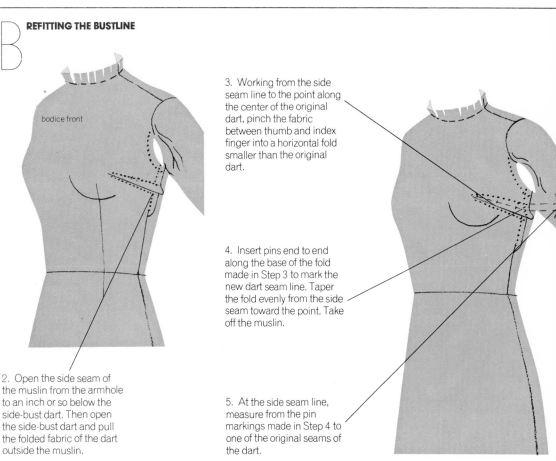

bodice front

2. Open the side seam of the muslin from the armhole to an inch or so below the side-bust dart. Then open the side-bust dart and pull the folded fabric of the dart outside the muslin.

3. Working from the side seam line to the point along the center of the original dart, pinch the fabric between thumb and index finger into a horizontal fold smaller than the original dart.

4. Insert pins end to end along the base of the fold made in Step 3 to mark the new dart seam line. Taper the fold evenly from the side seam toward the point. Take off the muslin.

5. At the side seam line, measure from the pin markings made in Step 4 to one of the original seams of the dart.

C ADJUSTING THE PATTERN

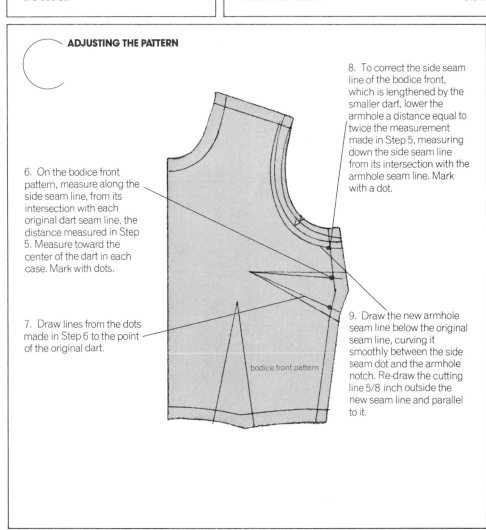

bodice front pattern

6. On the bodice front pattern, measure along the side seam line, from its intersection with each original dart seam line, the distance measured in Step 5. Measure toward the center of the dart in each case. Mark with dots.

7. Draw lines from the dots made in Step 6 to the point of the original dart.

8. To correct the side seam line of the bodice front, which is lengthened by the smaller dart, lower the armhole a distance equal to twice the measurement made in Step 5, measuring down the side seam line from its intersection with the armhole seam line. Mark with a dot.

9. Draw the new armhole seam line below the original seam line, curving it smoothly between the side seam dot and the armhole notch. Re-draw the cutting line 5/8 inch outside the new seam line and parallel to it.

IF THE DRESS BUSTLINE IS TOO FLAT...

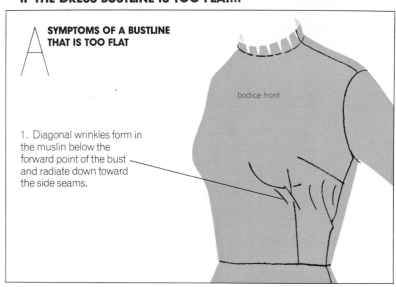

A SYMPTOMS OF A BUSTLINE THAT IS TOO FLAT

1. Diagonal wrinkles form in the muslin below the forward point of the bust and radiate down toward the side seams.

B REFITTING THE BUSTLINE

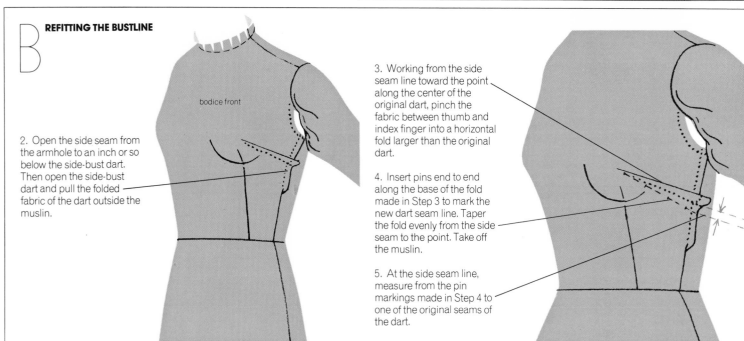

2. Open the side seam from the armhole to an inch or so below the side-bust dart. Then open the side-bust dart and pull the folded fabric of the dart outside the muslin.

3. Working from the side seam line toward the point along the center of the original dart, pinch the fabric between thumb and index finger into a horizontal fold larger than the original dart.

4. Insert pins end to end along the base of the fold made in Step 3 to mark the new dart seam line. Taper the fold evenly from the side seam to the point. Take off the muslin.

5. At the side seam line, measure from the pin markings made in Step 4 to one of the original seams of the dart.

C ADJUSTING THE PATTERN

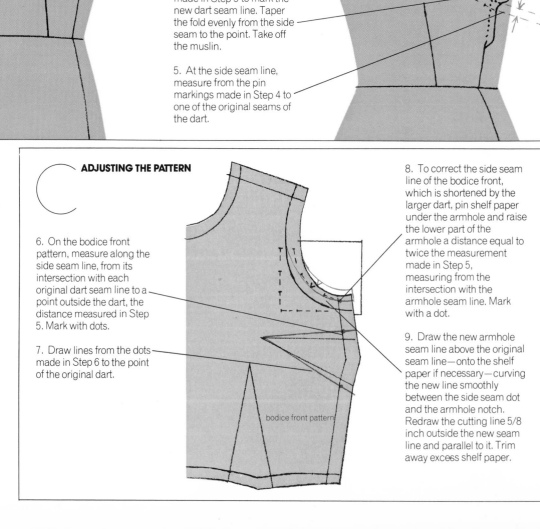

6. On the bodice front pattern, measure along the side seam line, from its intersection with each original dart seam line to a point outside the dart, the distance measured in Step 5. Mark with dots.

7. Draw lines from the dots made in Step 6 to the point of the original dart.

8. To correct the side seam line of the bodice front, which is shortened by the larger dart, pin shelf paper under the armhole and raise the lower part of the armhole a distance equal to twice the measurement made in Step 5, measuring from the intersection with the armhole seam line. Mark with a dot.

9. Draw the new armhole seam line above the original seam line—onto the shelf paper if necessary—curving the new line smoothly between the side seam dot and the armhole notch. Redraw the cutting line 5/8 inch outside the new seam line and parallel to it. Trim away excess shelf paper.

IF THE LOWER DRESS BACK IS TOO LONG...

A SYMPTOMS OF THE LOWER BACK THAT IS TOO LONG

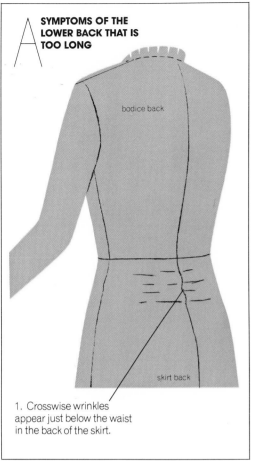

1. Crosswise wrinkles appear just below the waist in the back of the skirt.

B REFITTING THE SKIRT BACK

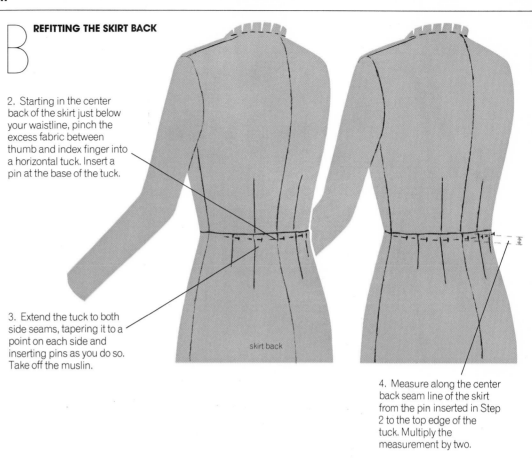

2. Starting in the center back of the skirt just below your waistline, pinch the excess fabric between thumb and index finger into a horizontal tuck. Insert a pin at the base of the tuck.

3. Extend the tuck to both side seams, tapering it to a point on each side and inserting pins as you do so. Take off the muslin.

4. Measure along the center back seam line of the skirt from the pin inserted in Step 2 to the top edge of the tuck. Multiply the measurement by two.

C ADJUSTING THE PATTERN

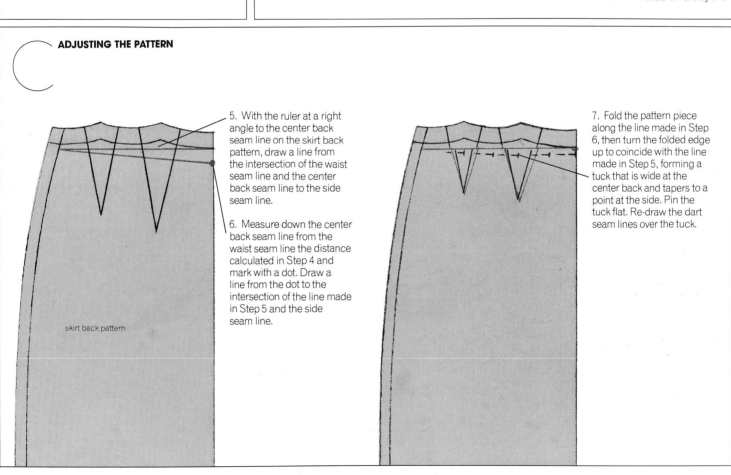

5. With the ruler at a right angle to the center back seam line on the skirt back pattern, draw a line from the intersection of the waist seam line and the center back seam line to the side seam line.

6. Measure down the center back seam line from the waist seam line the distance calculated in Step 4 and mark with a dot. Draw a line from the dot to the intersection of the line made in Step 5 and the side seam line.

7. Fold the pattern piece along the line made in Step 6, then turn the folded edge up to coincide with the line made in Step 5, forming a tuck that is wide at the center back and tapers to a point at the side. Pin the tuck flat. Re-draw the dart seam lines over the tuck.

IF THE SKIRT FRONT IS TIGHT...

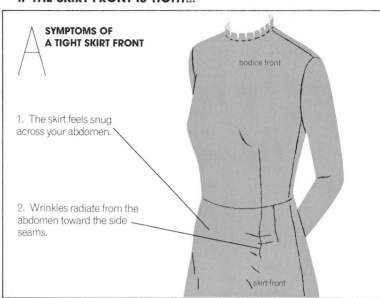

A SYMPTOMS OF
A TIGHT SKIRT FRONT

1. The skirt feels snug across your abdomen.

2. Wrinkles radiate from the abdomen toward the side seams.

bodice front

skirt front

B REFITTING
THE SKIRT FRONT

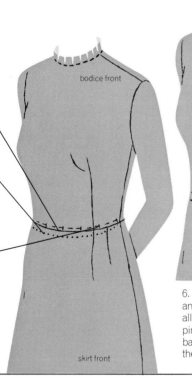

bodice front

3. Open the front waist seam from one side seam to the other.

4. Slide the skirt front down away from the bodice until the wrinkles below the darts disappear.

5. Starting from the center front and tapering evenly into the original waist seam line toward the sides, pin the seam allowance of the skirt waist to the bodice waist seam line.

skirt front

6. Open the skirt front darts and shorten the darts until all wrinkles disappear. Insert pins end to end along the base of each dart. Take off the muslin.

7. At the center front of the skirt, measure from the new waist seam line to the original one.

8. Measure the length of each shortened dart.

C ADJUSTING THE PATTERN

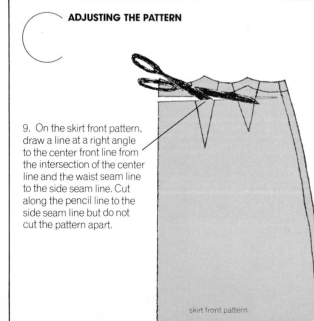

9. On the skirt front pattern, draw a line at a right angle to the center front line from the intersection of the center line and the waist seam line to the side seam line. Cut along the pencil line to the side seam line but do not cut the pattern apart.

skirt front pattern

10. Slide an insert of shelf paper under the slash and spread the sections of the pattern apart at the center line to the distance measured in Step 7 and pin them to the shelf paper.

11. Draw a line to connect the original center front line of the two edges. Trim away excess shelf paper.

12. On both original darts, measure down the center from the waist seam line a distance equal to that measured in Step 8 and mark with dots.

13. Draw new seam lines from the dots made in Step 12 to the base of the original darts at the waist seam line.

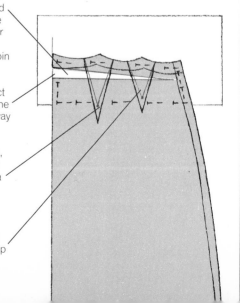

IF THE SIDE SEAM IS CROOKED...

A SYMPTOMS OF A CROOKED SIDE SEAM

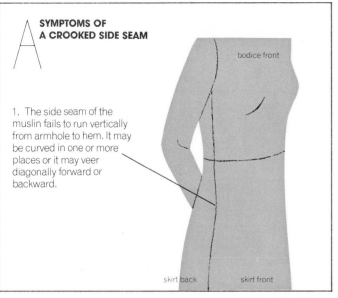

1. The side seam of the muslin fails to run vertically from armhole to hem. It may be curved in one or more places or it may veer diagonally forward or backward.

B REFITTING THE SIDE SEAM

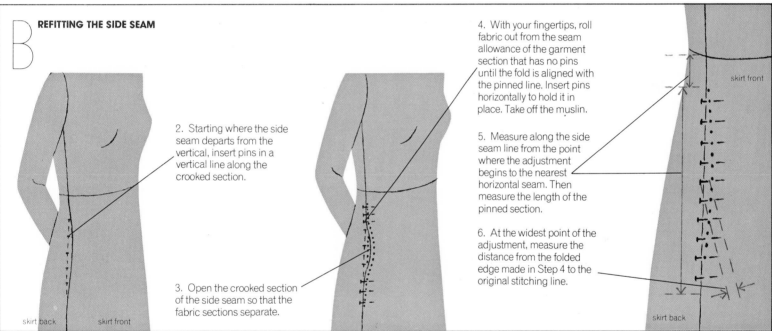

2. Starting where the side seam departs from the vertical, insert pins in a vertical line along the crooked section.

3. Open the crooked section of the side seam so that the fabric sections separate.

4. With your fingertips, roll fabric out from the seam allowance of the garment section that has no pins until the fold is aligned with the pinned line. Insert pins horizontally to hold it in place. Take off the muslin.

5. Measure along the side seam line from the point where the adjustment begins to the nearest horizontal seam. Then measure the length of the pinned section.

6. At the widest point of the adjustment, measure the distance from the folded edge made in Step 4 to the original stitching line.

C ADJUSTING THE PATTERN

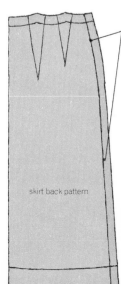

7. On the pattern corresponding to the unfolded edge of the seam, measure along the side seam line from the horizontal seam line that corresponds to the one used in Step 5, using the measurements made in Step 5, and mark with dots to indicate where the adjustment begins and ends.

8. Repeat Step 7 on the pattern corresponding to the folded edge of the seam.

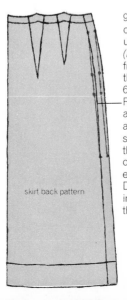

9. On the pattern piece corresponding to the unfolded edge of the seam (left in drawing), measure in from the original seam line the distance figured in Step 6 and mark with a dot. Repeat at 2-inch intervals along the middle of the adjustment. Draw a new side seam line that connects the dots and tapers into the original seam line at both ends of the adjustment. Draw a new cutting line 5/8 inch outside and parallel to the new seam line.

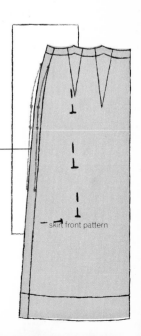

10. With the pattern piece corresponding to the folded edge of the seam (right in drawing), slip shelf paper under the seam line and measure the distance figured in Step 6 out from the original side seam line and mark with a dot. Repeat at 2-inch intervals along the middle of the adjustment. Draw a new side seam line that connects the dots and tapers into the original seam line at both ends of the adjustment. Draw a new cutting line 5/8 inch outside the new seam line and parallel to it.

Styles vary, but flawless work marks both the complex Balenciaga gown (*left*) and simpler House of Norell dress.

4
COUTURIER TECHNIQUES

Many couturiers' creations are deceptively simple. Consider the superb House of Norell dress shown on the preceding page, an example of couture at its uncluttered best. The dress flows like a sinuous white column of fabric from the soft drape of its shoulder line, past impeccably formed and fitted sleeves into a gracefully draped long skirt. Its elegant simplicity, however, is achieved because each

DISTINCTION IN STRUCTURE AND DETAIL

element of the dress has been stitched and finished with painstaking care. The House of Norell lavishes the highest quality of craftsmanship on its clothes, and a dress such as this might well be considered a House of Norell signature.

Now compare the Norell dress with the green Balenciaga at the left of the picture. Although it was designed about 1966, today such a design seems extreme and vaguely unwearable. It has rather the air of a museum piece (and indeed a museum is where it was photographed, along with the other classic Balenciagas shown on pages 94-97 —at The Costume Institute of The Metropolitan Museum of Art in New York City). But the Balenciaga dress, too, has been crafted with details that are distinct and impressive. The difference between the two garments is one of style—not craftsmanship, which is the hallmark of the custom look.

Regardless of style differences, the work of both designers points up the two major aspects of custom sewing that distinguish it from basic sewing: construction and detailing. The House of Norell's contemporary designs place heavy emphasis on meticulous detailing; the more flamboyant style of the Balenciaga dress was achieved primarily by the use of construction methods that involved cut as well as dramatic draping to create extraordinary shapes.

Balenciaga's fascination with exaggerated shaping techniques is not a new phenomenon. In mid-19th Century France, to cite one celebrated example, the taste in fashion ran to tiny waists set above enormously wide skirts. At first these skirts were held out from the body by a variety of starched petticoats. Later, hip pads and underskirts of horsehair were added to keep the material afloat. Then in the latter 19th Century a wired underskirt called the Thomson crinoline (presumably invented by a man named Thomson, though his precise identity is lost to history) appeared on the scene, and Charles Worth, the English father of French couture, adopted it with delight—for a while, at least.

The word crinoline derives from "crin," meaning horsehair, and "linum," meaning cotton or linen thread, the materials used in the first so-called crinoline. The Thomson crinoline carried the idea to its engineering extreme. It was made from hoops of whalebone and metal, placed horizontally one above another and held in place with a series of curved vertical ribs.

Standing alone, this creation resembled nothing so much as a huge bird cage; when worn by a Second Empire lady of fashion, the cage supported her voluminous skirts in such a way that not a hint of leg movement was discernible and the material of the skirt arched gracefully to the floor in a great, smooth bell shape.

But though the crinoline enjoyed great popularity and the skirts that covered it grew more sumptuous—Empress Eugénie wore one with 103 overlapping flounces cascading to the floor—there were distinct and quite serious drawbacks to its continued use. As the crinoline left the ballroom and moved into daily life, physical hazards began to loom. Sauntering in a brisk wind or getting in and out of a carriage, a lady found both skirts and crinoline unmanageable. And if she ventured too near a fire, she might discover to her horror that her skirts were beginning to smoke; impeded by countless fasteners in shucking her bulky, tightly fastened garment, she risked suffering a nasty singeing before help arrived.

Worth himself, after his first flush of enthusiasm, found the crinoline not only awkward but all too limiting as a fashion idea and in 1869 was able to dispatch it to oblivion by substituting another figure-distorting design—the bustle. In the front of his dresses Worth replaced the large folds and gathers of the crinoline-supported gowns with gores and darts to make the dresses flat and form-fitting. But in the back he more than made up for his improvement, cantilevering yards of trailing fabric in thin air by means of horsehair pads or springs. The bustle, however, had a fairly brief existence before it succumbed to fashion's whims. By 1890 it had disappeared, supplanted by the hourglass figure made popular by the illustrator Charles Dana Gibson. Even though the Gibson Girl's 18-inch wasp-waist was achieved with a heavily boned corset, it afforded its wearer more freedom and grace than the bustle had. By then women had moved onto the sporting fields, and there the bustle simply could not compete. Thereafter, fashion moved to the rakish "flapper" style of the 1920s then to the somber, straight-skirted look of the 1930s.

In the not-so-distant past, another designer temporarily revolutionized high fashion by reverting to startling exaggerations of woman's natural form. It was in 1947 that Christian Dior introduced his wasp-waisted, padded-hipped New Look, which was supported by the structural devices shown at right. Dropping hemlines toward the ankles, constricting or rounding out natural female curves, he seemed to be taking fashion back to the 19th Century idea of shaping the garment to a dramatic form, then shaping the wearer to the garment.

Although today's designers generally spurn such things as stays and heavy padding, they have by no means given up the principle of shape in the clothes they create. What distinguishes the work of today's couturiers from their predecessors is simply a difference in the degree of emphasis placed on construction, and in the nature of the techniques employed. As the drawings on pages 135-137 illustrate, seams, for example, often do more than simply connect two pattern pieces; they can actually take the place of old-fashioned understructures to support and shape a dress, holding the gown away from the body as required to achieve the form conceived by the designer. Similarly, an underlining, made from a tightly woven fabric, can be used to stabilize the shape of a gown. After the underlining pieces have been basted to those cut out of the dress fabric, the two thicknesses are treated as one. The basic fabric will stretch no more than the underlining.

Less obvious but equally important shaping and strengthening techniques involve the use of small pieces of tightly woven fabric, such as a scrap of underlining fabric or seam tape, to hold the shape of a garment at strategic points. In custom-made clothes such pieces are often inserted into the seam lines at a number of points of stress or stretch: at the sharply angled points of an underarm gusset (a diamond-shaped insert that eases freedom of movement in some designs) or at the upper point of a godet (a triangular insert that gives flare to a skirt). These are places where stitching needs to be reinforced to avoid being pulled out. Curved seam lines, particularly if they also perform a structural function, lie more smoothly and follow the body's form better when small pieces of tightly woven fabric are sewn along the stitching line.

All this depends upon meticulous hand work—beginning with the preparation of the pieces, the molding and shaping of the fabric, the hand basting and stitching—that accounts for the perfection of detailing in custom garments. In one dress the hem may have to be eased, or gently gathered, to do away with extra fullness; in another it may have to be stiffened with light interfacing so it will not droop or cling. A buttonhole may need to be worked vertically one time, horizontally or on the bias the next. All of these techniques require skillful manipulation of the fabric and the use of tiny, often invisible stitches that can be produced only by nimble fingers.

The garment's lining—silk or some similarly luxurious fabric to make the inside as elegant as the outside—will discreetly cover the myriad custom construction details. But their effect will be seen nonetheless. Wherever you choose to apply these techniques, whether on a sumptuous evening gown or on a plain A-line dress, the quality will always be apparent.

It is this quality of custom sewing, in its most glamorous heyday, that is epitomized by the Balenciaga museum-piece gowns. In the sections that follow, superb craftsmanship in the style of the 1970s is shown in close-ups of House of Norell gowns that precede step-by-step explanations of the tech-

Intricate construction undergirded Christian Dior's New Look of 1947. *Left to right:* a jersey dress shaped by sloping shoulder pads and a waist-flattening muslin belt; a suit with a whalebone waistband to cinch in the waist, and muslin bust and hip padding in the hourglass jacket; a jacket with shoulder pads to top a pleated skirt whose inner ruffled waistband flares it out over the hips; and a skirt stiffened with calico at the waist and hem.

niques of custom sewing. As you try your hand at some of these techniques, you will acquire a feeling of how the House of Norell works and you will have an idea of what the finished product should look like. There could be no better teacher.

Balenciaga: architect of elegance

Cristobal Balenciaga created nearly every major silhouette that women wore through the 1950s and '60s. The architecture of his clothes was striking: he revealed the neck, widened the shoulders, drew attention to the back, ignored the waist. Among the styles he introduced were the sack dress, the tunic dress, the semifitted suit or coat with a "tortoise" look (a round back and arms, a cutaway neck with a mounted collar), balloon-shaped skirts and body stockings covered by loose-fitting lightweight gowns. Balenciaga's last creation, in 1972, was a wedding gown for Generalissimo Francisco Franco's granddaughter Maria. For this grand finale, Balenciaga eschewed dramatic shapes—and designed a princess dress. A year after his death, New York's Metropolitan Museum of Art mounted an exhibit of Balenciaga's work, "to honor a giant of haute couture," as the museum director put it. The pictures on the following pages were taken at that exhibit.

Billowing Balenciaga skirts puff out over hemlines that rise and dip.

Back interest, a hallmark of Balenciaga's clothes, is provided by the insouciant drape of the overblouse that tops the slightly shirred skirt of this silk day dress. Balenciaga created this timelessly simple design in 1967.

Balenciaga's extravagantly shaped evening creations included gowns with a petal front and train *(above)*, flamenco ruffles *(right background)*, a voluminous bustle *(right)* and a kimono-sleeved evening coat *(far right)*.

The basic stitches of the couturier

Versatile as the modern sewing machine is, it still cannot replace hand stitching in some fine work—even for tasks ordinarily done by machine, such as seaming and topstitching. Firm, neat work like the half backstitch and backstitch *(right)* sews strong seams in awkward places a machine cannot readily reach. And these two stitches, along with the prick stitch and saddle stitch *(right)*, also make lines of decorative topstitching that are more elegant and less likely to harm delicate fabrics than machine stitches. For finishing edges, the blanket stitch adds elegance and precision.

There are, of course, places and purposes for which only a hand stitch will suffice. To make hems on knits and folded-over edges of belts neat, use a blind hemming stitch *(page 101)*. Underlining is held to fabric with strong diagonal basting stitches *(page 100)* to enable you to treat the two fabrics as one, and designs are precisely matched with slip basting *(pages 100-101)*.

In all cases, use a single strand of thread no more than 18 inches long for permanent stitches and no more than 30 inches long for temporary basting stitches. The thread should the same color as the garment unless a contrasting effect is desired, as in topstitching.

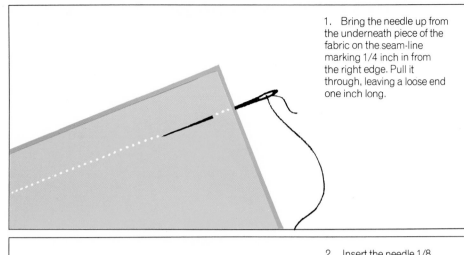

1. Bring the needle up from the underneath piece of the fabric on the seam-line marking 1/4 inch in from the right edge. Pull it through, leaving a loose end one inch long.

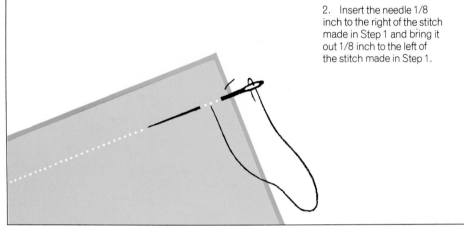

2. Insert the needle 1/8 inch to the right of the stitch made in Step 1 and bring it out 1/8 inch to the left of the stitch made in Step 1.

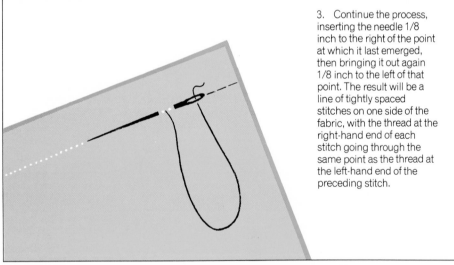

3. Continue the process, inserting the needle 1/8 inch to the right of the point at which it last emerged, then bringing it out again 1/8 inch to the left of that point. The result will be a line of tightly spaced stitches on one side of the fabric, with the thread at the right-hand end of each stitch going through the same point as the thread at the left-hand end of the preceding stitch.

4. End the row of stitches by inserting the needle back over the last completed stitch on the underneath piece of fabric, then make another stitch directly over this one.

IF YOU ARE LEFT-HANDED...
Follow the directions in Steps 1-4, proceeding from left to right as shown.

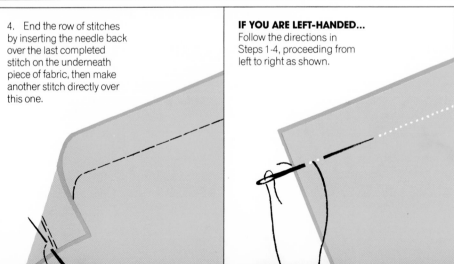

THE HALF BACKSTITCH For topstitching and hard-to-reach seams

1. Using a knotted thread, draw the needle up from the underneath piece of fabric on the seam-line markings about 1/4 inch from the right-hand edge and pull it through.

2. Insert the needle 1/16 to 1/8 inch to the right of the stitch made in Step 1 and bring the needle out 1/16 to 1/8 inch to the left of the stitch made in Step 1.

3. Continue the process, pulling the thread through firmly but loosely enough to keep the fabric from puckering. The stitches will be evenly spaced on top of the fabric and overlap on the back.

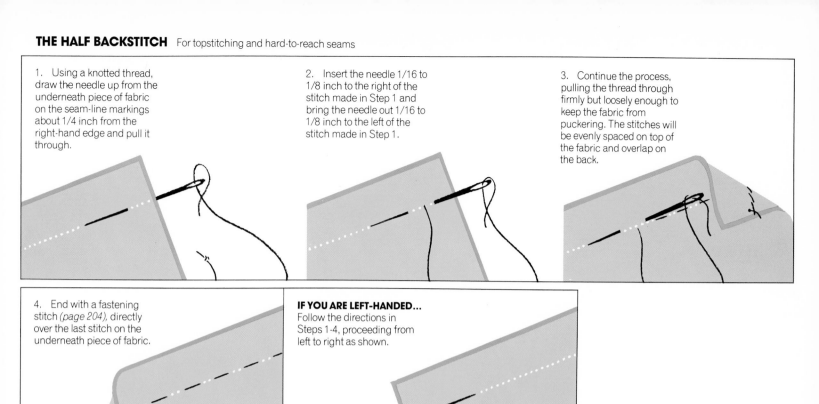

4. End with a fastening stitch (*page 204*), directly over the last stitch on the underneath piece of fabric.

IF YOU ARE LEFT-HANDED...
Follow the directions in Steps 1-4, proceeding from left to right as shown.

THE PRICK STITCH For topstitching and sewing zippers in place

1. Using a knotted thread, draw the needle up from the underneath piece of fabric to the top about 1/16 inch from the right edge and pull it through.

2. Insert the needle to the right three or four threads and bring it out 1/4 to 3/8 inch to the left of the stitch made in Step 1.

3. Continue the process, smoothing the fabric every few stitches.

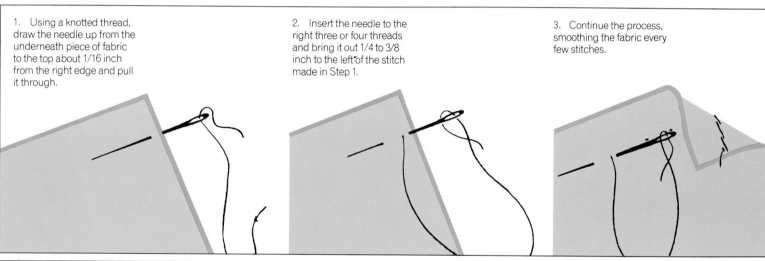

4. End with a fastening stitch (*page 204*), catching only the underneath piece of the fabric.

IF YOU ARE LEFT-HANDED...
Follow the directions in Steps 1-4, proceeding from left to right as shown.

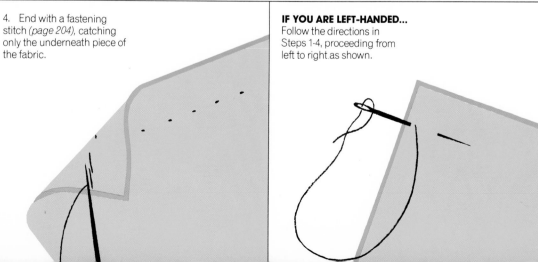

THE SADDLE STITCH: For bold topstitching

1. Draw the needle up from the underneath piece of fabric, about 1/8 inch in from the right edge.

2. Weave the needle in and out of the fabric two or three times in evenly spaced stitches, each at least 1/4 inch long.

3. Pull the thread through the fabric firmly but loosely enough to keep the fabric from puckering; repeat the process.

4. End with a fastening stitch *(page 204)* that catches only the underneath piece of fabric.

IF YOU ARE LEFT-HANDED... Follow the directions in Steps 1-4, proceeding from left to right as shown.

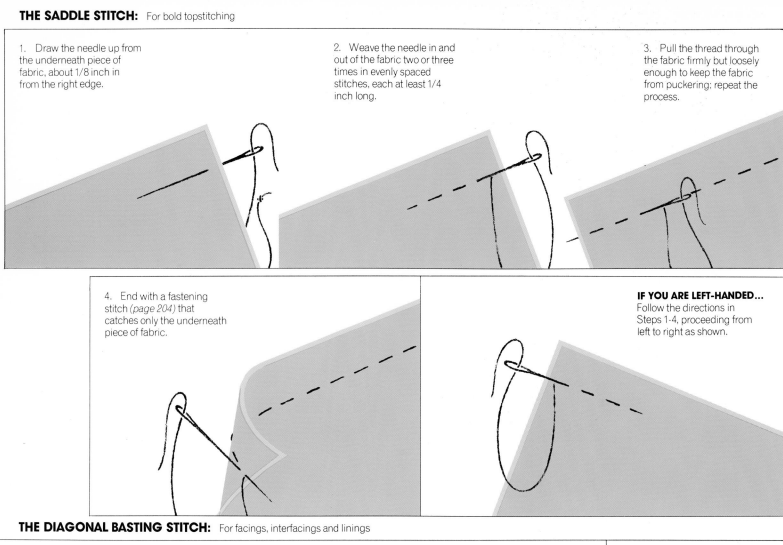

THE DIAGONAL BASTING STITCH: For facings, interfacings and linings

1. Anchor the basting with a 3/8-inch-long fastening stitch *(page 204)* through all fabric thicknesses. Bring the needle down 1 inch, and keeping the thread to the right of the needle, take a 3/8-inch stitch from right to left, directly under the fastening stitch.

2. Continue the process, bringing the needle down 1 inch and taking a 3/8-inch stitch from right to left under the stitch made in Step 1; smooth the fabric as you work your way down.

3. If the basting is to be left in, end with a backstitch. If the basting will be removed, end with a loose end 4 inches long.

IF YOU ARE LEFT-HANDED... Follow the directions in Steps 1-3, inserting the needle from left to right as shown.

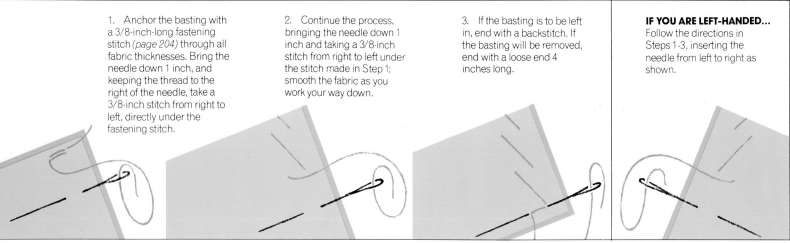

THE SLIP BASTING STITCH: For matching designs

1. Unless you have already done so, run a line of basting stitches along the seam lines where the design is to be matched.

2. Press under the seam allowance of one section. Place the folded edge on top of the seam line of the other section's right side, carefully matching the design. Pin through all fabric thicknesses at 1/2-to 1-inch intervals.

3. Using a knotted thread, draw the needle up from the back of the single thickness of fabric just below the fold; pull it through.

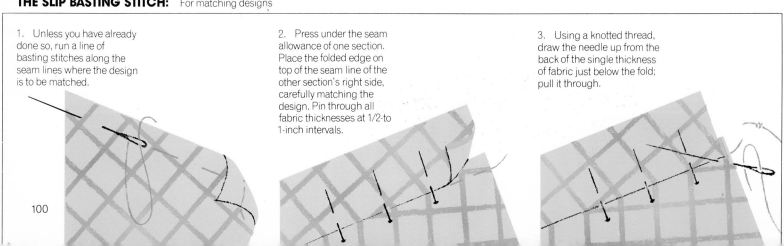

100

4. Insert the needle into the folded seam allowance just above the fold and directly above the stitch made in Step 3. Bring the needle out just below the fold and 1/4 to 1 inch to the left of the first stitch, depending on the size of the design to be matched.

5. Continue the process, removing the pins as you go. End with a loose fastening stitch *(page 204)* through all layers of fabric.

6. When you are finished and the folded seam allowance is opened out, long slanted stitches will appear on one side, and a row of small stitches will appear on the other side. The machine stitching for the seam will run directly over the small stitches.

IF YOU ARE LEFT-HANDED…
Follow the directions in Steps 1-5, proceeding from left to right as shown below.

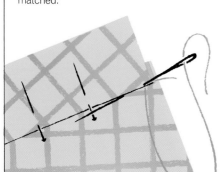

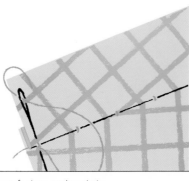

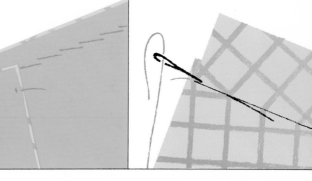

THE BLIND HEMMING STITCH: For hems, facings and pockets

1. Prepare the hem *(pages 123-127)*, then baste the hem to the garment 1/4 inch from the edge.

2. Fold the hem along the basting made in Step 1 so that the hem lies underneath the garment and the unstitched edge projects above the garment. Using knotted thread, insert the needle through one or two threads of the garment just below the fold and pull the thread through.

3. Pick up one or two threads just above the fold and 1/2 inch to the left of the first stitch; pull the thread through. End with a fastening stitch *(page 204)* on the hem fabric.

IF YOU ARE LEFT-HANDED…
Follow the directions in Steps 1-3, proceeding from left to right as shown.

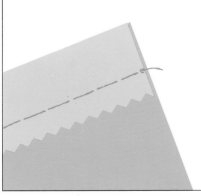

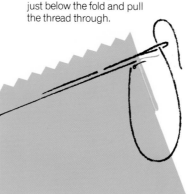

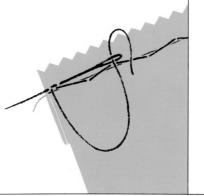

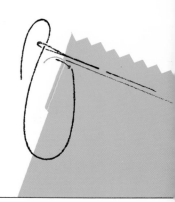

THE BLANKET STITCH: For decorating and protecting the edges of fine fabrics

1. Draw a guide line with chalk 1/4 inch above the edge to be sewn. Using a knotted thread, insert the needle from the bottom piece of fabric to the top, at the far left edge of the line.

2. Holding the thread with your left thumb, insert the needle 1/4 inch to the right of the stitch made in Step 1. Keep the thread behind the needle, and pull the needle through the loop.

3. Continue the process, ending with a fastening stitch *(page 204)* on the underneath piece only of the fabric.

IF YOU ARE LEFT-HANDED…
Follow the directions in Steps 1-3, proceeding from left to right as shown.

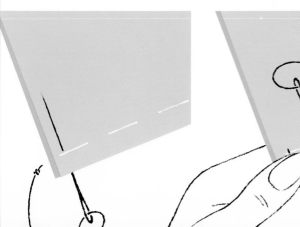

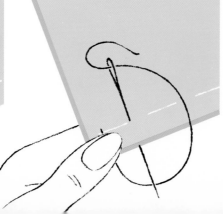

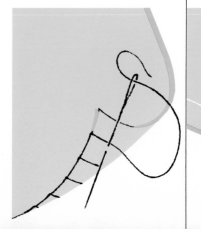

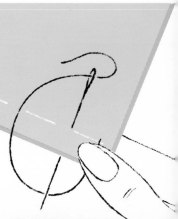

Collars: standing, rolled or flat

All collars fall into one of three basic shapes: standing, rolled or flat. Within each of these categories, great couturiers have perfected a number of variations; three of the most frequently used are demonstrated on the following pages.

The House of Norell's shaped standing collar shown at left, an example of the first type, rises crisply up and away from the dress because of a layer of interfacing attached to the outer collar. Special care must be taken in trimming this interfacing down to 1/16 inch inside the outer collar seam line to reduce bulk as much as possible *(Box A, opposite)*.

The shape of the second type, a soft, rolled collar, is provided by diagonal basting along the top edges of the collar. A feature of this collar is that it is made in two halves, with each half consisting of three pieces. The two halves are joined together at the center, and then the assembly is attached to the dress.

The tie collar is a custom variation on the basic flat shape. It should be made up in a soft fabric, such as silk, that will hold a bow attractively. The tie must be cut on the bias, like a man's necktie. This type of collar has no interfacing at all.

THE SHAPED STANDING COLLAR

A. MAKING AND INTERFACING THE OUTER COLLAR

1. Using the pattern piece provided for the collar, cut out two identical pieces of garment fabric and one piece of special interfacing fabric.

2. Place the piece for the outer collar wrong side up and make a row of basting stitches along the pattern markings to indicate the center line.

3. Run another row of basting stitches along the seam line of the lower neck edge. These two rows of bastings will aid you in attaching the collar to the garment accurately.

4. Place the interfacing over the wrong side of the outer collar and insert pins at the corners, inside the seam line, to hold it in place.

5. Trim away the seam allowances of the interfacing, cutting 1/16 inch inside the outer collar seam line to create a margin for rolling the inner collar out of sight later.

6. Pin the interfacing to the outer collar at 1-inch intervals around all four edges.

7. Baste the interfacing into place, sewing 1/4 inch inside the outer collar seam lines. Remove the pins.

8. Attach the interfacing permanently to the outer collar using a catch stitch (*page 204*), picking up a thread of the seam allowance of the outer collar and then a thread of the interfacing just outside the bastings made in Step 7. Remove these bastings.

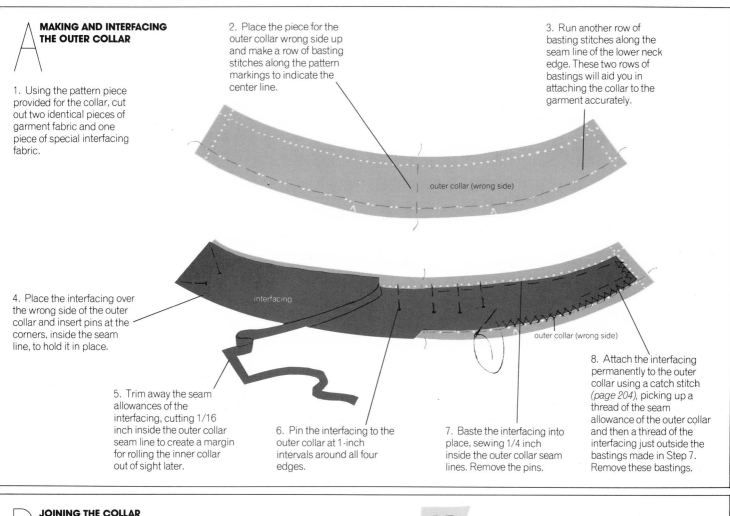

B. JOINING THE COLLAR SECTIONS

9. Make two rows of basting stitches on the inner collar as in Box A, Steps 2 and 3.

10. Place the inner collar wrong side down and pin the interfaced outer collar, wrong side up, to the inner collar. Match the notches, the seam intersections and the bastings.

11. Baste the outer collar to the inner collar at each end and along the upper edge, sewing just outside the seam line into the seam allowance. Remove the pins.

12. Machine stitch on the seam line around the three basted edges. Remove the basting stitches holding the collar sections together.

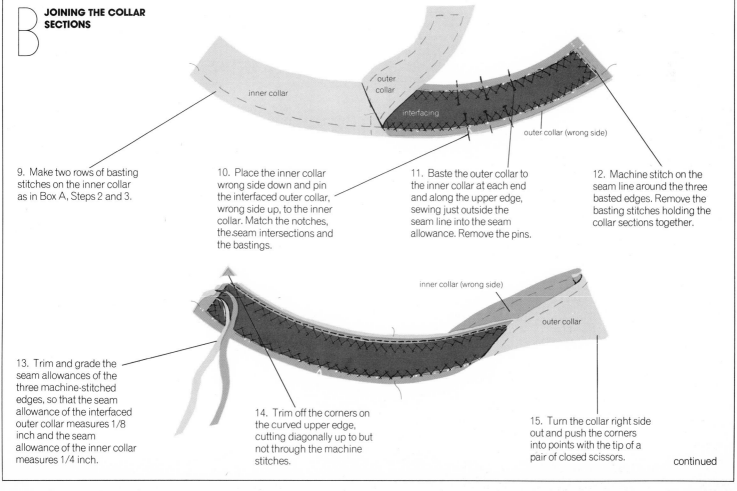

13. Trim and grade the seam allowances of the three machine-stitched edges, so that the seam allowance of the interfaced outer collar measures 1/8 inch and the seam allowance of the inner collar measures 1/4 inch.

14. Trim off the corners on the curved upper edge, cutting diagonally up to but not through the machine stitches.

15. Turn the collar right side out and push the corners into points with the tip of a pair of closed scissors.

continued

CONCEALING THE INNER COLLAR

16. Starting at one open corner, roll the inner and outer collar fabric lightly between your fingers all along the three machine-stitched edges to bring the line of seam stitching out to the edge.

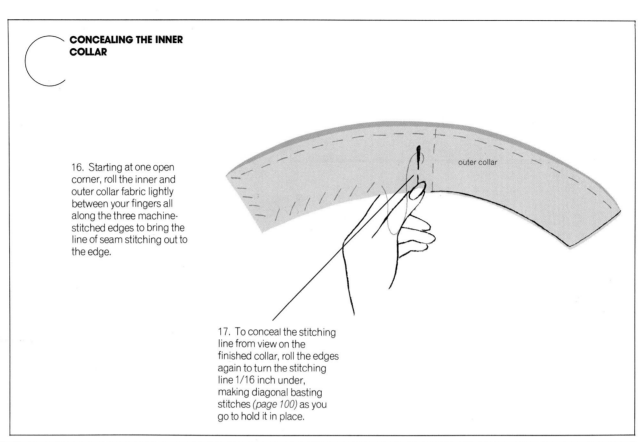

outer collar

17. To conceal the stitching line from view on the finished collar, roll the edges again to turn the stitching line 1/16 inch under, making diagonal basting stitches *(page 100)* as you go to hold it in place.

PREPARING THE NECKLINE

18. Complete the body section of the garment according to the pattern instructions, marking the center front of the garment with a row of basting stitches.

19. To aid in positioning the collar correctly, make another row of bastings along the seam line at the neck edge of the garment.

20. Machine stitch—setting the machine at 10 stitches per inch—around the neckline of the garment to hold the neckline in shape and prevent possible fraying. Sew just outside the basted seam line into the seam allowance.

21. Turn under the seam allowances of the placket opening at the back of the garment and finish the closure with a zipper *(pages 142-143)*.

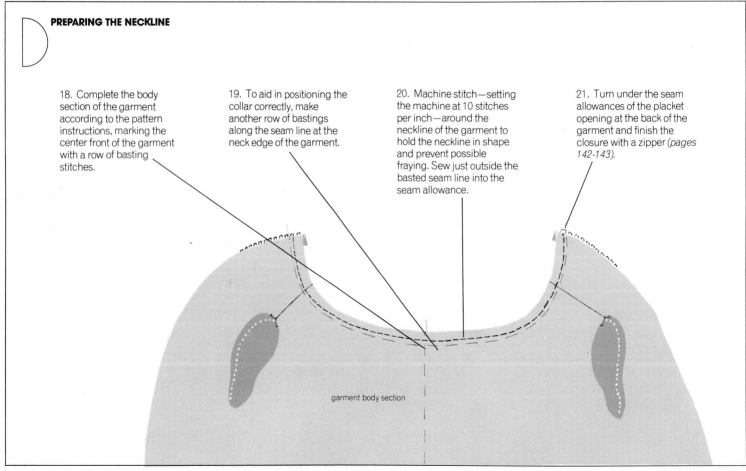

garment body section

ATTACHING THE COLLAR

22. With the right side of the garment—the side that will be visible in the finished garment—facing you, position the collar so that the inner collar is facing up and the unstitched neck edge of the collar is aligned with the neck edge of the garment. Spread the unstitched edges apart so that the wrong side of the interfaced outer collar is visible.

23. Match and pin together the notches, center front bastings and the bastings along the seam line of the outer collar and the neckline of the garment. Then add more pins at 1-inch intervals all around the neckline.

24. Baste the outer collar to the garment, sewing into the seam allowance just outside the basted seam line of the outer collar. Remove the pins.

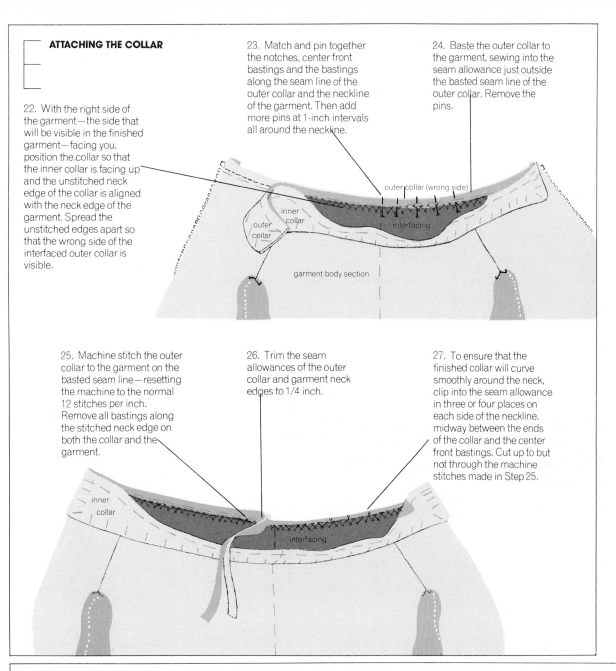

25. Machine stitch the outer collar to the garment on the basted seam line—resetting the machine to the normal 12 stitches per inch. Remove all bastings along the stitched neck edge on both the collar and the garment.

26. Trim the seam allowances of the outer collar and garment neck edges to 1/4 inch.

27. To ensure that the finished collar will curve smoothly around the neck, clip into the seam allowance in three or four places on each side of the neckline, midway between the ends of the collar and the center front bastings. Cut up to but not through the machine stitches made in Step 25.

FINISHING THE COLLAR

28. Place the garment wrong side up. Turn the collar upward so that the inner collar is facing you. Lift up the unstitched edge of the inner collar and, using an iron, press the machine-stitched and trimmed seam allowance of the neck edge away from the garment toward the interfaced outer collar.

29. Fold under the unstitched edge of the inner collar along its basted seam line, wrong sides together. Press the folded edge flat.

30. Position the pressed edge of the inner collar over the neck edge of the garment so that it covers the two lines of machine stitching. Then pin the inner collar in place and baste close to the fold. Remove the pins.

31. Attach the inner collar to the garment using a slip stitch (page 204). Pick up a thread of the machine stitching around the neckline made in Box E, Step 25, so that the slip stitches will not show on the finished garment.

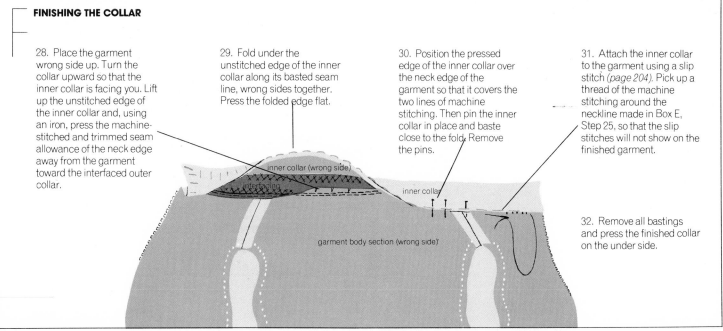

32. Remove all bastings and press the finished collar on the under side.

THE ROLLED POINTED COLLAR

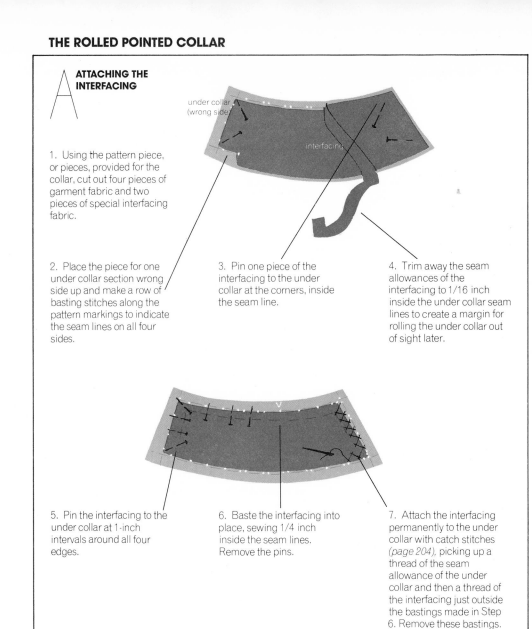

A ATTACHING THE INTERFACING

1. Using the pattern piece, or pieces, provided for the collar, cut out four pieces of garment fabric and two pieces of special interfacing fabric.

2. Place the piece for one under collar section wrong side up and make a row of basting stitches along the pattern markings to indicate the seam lines on all four sides.

3. Pin one piece of the interfacing to the under collar at the corners, inside the seam line.

4. Trim away the seam allowances of the interfacing to 1/16 inch inside the under collar seam lines to create a margin for rolling the under collar out of sight later.

5. Pin the interfacing to the under collar at 1-inch intervals around all four edges.

6. Baste the interfacing into place, sewing 1/4 inch inside the seam lines. Remove the pins.

7. Attach the interfacing permanently to the under collar with catch stitches (page 204), picking up a thread of the seam allowance of the under collar and then a thread of the interfacing just outside the bastings made in Step 6. Remove these bastings.

B JOINING THE COLLAR SECTIONS

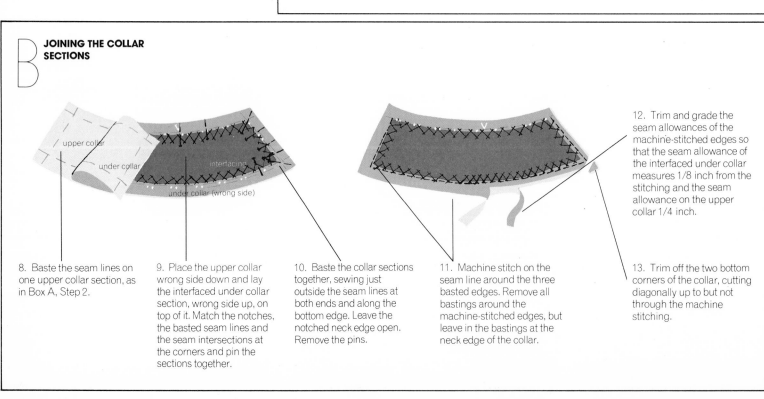

8. Baste the seam lines on one upper collar section, as in Box A, Step 2.

9. Place the upper collar wrong side down and lay the interfaced under collar section, wrong side up, on top of it. Match the notches, the basted seam lines and the seam intersections at the corners and pin the sections together.

10. Baste the collar sections together, sewing just outside the seam lines at both ends and along the bottom edge. Leave the notched neck edge open. Remove the pins.

11. Machine stitch on the seam line around the three basted edges. Remove all bastings around the machine-stitched edges, but leave in the bastings at the neck edge of the collar.

12. Trim and grade the seam allowances of the machine-stitched edges so that the seam allowance of the interfaced under collar measures 1/8 inch from the stitching and the seam allowance on the upper collar 1/4 inch.

13. Trim off the two bottom corners of the collar, cutting diagonally up to but not through the machine stitching.

CONCEALING THE UNDER COLLAR

14. Turn the collar piece right side out, pulling the bottom edge out through the open neck edge so that the interfacing lies inside

15. Push out the two machine-stitched corners of the collar with the tip of a pair of closed scissors.

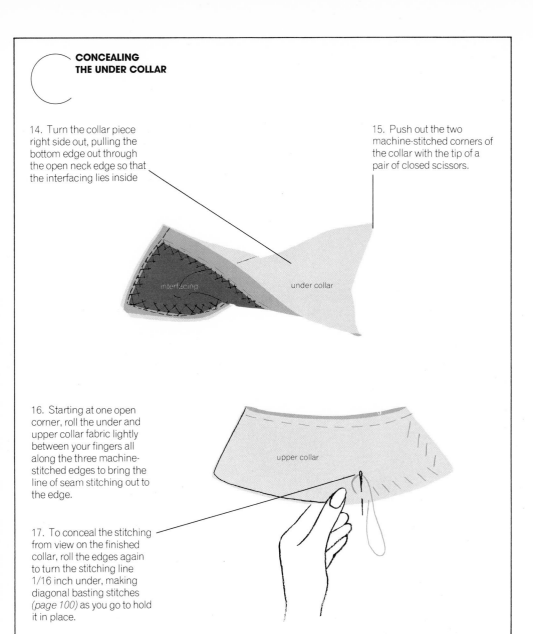

16. Starting at one open corner, roll the under and upper collar fabric lightly between your fingers all along the three machine-stitched edges to bring the line of seam stitching out to the edge.

17. To conceal the stitching from view on the finished collar, roll the edges again to turn the stitching line 1/16 inch under, making diagonal basting stitches (page 100) as you go to hold it in place.

SHAPING THE COLLAR

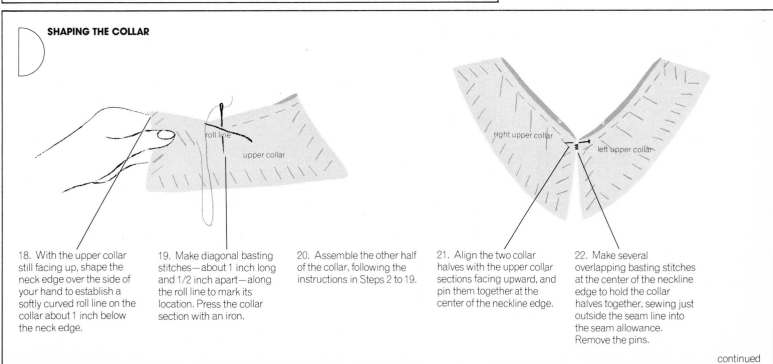

18. With the upper collar still facing up, shape the neck edge over the side of your hand to establish a softly curved roll line on the collar about 1 inch below the neck edge.

19. Make diagonal basting stitches—about 1 inch long and 1/2 inch apart—along the roll line to mark its location. Press the collar section with an iron.

20. Assemble the other half of the collar, following the instructions in Steps 2 to 19.

21. Align the two collar halves with the upper collar sections facing upward, and pin them together at the center of the neckline edge.

22. Make several overlapping basting stitches at the center of the neckline edge to hold the collar halves together, sewing just outside the seam line into the seam allowance. Remove the pins.

continued

ATTACHING THE COLLAR

23. Complete the body section of the garment according to the pattern instructions, marking the center front of the garment with a row of basting stitches. Following the instructions for The Shaped Standing Collar, Box D, Steps 19-20, baste and machine stitch the neckline of the garment.

24. Place the collar halves on the neckline, centering them over the bastings at the center front of the garment.

25. Match the notches and the basted seam lines on the collar halves to those on the garment. Pin at the notches and at the center, then add pins at 1-inch intervals all around the neckline.

26. Baste each collar half to the garment separately, working from the center out and sewing through all layers of fabric. Baste into the seam allowance just outside the basted seam line of the upper collar sections. Remove the pins.

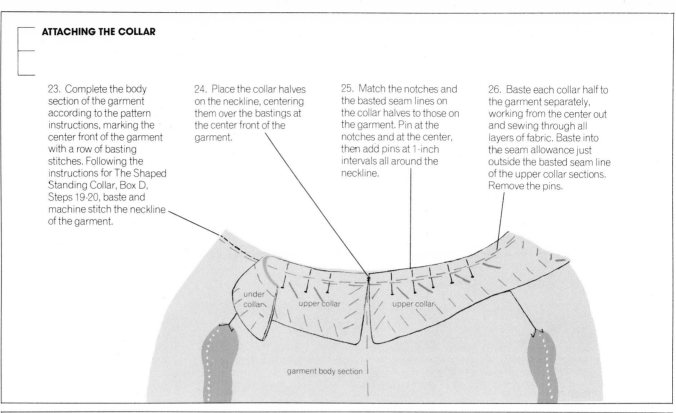

PREPARING AND ATTACHING THE FACING

27. If you have not already done so, cut out the collar facing according to the pattern instructions and mark the seam lines and the notches.

28. Hand overcast (page 204) the long curved outer edge of the facing or finish with machine zigzag stitches.

29. Place the facing, wrong side up, over the upper collar halves.

30. Match the notches and the bastings on the seam lines of the two collar halves to the notches and the seam line of the facing. Pin the facing to the collar halves and the garment at 1-inch intervals all around the neck edge.

31. Baste the facing to the collar halves and the garment, sewing through all layers of fabric just outside the seam line into the seam allowance. Remove the pins.

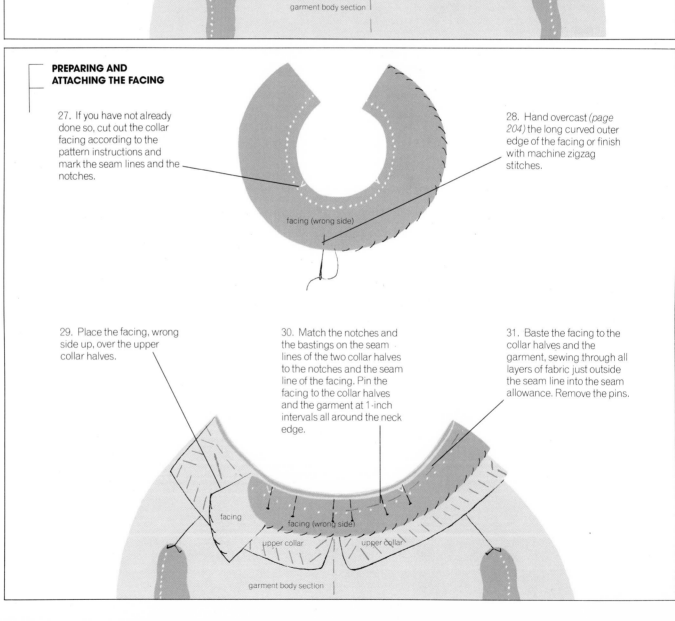

COMPLETING THE FACING

32. Machine stitch through all layers of fabric on the seam line of the facing.

33. Remove all visible bastings.

34. Trim and grade the seam allowances at the neckline, trimming the facing up to but not through the machine stitching made in Step 32. Trim the seam allowances of the two collar halves to within 1/8 inch of the machine stitching. Trim the garment neck edge to 1/4 inch.

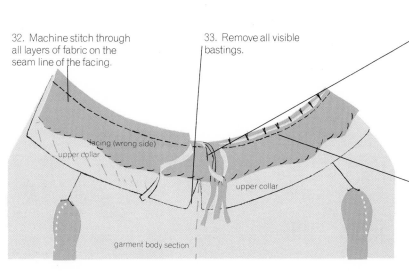

35. To ensure that the finished collar will curve smoothly around your neck, clip into the seam allowances of the garment and the collar halves at 1/2-inch intervals around the neck edge. Cut up to but not through the machine stitches.

36. Turn the garment section and the facing wrong sides up.

37. Press the seam allowances at the neckline up toward the extended facing.

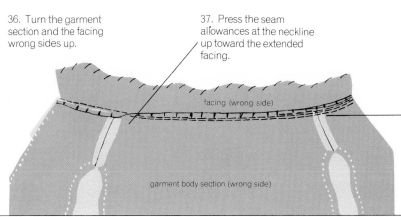

38. To prevent the facing from rolling out and showing on the finished garment, machine stitch the facing to the neckline seam allowances—a process called understitching —sewing into the seam allowance just outside the line of machine stitching made in Box E, Step 23.

FINISHING THE NECK EDGE

39. Turn the finished edge of the facing down so that it covers the neckline seam allowances. Press the facing.

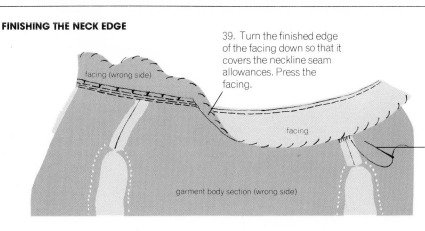

40. Hem stitch (page 204) the finished edge of the facing to the seam allowances at the garment shoulder seams. Pick up a few threads of the seam allowance fabric and the facing, making sure not to sew through to the main garment fabric.

41. Turn under the seam allowances of the placket opening at the back of the garment and finish the closure with a zipper (page 142-143).

42. Open up the zipper tab to free the opening at the back of the garment. Fold under each end of the facing, wrong sides together, and pin the folded edges out of the way of the zipper teeth.

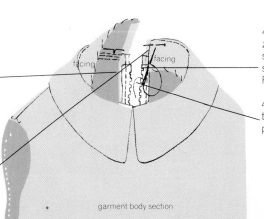

43. Baste the facing to the zipper tape and the placket seam allowance on both sides of the opening. Remove the pins.

44. Slip stitch (page 204) the ends of the facing in place. Remove the basting.

THE TIE COLLAR

A. MAKING THE TIE

1. Cut out the tie according to your pattern instructions, place it wrong side up and mark all the notches, seam lines and pattern markings indicating the points at which the tie will be attached to the garment. Baste a row of guide markings down the center line to aid in positioning the tie on the garment correctly.

2. Make another row of bastings along the fold line that runs the length of the tie.

3. Fold the tie along the fold line, wrong sides facing out. Match the seam lines, the center line bastings and the pattern markings, and pin at 2- to 3-inch intervals along the fold line to hold the tie in place.

4. Match the seam lines and seam intersections at either end of the tie and pin at 1-inch intervals at both ends. Then pin along the open edge at the bottom of the tie on each side up to the pattern markings indicating the points at which the tie will be attached to the garment.

5. Baste just outside the seam line into the seam allowance, from the fold line to the bottom edge at each end and across the bottom of the tie to the pins at the pattern markings indicating the attachment points. Remove all of the pins.

6. Machine stitch on the seam line at each end of the tie beginning at the fold line, pivoting at the corner and continuing to the end of the bastings. Remove these bastings, but leave in the bastings at the center line and along the fold line.

7. At the pattern markings indicating the attachment points, cut into the seam allowance from the bottom edge of the tie to within 1/4 inch of the machine stitching.

8. Starting from the cuts made in Step 7, trim the seam allowances at the bottom and sides of each end of the tie, to within 1/4 inch of the machine stitching.

9. Clip off the four corners of the tie diagonally, cutting up to but not through the machine stitches.

10. Turn the collar right side out, pushing one end at a time through the open edges in the center. Push out the four corners with the tip of a pair of closed scissors. Press, and remove the fold-line bastings.

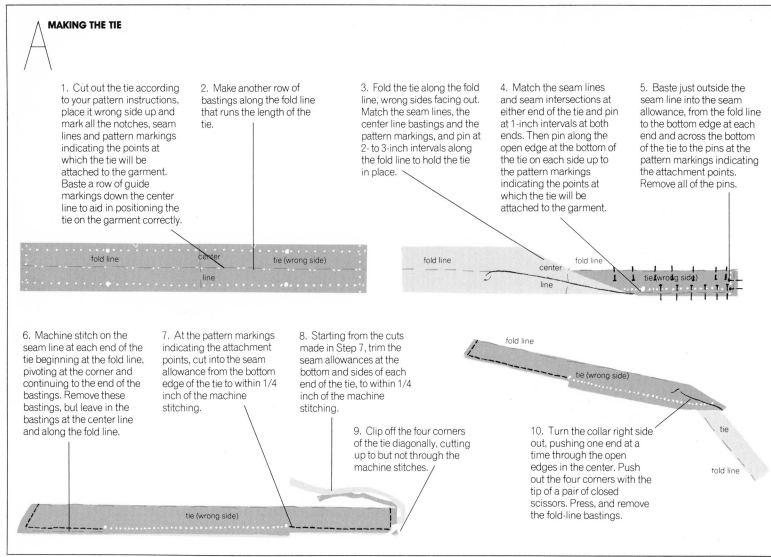

B. PREPARING THE NECKLINE OF THE GARMENT

11. Complete the body section of the garment according to the pattern instructions. Make sure that the front facings are turned to the wrong side of the garment.

12. To determine the center back line on the garment, spread it wrong side up and measure in halfway from the intersection of the underarm seam lines with the garment side seam and halfway between the notches indicating the attachment points of the tie. Mark the points with chalk and draw a line connecting these points. Run a line of basting stitches along the center back line.

13. Baste around the neck edge of the garment along the seam line to aid you in positioning the collar correctly.

14. Machine stitch the neckline of the garment —setting the machine at 10 stitches per inch—to hold the neckline in shape and prevent possible fraying. Stitch just outside the seam line into the seam allowance.

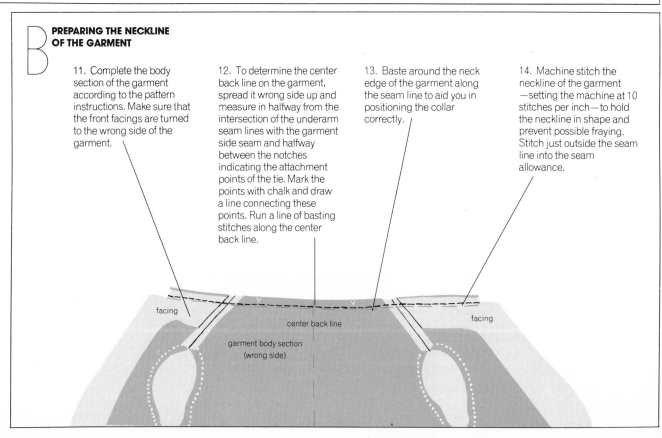

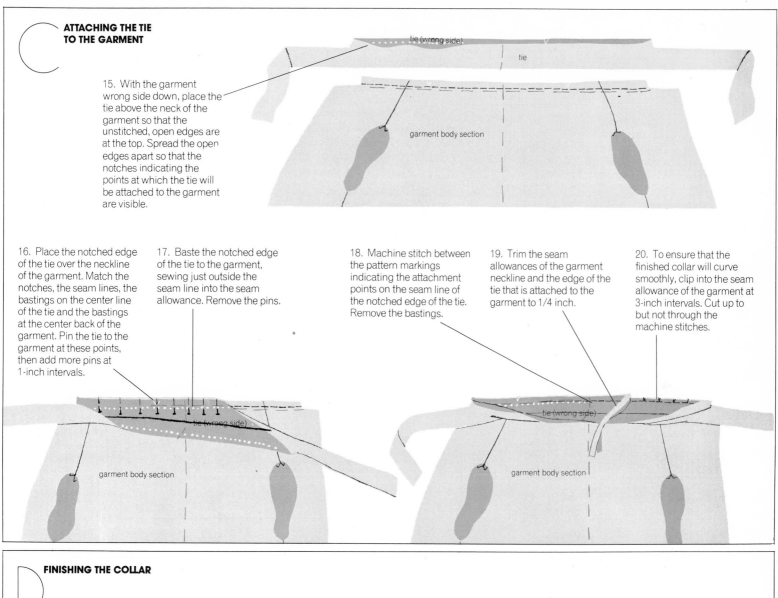

ATTACHING THE TIE TO THE GARMENT

15. With the garment wrong side down, place the tie above the neck of the garment so that the unstitched, open edges are at the top. Spread the open edges apart so that the notches indicating the points at which the tie will be attached to the garment are visible.

16. Place the notched edge of the tie over the neckline of the garment. Match the notches, the seam lines, the bastings on the center line of the tie and the bastings at the center back of the garment. Pin the tie to the garment at these points, then add more pins at 1-inch intervals.

17. Baste the notched edge of the tie to the garment, sewing just outside the seam line into the seam allowance. Remove the pins.

18. Machine stitch between the pattern markings indicating the attachment points on the seam line of the notched edge of the tie. Remove the bastings.

19. Trim the seam allowances of the garment neckline and the edge of the tie that is attached to the garment to 1/4 inch.

20. To ensure that the finished collar will curve smoothly, clip into the seam allowance of the garment at 3-inch intervals. Cut up to but not through the machine stitches.

FINISHING THE COLLAR

21. Place the garment wrong side up. Turn the tie up away from the garment. Lift up the remaining open edge of the tie and, using an iron, press the machine-stitched and trimmed seam allowances of the tie and the garment toward the tie.

22. Fold under the unstitched edge of the tie along its seam line, wrong sides together, and press the folded edge.

23. Place the folded edge of the tie over the machine stitching made in Box C, Step 18, and pin it. Baste close to the fold and remove the pins.

24. Slip stitch (page 204) along the fold, picking up threads of the machine stitching on the garment so that the stitches do not show through to the outside.

25. Turn the garment right side out. Remove all remaining bastings. Press the tie on both sides.

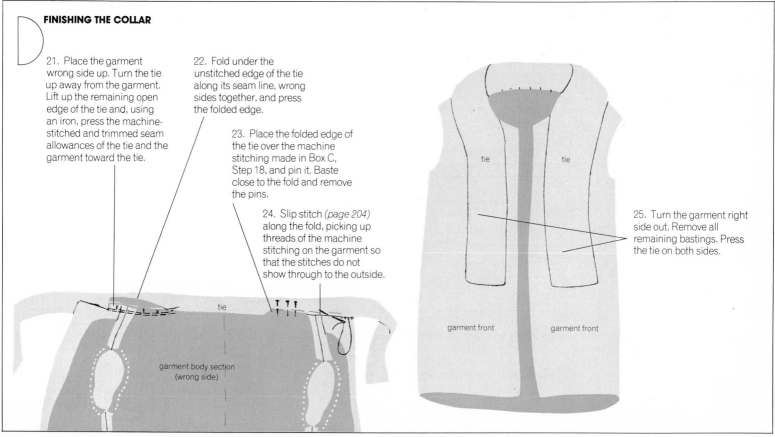

Linings: visible and invisible

Nothing sets apart a garment as custom-made more distinctly than a lining or an underlining.

An underlining, which gives support to the fabric, is cut in the shape of the main pieces of the garment from tightly woven synthetic fabric especially made for this purpose. The underlining is sewn to each piece of the garment, and the two layers are then treated as one when the garment is constructed.

A lining is constructed independently of special lining fabric, such as rayon, polyester blends or even silk. It is then installed inside the assembled garment as a layer to separate the garment from the body. This prevents the garment from clinging and allows it to retain its own shape, as seen in the lined House of Norell skirt at left. Lining also has other purposes that cannot be seen: to finish the garment as perfectly on the inside as on the outside and to conceal construction details such as darts and seam allowances.

Because lining fabrics are tightly woven and do not "give," it is important to pin the lining to the garment just loosely enough to cause the lining to wrinkle slightly. Then, when the outer fabric stretches a bit, the lining will not be too tight.

MAKING AND ATTACHING UNDERLINING

1. Before constructing the garment, cut out the underlining from special underlining fabric, using the main pieces of your pattern, exactly as you cut out the garment fabric. Do not cut out underlinings for garment pieces that will be interfaced or for those that will be on the underside of the garment, such as facings.

2. Transfer all pattern markings to either side of the underlining; do not transfer any pattern markings to the garment fabric pieces to be underlined.

3. Working on one section at a time (a skirt front in this drawing) lay the underlining marked side down, and cover it with the corresponding garment section, wrong side down. Pin the two pieces of fabric together around all the edges, keeping them as flat as possible.

4. On large pattern pieces, run parallel rows of diagonal basting stitches (page 100) about 3 inches apart down the length of the section, smoothing the two fabrics as you go to eliminate puckers and wrinkles.

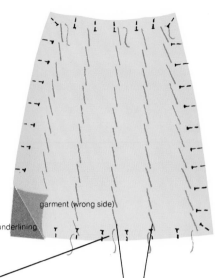

garment (wrong side)

underlining

5. Turn each section over so that the underlining faces up. Run hand bastings along all seam lines and pattern markings, stitching through both garment and underlining. Smooth the layers of fabric outward from the diagonal bastings so that both layers lie as flat as possible. Start at one corner or seam intersection and stitch to the opposite corner; stop, leaving 2 or 3 inches of thread loose. Begin again in the next direction with a new thread. Remove the pins.

6. Check the underlining and garment fabric to be sure they are smooth. If either layer pulls or wrinkles, clip the nearby bastings and re-baste.

7. Repeat Steps 1-6 on all pattern pieces that are to be underlined.

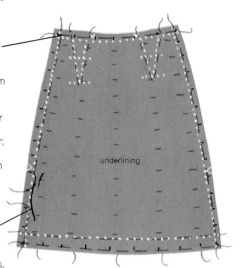

underlining

8. Sew the garment, but do not remove the basting stitches holding the underlinings to each section until the garment is completed.

MAKING LINING

LINING FOR A DRESS WITHOUT FACINGS

1. If your pattern does not provide separate pattern pieces for the lining—as in the example shown, a dress with a waistline seam—cut out the lining fabric exactly as you did the garment fabric, using only the main pattern pieces.

2. Transfer the pattern markings to the wrong sides of the lining.

3. Machine stitch the darts and all the seams except the waistline seam and armhole seams to complete the lining for each section of the garment, making any fitting adjustments you made on the garment. Press the darts and seams.

4. Machine stitch along the neckline and armhole seam lines to prevent stretching. Also stitch along the waist seam line on the skirt.

5. Machine baste—at six stitches per inch—two parallel lines 1/4 inch apart along the top of the sleeves, between the notches, leaving loose threads at both ends for easing.

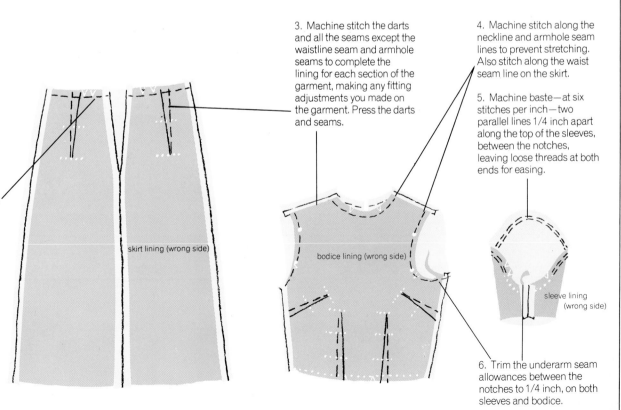

skirt lining (wrong side)

bodice lining (wrong side)

sleeve lining (wrong side)

6. Trim the underarm seam allowances between the notches to 1/4 inch, on both sleeves and bodice.

LINING FOR A DRESS WITH FACINGS

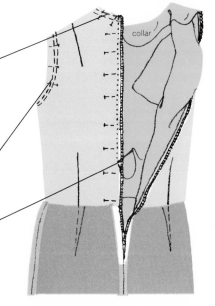

facing pattern piece

facing pattern piece

lining (wrong side)

1. Cut out, mark and machine stitch the lining as shown in Steps 1-3 for making a lining for a dress without facings *(page 113)*. Stitch the waist seam line on the skirt lining.

2. Pin the patterns for the facings over the wrong side of the appropriate lining pieces, matching the seam lines at the edges.

3. Draw a line with chalk or a dressmaker's marking pencil on the lining along the inside edge of each facing pattern. Remove the pins and the facing pattern pieces.

4. Run a line of machine stitching on the edge of the lining 5/8 inch from the chalk line made in Step 3.

5. Trim the edge of the lining 5/8 inch from the machine stitching made in Step 4; then clip at 1/2-inch intervals into the trimmed edge at the curves to within 1/8 inch of the stitching line.

ATTACHING LINING TO A BODICE

LINING A BODICE WITHOUT FACINGS

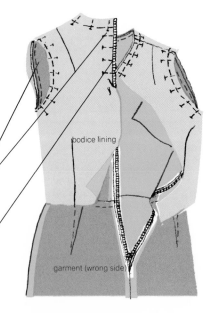

bodice lining

garment (wrong side)

collar

1. Turn the bodice wrong side out and tuck the sleeves inside the bodice armholes.

2. Place the bodice lining over the garment with the wrong sides facing in. Pin the lining to the garment around the armholes and neckline at 2-inch intervals, matching seam lines and pattern markings.

3. Fold under the lining along the zipper opening so that the folded edge is 1/4 inch from the teeth of the zipper, and pin.

4. Check to be sure the lining does not bind or pull the garment fabric out of shape. If it does, re-pin, even if this means that the folded edge of the lining may have to be drawn back slightly from its original position.

5. Baste the garment and the lining together along the line of machine stitching at the neckline of the garment.

6. Hand stitch a row of running stitches around the armholes, going through both lining and garment layers as closely as possible to the outside of the seam line of the armholes.

7. Slip stitch *(page 204)* the folded edge of the lining at the zipper. Remove all pins.

8. Attach the collar, neckband or other neckline finish as the pattern instructs.

LINING A BODICE WITH FACINGS

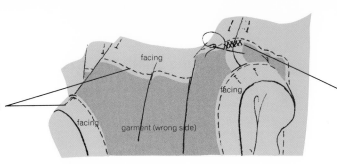

1. Run a line of machine stitching around the facings 1/4 inch away from the unfinished edges.

2. Hand sew the machine-stitched edge of the facing to the garment at the shoulder seams, underarm seams and waistline seam, using a catch stitch *(page 204)*.

3. Place the garment on a wooden or padded hanger, wrong side out, and drop the bodice lining over it, wrong side in. Pin the lining to the garment along the neckline, armholes and front or back opening, placing pins 1 1/2 inches from the edges at 2- to 3-inch intervals, matching the lining seam lines to those of the garment at the shoulder and side seams.

4. Check to be sure the lining does not bind or pull the garment fabric out of shape. If it does, re-pin, even if this means that the folded edge of the lining may have to be drawn back slightly from its original position.

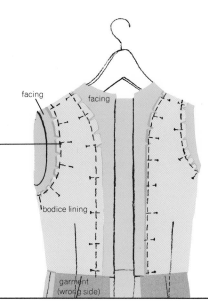

5. Remove one of the pins holding the lining to the bodice, and fold under the edge of the lining so that the machine stitching along the edge is hidden, then replace the pin 1/2 inch from the folded edge. Repeat—removing, folding and replacing one pin at a time—around the lining edge at the neckline, armholes and bodice opening.

6. Slip stitch *(page 204)* the folded edge of lining to the garment facing around the neckline and armholes and along the front or back opening. Remove the pins.

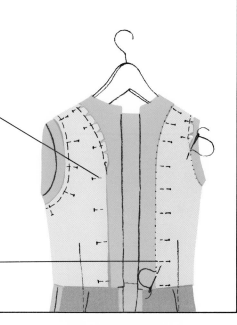

ATTACHING LINING AT A WAISTLINE

A ATTACHING THE SKIRT LINING

1. Turn the garment wrong side out and fold the lined bodice down inside the skirt, leaving the waistline seam uppermost.

2. Place the skirt lining, wrong side in, over the skirt, and pin the two together around the waistline, aligning the seam lines at the waist and matching all pattern markings.

3A. If the garment opening has a zipper, fold under the seam allowances of the skirt lining along the opening so that the folded edges are 1/4 inch from the teeth of the zipper. Pin.

3B. If the skirt opening has a facing, prepare it and attach it as you did for the bodice.

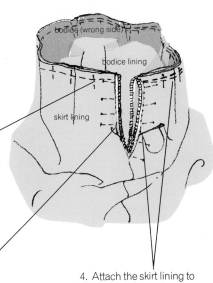

4. Attach the skirt lining to the garment along the waistline seam with a line of small, running stitches *(page 204)*; then slip stitch *(page 204)* the lining to the zipper or facing at the opening. Remove the pins.

B ATTACHING THE BODICE LINING TO THE SKIRT

5. Place the dress on a wooden or padded hanger, wrong side out. Push the bottom of the lining fabric up toward the shoulders about 1/4 inch, so that it blouses slightly, then pin the bodice lining to the bodice 1 1/2 inches above the waistline seam, matching the side seams of the lining and garment.

6. Fold under the bottom of the bodice lining so that the folded edge just covers the hand stitches made at the waistline seam in Step 4 and pin.

7. Remove the garment from the hanger and slip stitch the bodice lining to the skirt lining. Remove the pins. The lining will blouse slightly over the waistline, creating wearing ease.

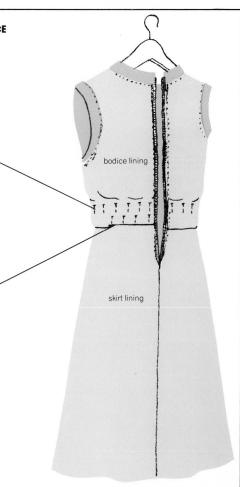

ATTACHING LINING TO A SLEEVE

A. PREPARING THE SLEEVE LINING

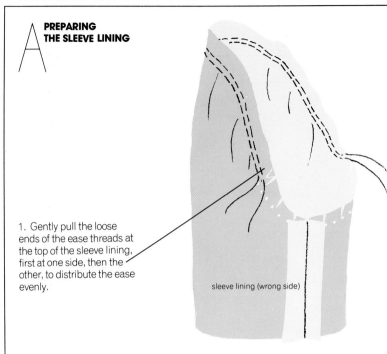

sleeve lining (wrong side)

1. Gently pull the loose ends of the ease threads at the top of the sleeve lining, first at one side, then the other, to distribute the ease evenly.

B. ATTACHING THE SLEEVE LINING TO A GARMENT AT THE SHOULDER

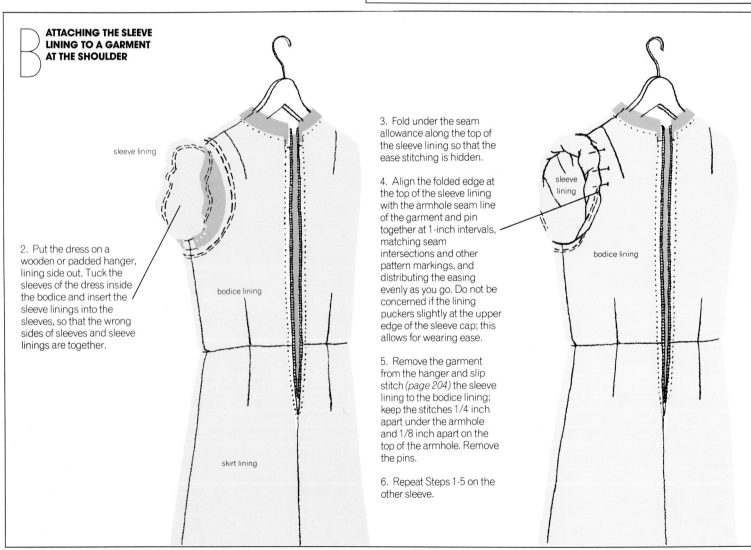

sleeve lining

bodice lining

skirt lining

sleeve lining

bodice lining

2. Put the dress on a wooden or padded hanger, lining side out. Tuck the sleeves of the dress inside the bodice and insert the sleeve linings into the sleeves, so that the wrong sides of sleeves and sleeve linings are together.

3. Fold under the seam allowance along the top of the sleeve lining so that the ease stitching is hidden.

4. Align the folded edge at the top of the sleeve lining with the armhole seam line of the garment and pin together at 1-inch intervals, matching seam intersections and other pattern markings, and distributing the easing evenly as you go. Do not be concerned if the lining puckers slightly at the upper edge of the sleeve cap; this allows for wearing ease.

5. Remove the garment from the hanger and slip stitch (*page 204*) the sleeve lining to the bodice lining; keep the stitches 1/4 inch apart under the armhole and 1/8 inch apart on the top of the armhole. Remove the pins.

6. Repeat Steps 1-5 on the other sleeve.

ATTACHING A SLEEVE LINING AT THE SLEEVE HEM

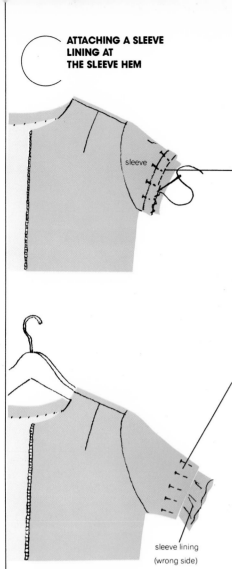

sleeve

sleeve lining
(wrong side)

7. Run a line of machine stitching 1/4 inch in from the bottom edge of the unhemmed sleeve. Fold up the sleeve to the desired length and pin. Stitch the hem, using a blind hemming stitch *(page 101)*. Remove pins; press.

8. Place the garment on a wooden or padded hanger, right side out, and pull out the sleeve lining so that it hangs below the bottom of the sleeve.

9A. If you are working on a short sleeve, pin the sleeve to the lining 3 inches above the bottom edge of the sleeve.

9B. If the sleeve reaches below the elbow, pin the lining as described in Step 9A. Baste and remove the pins. Try on the garment. If the lining causes strain when the elbow is bent, or if it causes the sleeve to ride up, clip the basting stitches, push the lining up slightly toward the shoulder and re-baste.

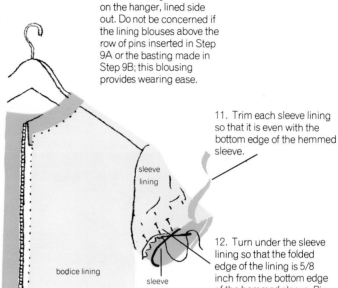

bodice lining

sleeve lining

sleeve

10. Place the garment back on the hanger, lined side out. Do not be concerned if the lining blouses above the row of pins inserted in Step 9A or the basting made in Step 9B; this blousing provides wearing ease.

11. Trim each sleeve lining so that it is even with the bottom edge of the hemmed sleeve.

12. Turn under the sleeve lining so that the folded edge of the lining is 5/8 inch from the bottom edge of the hemmed sleeve. Pin and hem with a blind hemming stitch *(page 101)*.

13. Remove the pins and any basting stitches. The sleeve lining will drop slightly (almost to the sleeve edge) when released; this is necessary for wearing ease. Press lightly at the hem.

ATTACHING LINING TO THE SKIRT OF A HEMMED GARMENT

A. HEMMING THE LINING

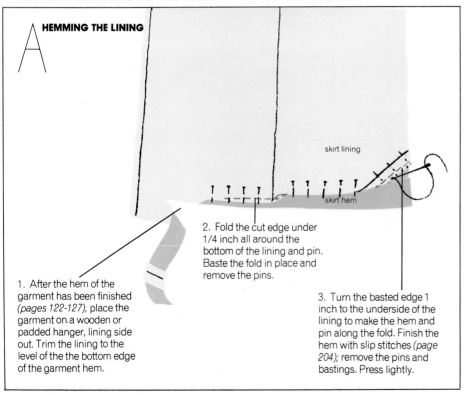

skirt lining

skirt hem

1. After the hem of the garment has been finished *(pages 122-127)*, place the garment on a wooden or padded hanger, lining side out. Trim the lining to the level of the bottom edge of the garment hem.

2. Fold the cut edge under 1/4 inch all around the bottom of the lining and pin. Baste the fold in place and remove the pins.

3. Turn the basted edge 1 inch to the underside of the lining to make the hem and pin along the fold. Finish the hem with slip stitches *(page 204)*; remove the pins and bastings. Press lightly.

B. ATTACHING THE LINING TO THE GARMENT

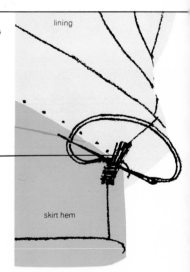

lining

skirt hem

4. Connect the hem of the lining to the hem of the garment at each vertical seam with a 1-inch-long chain of thread called a French tack. To make a French tack, begin by making a 1-inch "bar" of thread between the lining and the garment hem. Using a doubled thread knotted at the end, make a stitch in the middle of the lining hem, then draw the needle through and pick up a few threads of the under layer of the garment hem. Repeat this two or three times in the same place. End with a backstitch *(page 98)* on the hem of the garment.

5. Make the chain part of the French tack by inserting the needle through the loops of thread, as in the blanket stitch *(page 101)*, using the "bar" of thread formed in Step 4 as if it were a fabric edge.

117

Pockets: the discreet, flat welt

In a welt pocket, one of the more elegant variations on that essential clothing convenience, all but the top edge, or welt, of the pocket is entirely hidden inside the garment. Welt pockets are best suited to garments made from a firmly woven fabric that does not fray easily. The pocket should be of lightweight fabric and its color should harmonize with the garment. The welt itself is a straight strip made from the same fabric as the garment. For an added custom touch, make the interior of the pocket from the same fabric that you use to line the rest of the garment.

The well-made welt pocket should look crisp and the welt should lie absolutely flat like the House of Norell version at right. To achieve this effect, take special care to match all pattern markings precisely and to cut and stitch accurately when making the little triangles at each end of the pocket opening, as illustrated in Boxes E and G on pages 120-121.

THE WELT POCKET

A CUTTING OUT THE WELT INTERFACING

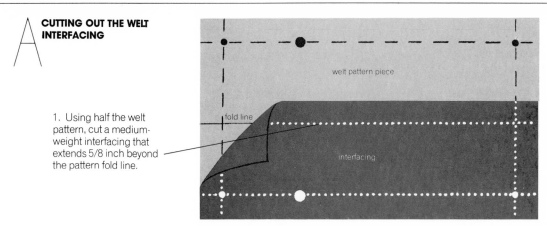

welt pattern piece

fold line

interfacing

1. Using half the welt pattern, cut a medium-weight interfacing that extends 5/8 inch beyond the pattern fold line.

B ATTACHING THE INTERFACING

2. Cut the welt from the garment material and pin the interfacing to the wrong side of the welt, matching the seam lines and other pattern markings.

3. Baste the left, upper and right edges of the interfacing to the welt just inside the seam lines. Remove the pins.

4. Just outside the fold line, attach the interfacing to the welt with small running stitches, about six to an inch. Use thread the same color as the garment and pick up only a thread of the welt fabric.

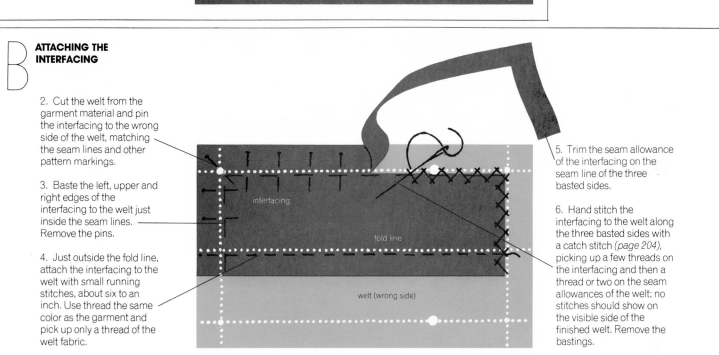

interfacing

fold line

welt (wrong side)

5. Trim the seam allowance of the interfacing on the seam line of the three basted sides.

6. Hand stitch the interfacing to the welt along the three basted sides with a catch stitch *(page 204)*, picking up a few threads on the interfacing and then a thread or two on the seam allowances of the welt; no stitches should show on the visible side of the finished welt. Remove the bastings.

C STITCHING AND FOLDING THE WELT

7. Fold the interfaced welt along the fold line, wrong side out.

8. Pin and baste the folded welt along the seam lines at left and right. Remove the pins.

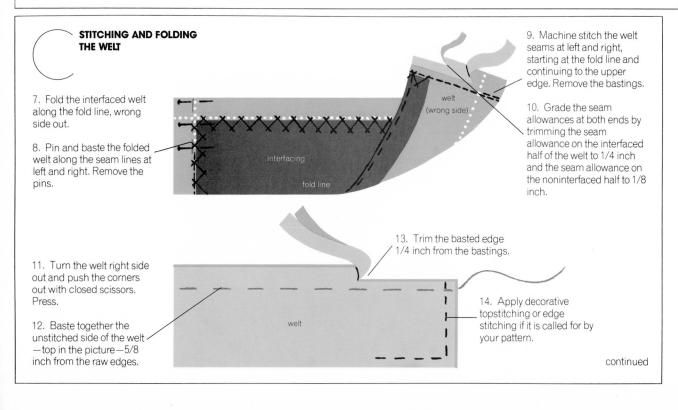

welt (wrong side)

interfacing

fold line

9. Machine stitch the welt seams at left and right, starting at the fold line and continuing to the upper edge. Remove the bastings.

10. Grade the seam allowances at both ends by trimming the seam allowance on the interfaced half of the welt to 1/4 inch and the seam allowance on the noninterfaced half to 1/8 inch.

11. Turn the welt right side out and push the corners out with closed scissors. Press.

12. Baste together the unstitched side of the welt —top in the picture—5/8 inch from the raw edges.

welt

13. Trim the basted edge 1/4 inch from the bastings.

14. Apply decorative topstitching or edge stitching if it is called for by your pattern.

continued

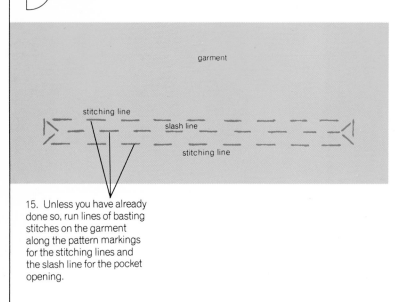

16. Pin the welt to the right side of the garment—the side that will be visible when the garment is finished —matching the basting made in Step 12 to the marking for the lower stitching line.

17. Baste the welt to the garment just below the basting made in Step 12 and remove the pins.

18. Machine stitch the welt to the garment between the two lines of basting. Remove both lines of basting.

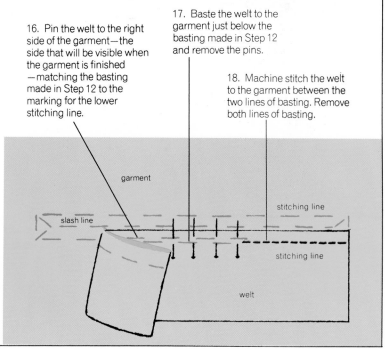

15. Unless you have already done so, run lines of basting stitches on the garment along the pattern markings for the stitching lines and the slash line for the pocket opening.

LINING THE POCKET

19. Unless you have already done so, run lines of basting stitches on the pocket lining along the pattern markings for the stitching lines and the slash line for the pocket opening.

20. With the larger part of the pocket lining at the top, place the lining wrong side up on the garment, matching the lower stitching line of the lining to the machine stitching on the welt made in Step 18.

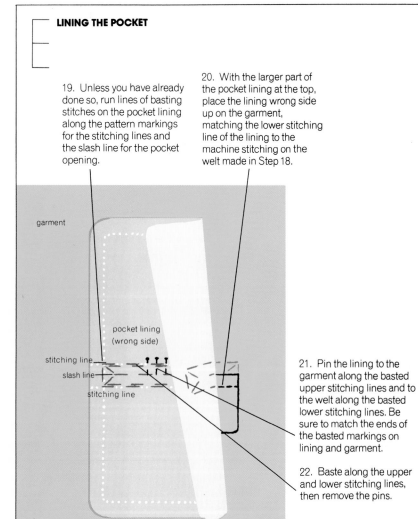

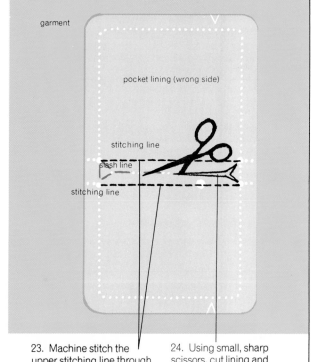

21. Pin the lining to the garment along the basted upper stitching lines and to the welt along the basted lower stitching lines. Be sure to match the ends of the basted markings on lining and garment.

22. Baste along the upper and lower stitching lines, then remove the pins.

23. Machine stitch the upper stitching line through pocket lining and garment; machine stitch the lower stitching line through pocket lining, garment and the two layers of welt fabric. Reinforce both ends of the stitching lines with backstitches. Do not machine stitch along the ends. Remove the bastings.

24. Using small, sharp scissors, cut lining and garment along the basted slash line, first to the apex of the triangular marking at one end and then to the apex of the triangular marking at the other.

25. Carefully clip along the triangle sides toward the ends of the stitching lines, cutting up to—but not into —the machine stitches made in Step 23.

F FORMING THE POCKET

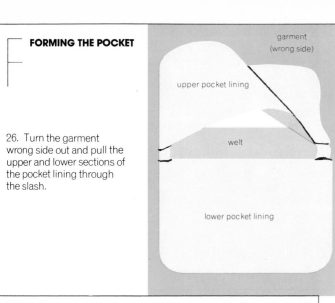

garment (wrong side)

upper pocket lining

welt

lower pocket lining

26. Turn the garment wrong side out and pull the upper and lower sections of the pocket lining through the slash.

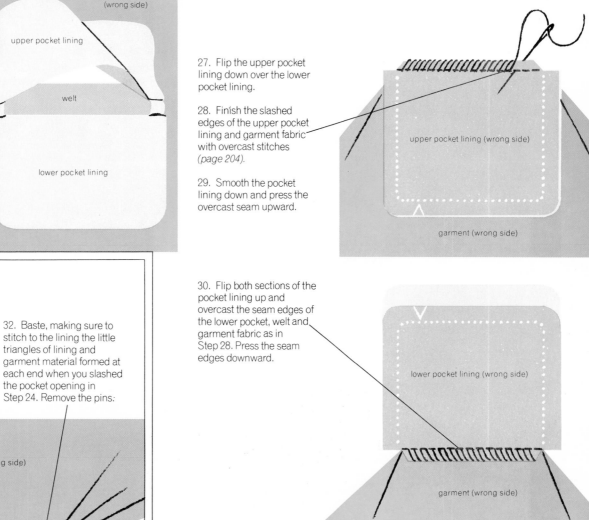

upper pocket lining (wrong side)

garment (wrong side)

lower pocket lining (wrong side)

garment (wrong side)

27. Flip the upper pocket lining down over the lower pocket lining.

28. Finish the slashed edges of the upper pocket lining and garment fabric with overcast stitches *(page 204)*.

29. Smooth the pocket lining down and press the overcast seam upward.

30. Flip both sections of the pocket lining up and overcast the seam edges of the lower pocket, welt and garment fabric as in Step 28. Press the seam edges downward.

G FINISHING THE POCKET

31. Turn the pocket lining sections down again and pin them together along the sides and bottom, matching seam lines and other pattern markings.

32. Baste, making sure to stitch to the lining the little triangles of lining and garment material formed at each end when you slashed the pocket opening in Step 24. Remove the pins:

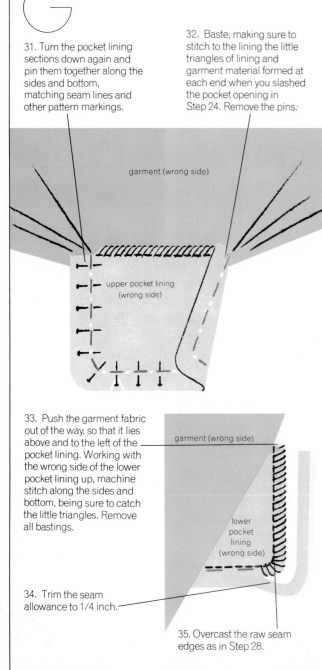

garment (wrong side)

upper pocket lining (wrong side)

33. Push the garment fabric out of the way, so that it lies above and to the left of the pocket lining. Working with the wrong side of the lower pocket lining up, machine stitch along the sides and bottom, being sure to catch the little triangles. Remove all bastings.

garment (wrong side)

lower pocket lining (wrong side)

34. Trim the seam allowance to 1/4 inch.

35. Overcast the raw seam edges as in Step 28.

H FINISHING THE WELT

36. Turn the garment right side out. Press the welt upward and pin the ends of the welt to the garment. Baste and remove the pins.

37. Slip stitch *(page 204)* the welt ends to the garment, picking up only a thread of the garment fabric close to the welt and sliding the needle through the fold of the welt. Remove the basting and press.

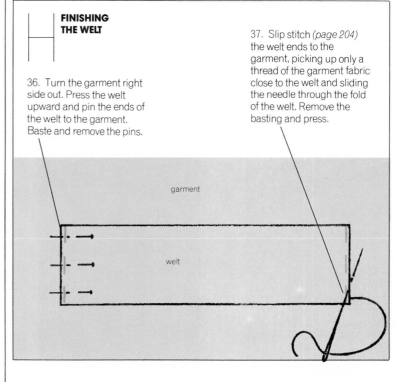

garment

welt

Hemlines: flared or reinforced

The lowly hem—often dashed off after the rest of the garment has been completed with care—has its own sewing techniques that help lend a look of elegance.

On most dresses a 2 1/2-inch hem is a good average, but the heavier the fabric and the more flare to the skirt the narrower the hem should be. If a skirt flares, the bottom raw edge will be wider than the hemline, which is 1 to 2 1/2 inches above that edge. The raw edge must be shrunk, or eased, to fit the circumference at the hemline, as illustrated opposite. Do not make little tucks as you hem a flared skirt. Unless your hem is properly eased it will never approach the professional look of the House of Norell skirt shown at left. A decorative variation on the basic eased hem is the scalloped edge, shown on pages 125 and 126.

A garment that has been underlined *(page 113)* requires a different technique—a hem with bias interfacing. This is a hem that has been stiffened slightly to reinforce the shape at the hemline, just as the underlining reinforces the shape of the garment as a whole.

All of these variations will be enhanced if you add a Hong Kong Finish *(page 127)* of the same material as the dress or its underlining—another custom touch.

THE EASED HEM

A PREPARING TO MAKE THE HEM

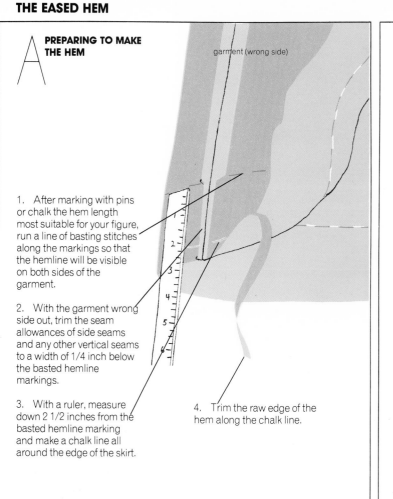

garment (wrong side)

1. After marking with pins or chalk the hem length most suitable for your figure, run a line of basting stitches along the markings so that the hemline will be visible on both sides of the garment.

2. With the garment wrong side out, trim the seam allowances of side seams and any other vertical seams to a width of 1/4 inch below the basted hemline markings.

3. With a ruler, measure down 2 1/2 inches from the basted hemline marking and make a chalk line all around the edge of the skirt.

4. Trim the raw edge of the hem along the chalk line.

B TURNING UP THE HEM

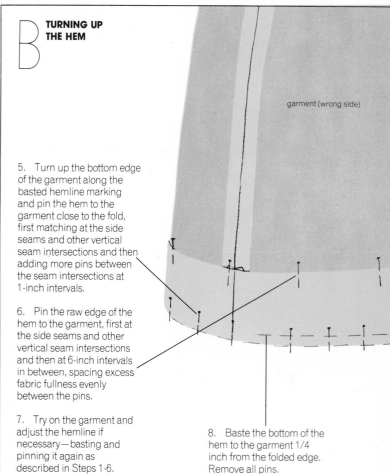

garment (wrong side)

5. Turn up the bottom edge of the garment along the basted hemline marking and pin the hem to the garment close to the fold, first matching at the side seams and other vertical seam intersections and then adding more pins between the seam intersections at 1-inch intervals.

6. Pin the raw edge of the hem to the garment, first at the side seams and other vertical seam intersections and then at 6-inch intervals in between, spacing excess fabric fullness evenly between the pins.

7. Try on the garment and adjust the hemline if necessary—basting and pinning it again as described in Steps 1-6.

8. Baste the bottom of the hem to the garment 1/4 inch from the folded edge. Remove all pins.

C EASING THE HEM

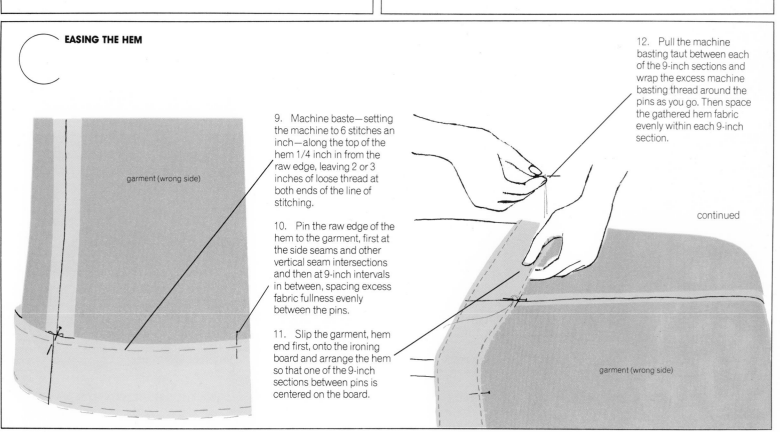

garment (wrong side)

garment (wrong side)

9. Machine baste—setting the machine to 6 stitches an inch—along the top of the hem 1/4 inch in from the raw edge, leaving 2 or 3 inches of loose thread at both ends of the line of stitching.

10. Pin the raw edge of the hem to the garment, first at the side seams and other vertical seam intersections and then at 9-inch intervals in between, spacing excess fabric fullness evenly between the pins.

11. Slip the garment, hem end first, onto the ironing board and arrange the hem so that one of the 9-inch sections between pins is centered on the board.

12. Pull the machine basting taut between each of the 9-inch sections and wrap the excess machine basting thread around the pins as you go. Then space the gathered hem fabric evenly within each 9-inch section.

continued

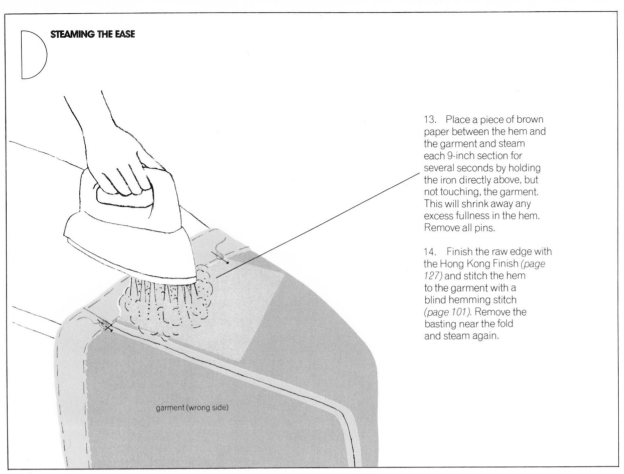

D STEAMING THE EASE

13. Place a piece of brown paper between the hem and the garment and steam each 9-inch section for several seconds by holding the iron directly above, but not touching, the garment. This will shrink away any excess fullness in the hem. Remove all pins.

14. Finish the raw edge with the Hong Kong Finish *(page 127)* and stitch the hem to the garment with a blind hemming stitch *(page 101)*. Remove the basting near the fold and steam again.

garment (wrong side)

THE BIAS INTERFACED HEM

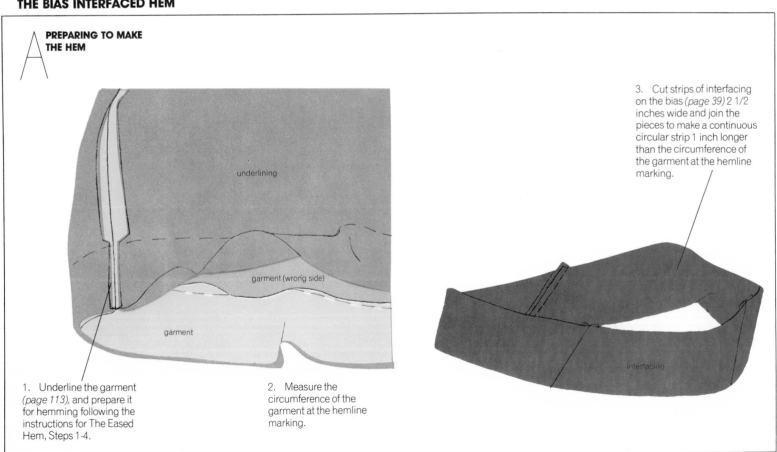

A PREPARING TO MAKE THE HEM

underlining

garment (wrong side)

garment

interfacing

1. Underline the garment *(page 113)*, and prepare it for hemming following the instructions for The Eased Hem, Steps 1-4.

2. Measure the circumference of the garment at the hemline marking.

3. Cut strips of interfacing on the bias *(page 39)* 2 1/2 inches wide and join the pieces to make a continuous circular strip 1 inch longer than the circumference of the garment at the hemline marking.

B ATTACHING THE BIAS STRIP

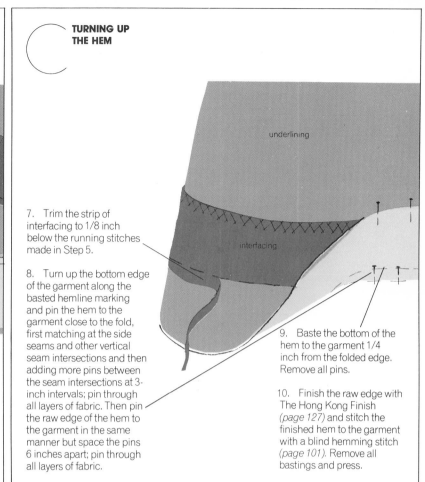

4. Pin the bias strip to the underlining of the garment with its lower edge 5/8 inch below the hemline marking.

5. Sew the bias strip to the underlining with a running stitch *(page 204)* a fraction of an inch below the hemline marking, making sure not to stitch through the garment fabric.

6. Sew the top edge of the strip to the underlining with a catch stitch *(page 204)*, making sure not to stitch through the garment fabric. Remove the pins.

C TURNING UP THE HEM

7. Trim the strip of interfacing to 1/8 inch below the running stitches made in Step 5.

8. Turn up the bottom edge of the garment along the basted hemline marking and pin the hem to the garment close to the fold, first matching at the side seams and other vertical seam intersections and then adding more pins between the seam intersections at 3-inch intervals; pin through all layers of fabric. Then pin the raw edge of the hem to the garment in the same manner but space the pins 6 inches apart; pin through all layers of fabric.

9. Baste the bottom of the hem to the garment 1/4 inch from the folded edge. Remove all pins.

10. Finish the raw edge with The Hong Kong Finish *(page 127)* and stitch the finished hem to the garment with a blind hemming stitch *(page 101)*. Remove all bastings and press.

THE SCALLOPED HEM

A PREPARING TO MAKE THE HEM

1. Prepare the garment for hemming following the instructions for The Eased Hem, Step 1.

2. Trim the raw edge of the garment evenly 1 inch below the hemline marking.

3. Measure the circumference of the garment along the bottom raw edge.

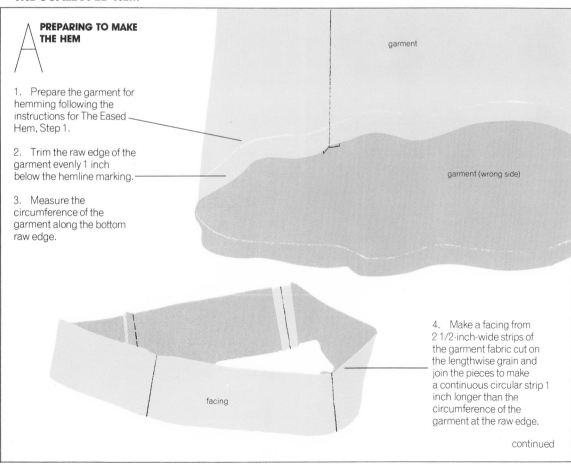

4. Make a facing from 2 1/2-inch-wide strips of the garment fabric cut on the lengthwise grain and join the pieces to make a continuous circular strip 1 inch longer than the circumference of the garment at the raw edge.

continued

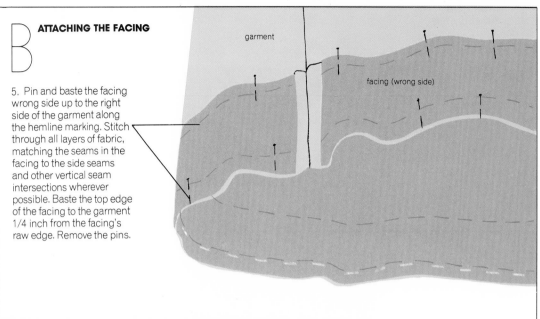

B ATTACHING THE FACING

garment

facing (wrong side)

5. Pin and baste the facing wrong side up to the right side of the garment along the hemline marking. Stitch through all layers of fabric, matching the seams in the facing to the side seams and other vertical seam intersections wherever possible. Baste the top edge of the facing to the garment 1/4 inch from the facing's raw edge. Remove the pins.

C MAKING THE SCALLOPS

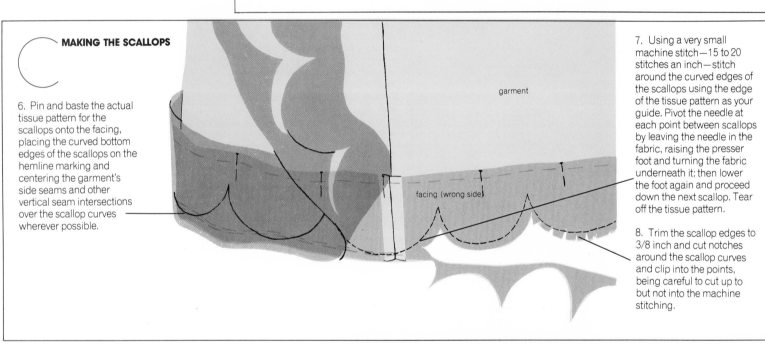

garment

facing (wrong side)

6. Pin and baste the actual tissue pattern for the scallops onto the facing, placing the curved bottom edges of the scallops on the hemline marking and centering the garment's side seams and other vertical seam intersections over the scallop curves wherever possible.

7. Using a very small machine stitch—15 to 20 stitches an inch—stitch around the curved edges of the scallops using the edge of the tissue pattern as your guide. Pivot the needle at each point between scallops by leaving the needle in the fabric, raising the presser foot and turning the fabric underneath it; then lower the foot again and proceed down the next scallop. Tear off the tissue pattern.

8. Trim the scallop edges to 3/8 inch and cut notches around the scallop curves and clip into the points, being careful to cut up to but not into the machine stitching.

D FINISHING THE SCALLOPS

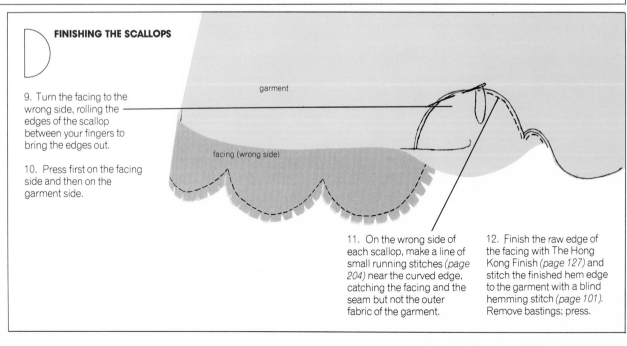

garment

facing (wrong side)

9. Turn the facing to the wrong side, rolling the edges of the scallop between your fingers to bring the edges out.

10. Press first on the facing side and then on the garment side.

11. On the wrong side of each scallop, make a line of small running stitches (page 204) near the curved edge, catching the facing and the seam but not the outer fabric of the garment.

12. Finish the raw edge of the facing with The Hong Kong Finish (page 127) and stitch the finished hem edge to the garment with a blind hemming stitch (page 101). Remove bastings; press.

THE HONG KONG FINISH

A PREPARING TO MAKE THE HEM

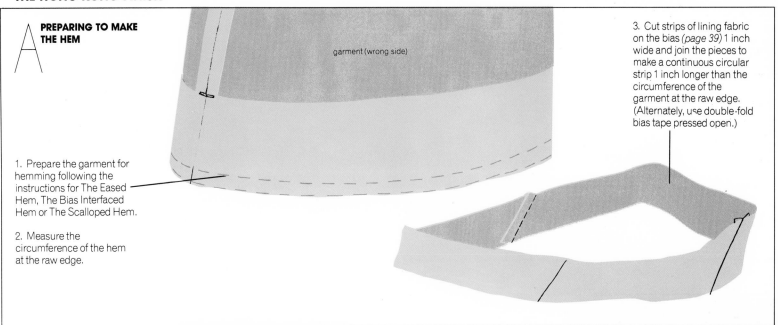

garment (wrong side)

1. Prepare the garment for hemming following the instructions for The Eased Hem, The Bias Interfaced Hem or The Scalloped Hem.

2. Measure the circumference of the hem at the raw edge.

3. Cut strips of lining fabric on the bias (page 39) 1 inch wide and join the pieces to make a continuous circular strip 1 inch longer than the circumference of the garment at the raw edge. (Alternately, use double-fold bias tape pressed open.)

B ATTACHING THE BIAS STRIP

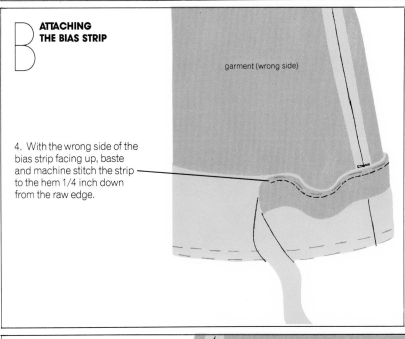

garment (wrong side)

4. With the wrong side of the bias strip facing up, baste and machine stitch the strip to the hem 1/4 inch down from the raw edge.

C TURNING THE BIAS STRIP

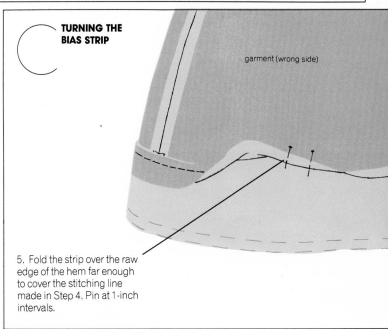

garment (wrong side)

5. Fold the strip over the raw edge of the hem far enough to cover the stitching line made in Step 4. Pin at 1-inch intervals.

D COMPLETING THE HEM

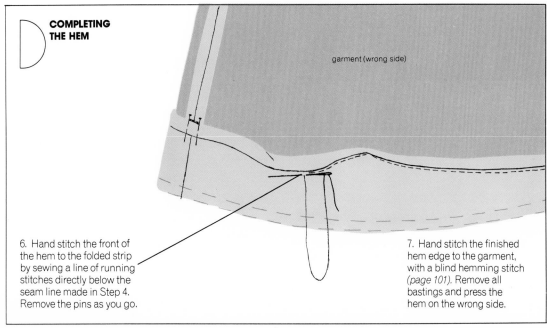

garment (wrong side)

6. Hand stitch the front of the hem to the folded strip by sewing a line of running stitches directly below the seam line made in Step 4. Remove the pins as you go.

7. Hand stitch the finished hem edge to the garment, with a blind hemming stitch (page 101). Remove all bastings and press the hem on the wrong side.

Waistlines: inset, contour or seamed

There are many ways for a garment to circle a waist. Some designs merely join the skirt to the bodice with a simple, unobtrusive seam; others emphasize it with an inset waistband, as in the House of Norell dress at right, or a contour belt cut to fit the curve of the body (overleaf).

In all cases the skirt and bodice should be fitted perfectly to your figure at the basting stage before you begin work on the waistline. Only if this is done in advance can you avoid two common pitfalls: a waistline seam that does not fall precisely at the wearer's waist or a seam that droops or puckers because the bodice and skirt are not exactly the same size at the waist.

A contour belt is designed to follow the contours of the waist and hipline and can add interest to any dress, with or without a simple waistline seam. The key to achieving the proper shape for the contour belt is hidden within it; the shaping is the result of many curved lines of parallel machine stitches that fuse together two pieces of interfacing, as shown on page 131.

THE BASIC SEAMED WAISTLINE

1. With the completed skirt turned wrong side out, run a line of machine stitching along the waist seam line to prevent the curved edge from stretching out of shape.

2. With the bodice turned right side out, insert it upside down into the skirt. The right sides of both pieces—the sides that will be visible in the finished garment—will then face together.

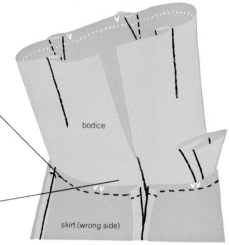

3. Pin the skirt to the bodice at the waistline, matching side seams and notches as well as center front and center back.

4. Baste the skirt and bodice together along the waist seam line. Remove the pins.

5. Machine stitch around the waist along the seam line. Remove the basting.

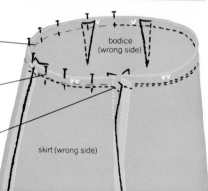

6. Pull out the bodice from inside the skirt and press the seam allowances upward toward the bodice.

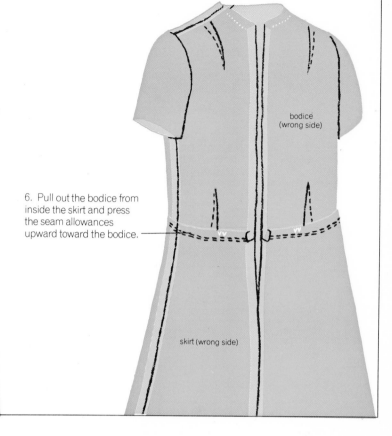

THE RIBBON-REINFORCED SEAMED WAISTLINE

1. Join the bodice and skirt, following the instructions for the basic seamed waistline. Finish the closure with a zipper or buttons (pages 139-143).

2. Close the zipper or buttons. Then turn the garment wrong side out.

3. Measure the circumference of the waist seam line, including the zipper or button closure facing.

4. Cut 5/8-inch-wide grosgrain ribbon 1 1/2 inches longer than the waistline circumference as measured in Step 3.

5. Fold 3/4 inch of the ribbon under at one end and pin the folded end to the waist seam line allowance of the garment, centering the ribbon on the seam line and aligning the folded end with the center of the closure.

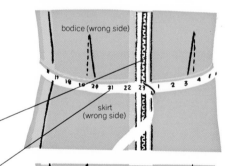

6. Fasten the remaining ribbon around the waistline along the seam, inserting pins at 2-inch intervals. Fold the loose end of the ribbon under at the center of the closure. Pin so that the two folded ends meet exactly.

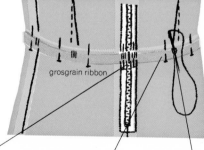

7. Using thread knotted at the end, stitch the ribbon to the waistline seam allowance just above the waist seam line by making three or four 1/4-inch-long overlapping stitches at each of the side seams and darts, at both edges of the zipper tape or closure facing, and finally at the center of the section of the garment directly opposite the closure. Remove the pins.

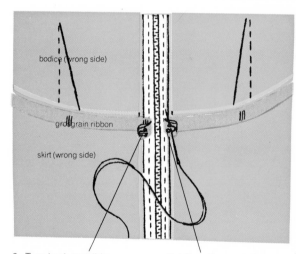

8. Turn back one ribbon end and place a hook as shown on the underside 1/8 inch from the folded end. Using a double strand of thread knotted at the end, stitch the hook to the ribbon by making three or four 1/4-inch-long overlapping stitches at the end of each metal ring and at the bend of the hook. Be sure to sew through both layers of the ribbon to hold the fold in place. Secure the end of the thread with a fastening stitch (page 204).

9. Lift up the opposite ribbon end and place an eye on the underside so that the rim of the eye protrudes just beyond the folded edge. Stitch the eye in place in the same way that you stitched the hook. The folded ribbon edges should meet exactly when hook and eye are fastened.

10. Try on the garment and if the ribbon pulls the waistline out of shape, clip out the fastening stitches made in Step 7. Re-pin the ribbon to the waistline as shown in Step 6 and sew in new fastening stitches.

THE INSET WAISTBAND

A PREPARING THE WAISTBAND

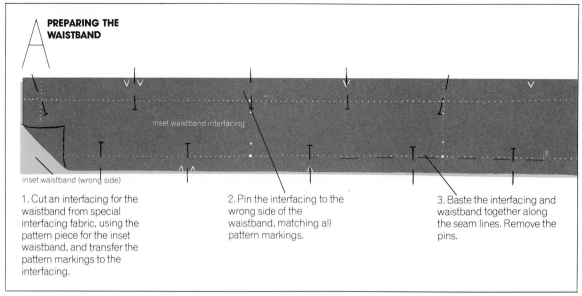

inset waistband interfacing

inset waistband (wrong side)

1. Cut an interfacing for the waistband from special interfacing fabric, using the pattern piece for the inset waistband, and transfer the pattern markings to the interfacing.

2. Pin the interfacing to the wrong side of the waistband, matching all pattern markings.

3. Baste the interfacing and waistband together along the seam lines. Remove the pins.

B ATTACHING THE WAISTBAND TO THE BODICE

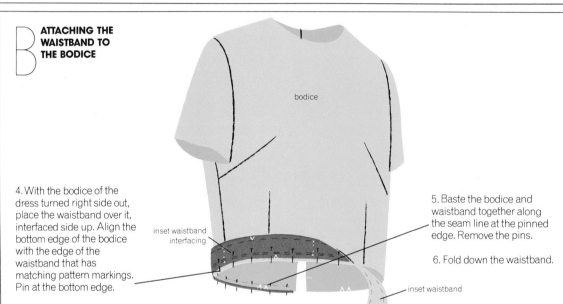

bodice

inset waistband interfacing

inset waistband

4. With the bodice of the dress turned right side out, place the waistband over it, interfaced side up. Align the bottom edge of the bodice with the edge of the waistband that has matching pattern markings. Pin at the bottom edge.

5. Baste the bodice and waistband together along the seam line at the pinned edge. Remove the pins.

6. Fold down the waistband.

C ATTACHING THE WAISTBAND TO THE SKIRT

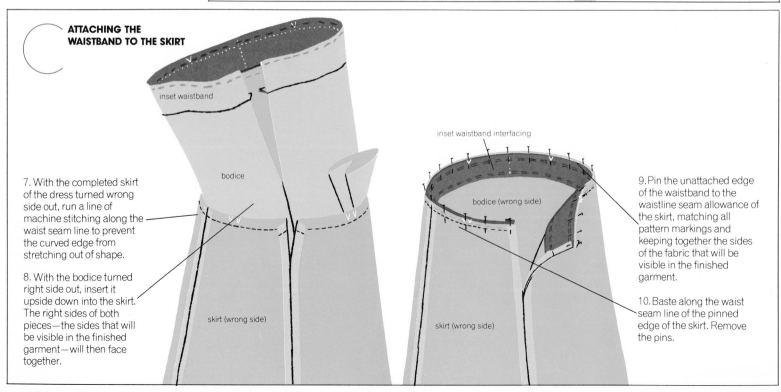

inset waistband

bodice

skirt (wrong side)

inset waistband interfacing

bodice (wrong side)

skirt (wrong side)

7. With the completed skirt of the dress turned wrong side out, run a line of machine stitching along the waist seam line to prevent the curved edge from stretching out of shape.

8. With the bodice turned right side out, insert it upside down into the skirt. The right sides of both pieces—the sides that will be visible in the finished garment—will then face together.

9. Pin the unattached edge of the waistband to the waistline seam allowance of the skirt, matching all pattern markings and keeping together the sides of the fabric that will be visible in the finished garment.

10. Baste along the waist seam line of the pinned edge of the skirt. Remove the pins.

FINISHING THE WAISTBAND

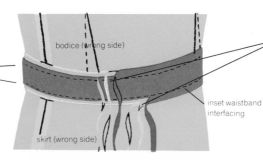

11. Pull out the bodice from inside the skirt and with the garment wrong side out, machine stitch the waistband first to the bodice and then to the skirt along the bastings made in Steps 5 and 10. Remove all bastings.

12. To reduce bulkiness, trim and grade the seam allowances at the top and bottom of the waistband —that is, trim the interfacing seam allowance to 1/8 inch, the waistband seam allowance to 1/4 inch, and the bodice and skirt seam allowances to 1/2 inch.

13. Press the seam allowances from the bodice waist seam line down to the waistband, and from the skirt waist seam line up to the waistband.

14. Using the pattern pieces for the inset waistband, cut out a lining for the waistband from lining fabric. Transfer the pattern markings to the wrong side of the lining.

15. Pin the lining to the garment, wrong sides together, matching all pattern markings and aligning the top and bottom seam lines of the lining with the waist seam lines of the bodice and skirt.

16. Remove one of the pins holding the lining to the bodice, and fold under the top edge of the lining so that it just covers the waist seam line of the bodice, then replace the pin. Repeat —removing, folding and replacing one pin at a time —all around the top edge of the waistband.

17. Repeat this process around the bottom edge of the waistband so that the folded edge of the bottom of the lining just covers the waist seam line of the skirt.

18. Slip stitch the lining to the garment (page 204) along the machine stitching made in Step 11. Remove the pins and press lightly.

19. Insert the zipper or finish the button closure (pages 139-143), then fold under the ends of the lining and slip stitch the folded edges to the zipper tape or closure facing.

THE CONTOUR BELT

A PREPARING THE INTERFACING

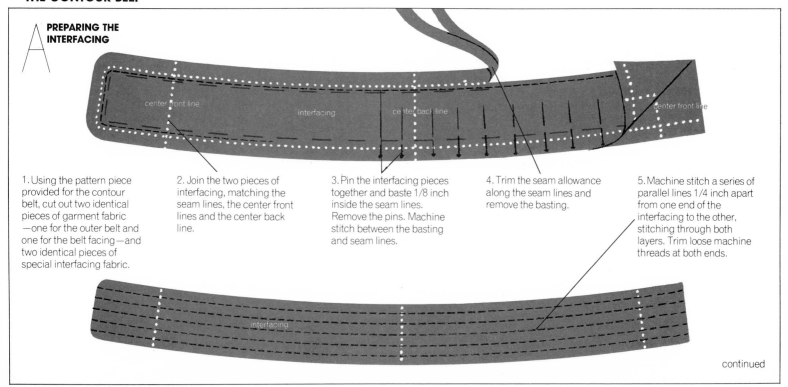

1. Using the pattern piece provided for the contour belt, cut out two identical pieces of garment fabric —one for the outer belt and one for the belt facing—and two identical pieces of special interfacing fabric.

2. Join the two pieces of interfacing, matching the seam lines, the center front lines and the center back line.

3. Pin the interfacing pieces together and baste 1/8 inch inside the seam lines. Remove the pins. Machine stitch between the basting and seam lines.

4. Trim the seam allowance along the seam lines and remove the basting.

5. Machine stitch a series of parallel lines 1/4 inch apart from one end of the interfacing to the other, stitching through both layers. Trim loose machine threads at both ends.

continued

B INTERFACING THE OUTER BELT

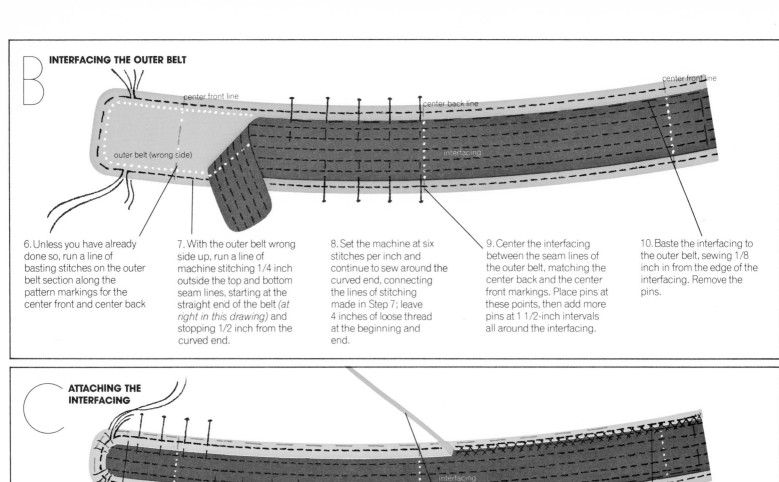

6. Unless you have already done so, run a line of basting stitches on the outer belt section along the pattern markings for the center front and center back

7. With the outer belt wrong side up, run a line of machine stitching 1/4 inch outside the top and bottom seam lines, starting at the straight end of the belt *(at right in this drawing)* and stopping 1/2 inch from the curved end.

8. Set the machine at six stitches per inch and continue to sew around the curved end, connecting the lines of stitching made in Step 7; leave 4 inches of loose thread at the beginning and end.

9. Center the interfacing between the seam lines of the outer belt, matching the center back and the center front markings. Place pins at these points, then add more pins at 1 1/2-inch intervals all around the interfacing.

10. Baste the interfacing to the outer belt, sewing 1/8 inch in from the edge of the interfacing. Remove the pins.

C ATTACHING THE INTERFACING

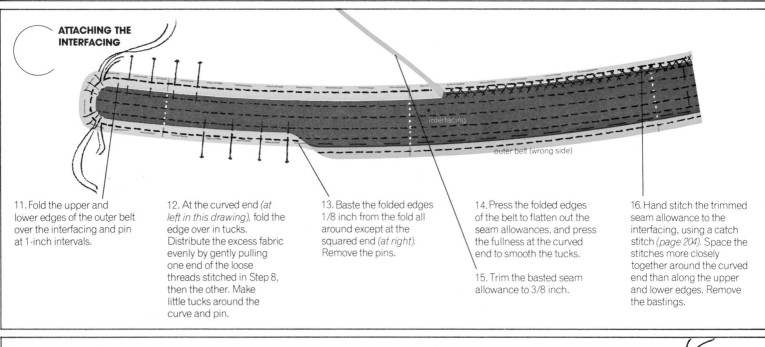

11. Fold the upper and lower edges of the outer belt over the interfacing and pin at 1-inch intervals.

12. At the curved end *(at left in this drawing)*, fold the edge over in tucks. Distribute the excess fabric evenly by gently pulling one end of the loose threads stitched in Step 8, then the other. Make little tucks around the curve and pin.

13. Baste the folded edges 1/8 inch from the fold all around except at the squared end *(at right)*. Remove the pins.

14. Press the folded edges of the belt to flatten out the seam allowances, and press the fullness at the curved end to smooth the tucks.

15. Trim the basted seam allowance to 3/8 inch.

16. Hand stitch the trimmed seam allowance to the interfacing, using a catch stitch *(page 204)*. Space the stitches more closely together around the curved end than along the upper and lower edges. Remove the bastings.

D PREPARING THE FACING

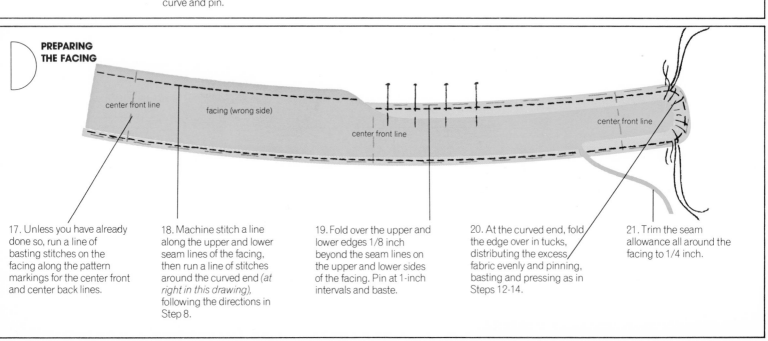

17. Unless you have already done so, run a line of basting stitches on the facing along the pattern markings for the center front and center back lines.

18. Machine stitch a line along the upper and lower seam lines of the facing, then run a line of stitches around the curved end *(at right in this drawing)*, following the directions in Step 8.

19. Fold over the upper and lower edges 1/8 inch beyond the seam lines on the upper and lower sides of the facing. Pin at 1-inch intervals and baste.

20. At the curved end, fold the edge over in tucks, distributing the excess fabric evenly and pinning, basting and pressing as in Steps 12-14.

21. Trim the seam allowance all around the facing to 1/4 inch.

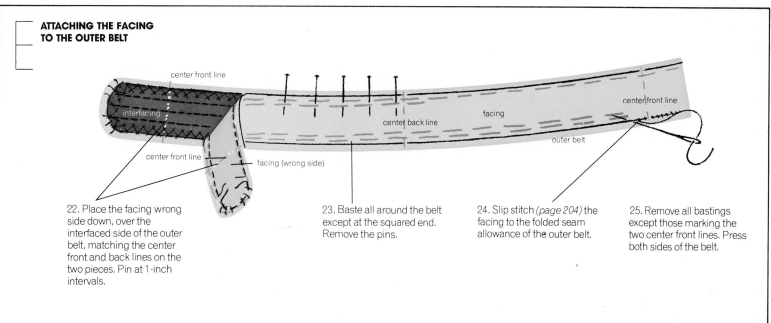

center front line

interfacing

center front line

facing (wrong side)

center back line

facing

outer belt

center front line

center front line

22. Place the facing wrong side down, over the interfaced side of the outer belt, matching the center front and back lines on the two pieces. Pin at 1-inch intervals.

23. Baste all around the belt except at the squared end. Remove the pins.

24. Slip stitch *(page 204)* the facing to the folded seam allowance of the outer belt.

25. Remove all bastings except those marking the two center front lines. Press both sides of the belt.

ATTACHING A SLIDE BUCKLE

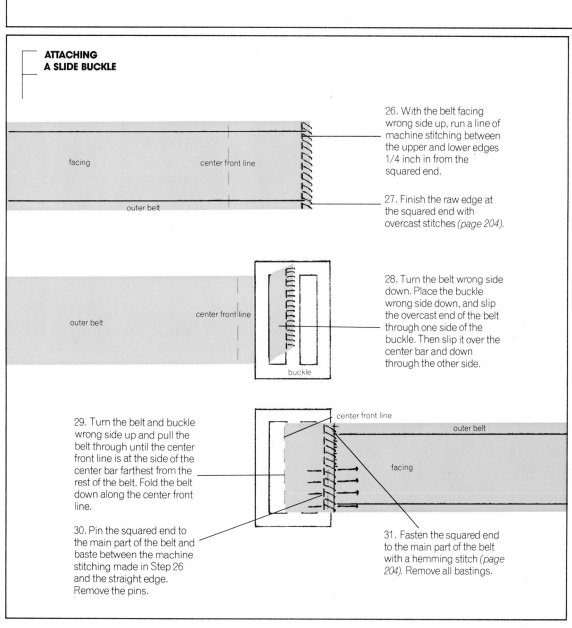

facing

center front line

outer belt

26. With the belt facing wrong side up, run a line of machine stitching between the upper and lower edges 1/4 inch in from the squared end.

27. Finish the raw edge at the squared end with overcast stitches *(page 204)*.

outer belt

center front line

buckle

28. Turn the belt wrong side down. Place the buckle wrong side down, and slip the overcast end of the belt through one side of the buckle. Then slip it over the center bar and down through the other side.

29. Turn the belt and buckle wrong side up and pull the belt through until the center front line is at the side of the center bar farthest from the rest of the belt. Fold the belt down along the center front line.

30. Pin the squared end to the main part of the belt and baste between the machine stitching made in Step 26 and the straight edge. Remove the pins.

center front line

outer belt

facing

31. Fasten the squared end to the main part of the belt with a hemming stitch *(page 204)*. Remove all bastings.

Seams: welt, slot or corner

Seams can do more than just join sections of fabric; in custom dressmaking they may emphasize the way a garment is made or even establish the style, as in the corner seam at the underarm of the House of Norell dress at left.

Some seams are purely decorative—used as accents on garments. Among the most interesting is the slot seam, which you can make by sewing a strip of fabric—its color matching or contrasting with that of the garment—under a seam that has been basted together. When the basting is removed and the "slot" opens, the final effect is of two even tucks with an underlay peeping through. You can heighten the impact further by hand topstitching the underlay with wool yarn of a contrasting color, using a prick stitch or saddle stitch *(pages 99-100).*

A welt seam's precisely spaced extra lines of machine stitching lend a kind of architectural quality to the dress, giving it a strong structure of its own that is seemingly independent of the fabric beneath.

All seams, whether decorative or functional, require the most careful execution—absolutely straight stitching and the precise matching of intersections.

JOINING A SEAM AT A CORNER

A REINFORCING THE CORNER

1. Make a reinforcement patch by cutting out a 3-inch square of fabric —using a piece of the underlining or lining fabric or organza—in a color that harmonizes with the garment. Cut on the bias, that is, diagonally across the threads forming the weave.

2. Place the garment piece wrong side down. Center the bias patch over the point of the garment corner and pin it to the garment piece.

3. Turn the garment piece wrong side up and baste the patch to the garment, sewing just inside the seam line as indicated by tracing wheel markings. Remove the pins.

4. Machine stitch—at 15 stitches per inch—as closely as possible to the outside of the seam line. Stitch around the point of the corner, pivoting the fabric sections.

5. Slash into the corner through both the patch and the garment fabric. Cut up to but not through the line of machine stitching. Remove the bastings.

6. Turn the garment fabric wrong side down. Turn the edges of the patch over toward the corner where the inset will be sewn, and press, covering the line of machine stitching made in Step 4. The center of the patch will bunch up.

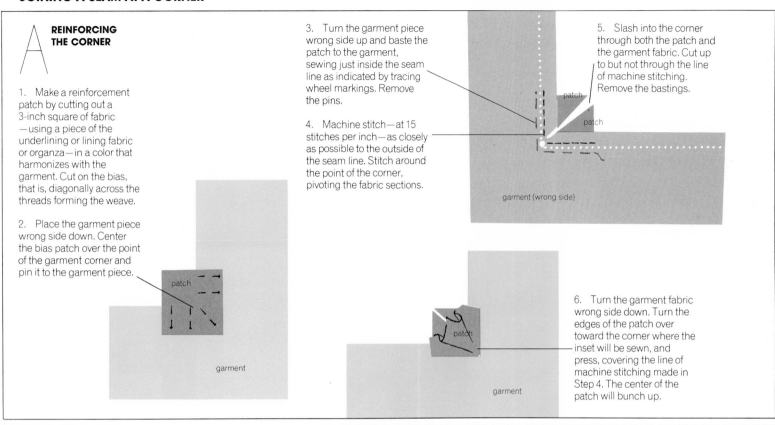

B JOINING THE INSET TO THE CORNER

7. Push a pin from the wrong side of the garment fabric through the point of the slashed corner. Then place the inset, wrong side up, over the garment piece and push the pin through the point where the inset seam lines intersect.

8. Turn the garment section over the inset so that the garment is wrong side up and the slashed corner is up at the top.

9. Spread the slash open. Match the seam lines of the garment and inset, and push the pin inserted in Step 7 parallel to one garment seam line (the left seam line in this drawing). Secure it on the seam line.

10. Insert a second pin on the other garment seam line (the right seam line in this drawing). The two pins will cross at the point of the corner.

11. Pin the garment piece to the inset along the seam lines, inserting these pins at right angles to the seam line.

12. Baste the garment to the inset just inside the seam line, and remove all the pins except the two crossed pins at the point of the corner.

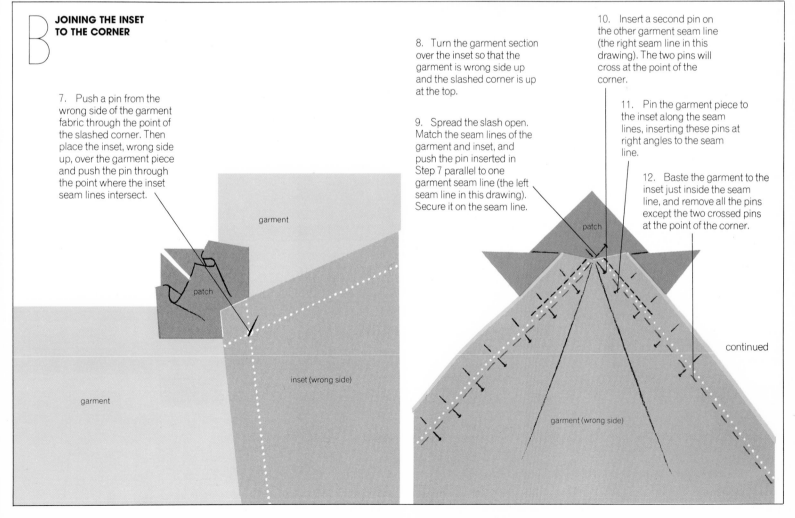

continued

STITCHING THE SEAM

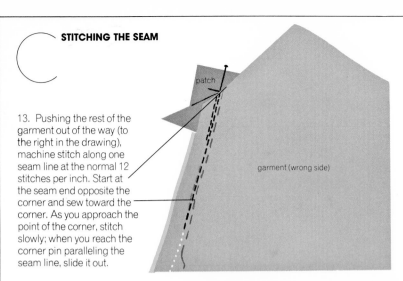

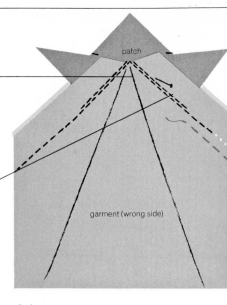

13. Pushing the rest of the garment out of the way (to the right in the drawing), machine stitch along one seam line at the normal 12 stitches per inch. Start at the seam end opposite the corner and sew toward the corner. As you approach the point of the corner, stitch slowly; when you reach the corner pin paralleling the seam line, slide it out.

14. At the point of the corner, stop the machine with the needle in the fabric and raise the presser foot of the machine. Flip the bunched-up fabric of the garment out of the way over the machine stitching done in Step 13. Pivot at the point and lower the presser foot again.

15. Now slide the second pin out and stitch down the length of the remaining seam. Remove all bastings.

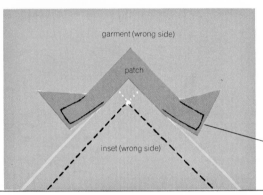

16. With the garment piece and inset spread open wrong side up, press the seam allowances of the inset section flat, over the patch and the garment piece.

17. Trim all extended edges of the patch so that they are even with the seam allowances.

MAKING A SLOT SEAM

A JOINING THE GARMENT SECTIONS

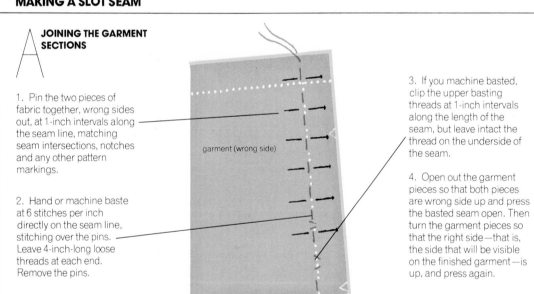

1. Pin the two pieces of fabric together, wrong sides out, at 1-inch intervals along the seam line, matching seam intersections, notches and any other pattern markings.

2. Hand or machine baste at 6 stitches per inch directly on the seam line, stitching over the pins. Leave 4-inch-long loose threads at each end. Remove the pins.

3. If you machine basted, clip the upper basting threads at 1-inch intervals along the length of the seam, but leave intact the thread on the underside of the seam.

4. Open out the garment pieces so that both pieces are wrong side up and press the basted seam open. Then turn the garment pieces so that the right side—that is, the side that will be visible on the finished garment—is up, and press again.

B ATTACHING THE UNDERLAY

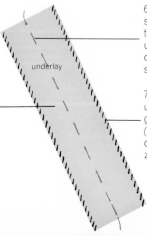

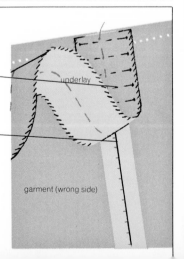

5. Cut a 2-inch-wide strip of fabric—the length of the seam to be slotted—along the lengthwise grain. Use either fabric left over after cutting out your pattern or, for a more dramatic effect, a fabric of similar weight and texture but contrasting color.

6. Hand baste a row of stitches lengthwise down the exact center of the underlay to aid you in correctly positioning the strip over the seam.

7. Finish the edges of the underlay as in the rest of the garment; hand overcast (page 204) as shown in the drawing, or use machine zigzag stitches.

8. With the wrong side of the garment pieces facing up, center the underlay, wrong side up, over the basted seam. Match the bastings along the center of the underlay to the seam. Pin carefully on each side of the bastings through all layers of fabric.

COMPLETING THE SLOT SEAM

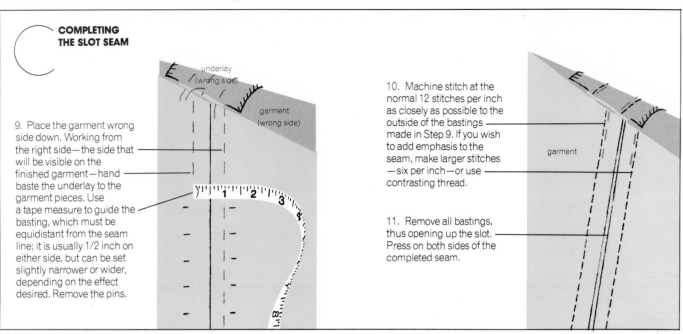

9. Place the garment wrong side down. Working from the right side—the side that will be visible on the finished garment—hand baste the underlay to the garment pieces. Use a tape measure to guide the basting, which must be equidistant from the seam line; it is usually 1/2 inch on either side, but can be set slightly narrower or wider, depending on the effect desired. Remove the pins.

10. Machine stitch at the normal 12 stitches per inch as closely as possible to the outside of the bastings made in Step 9. If you wish to add emphasis to the seam, make larger stitches —six per inch—or use contrasting thread.

11. Remove all bastings, thus opening up the slot. Press on both sides of the completed seam.

THE WELT SEAM

A STITCHING THE SEAM

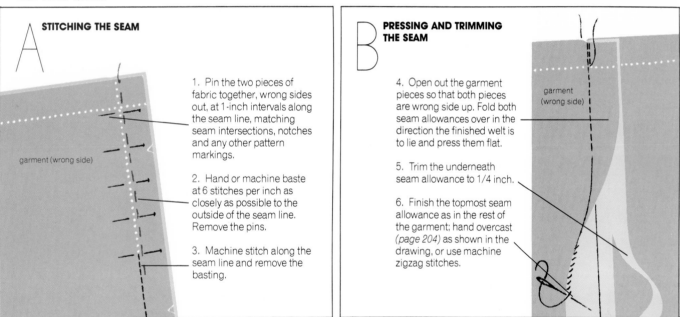

1. Pin the two pieces of fabric together, wrong sides out, at 1-inch intervals along the seam line, matching seam intersections, notches and any other pattern markings.

2. Hand or machine baste at 6 stitches per inch as closely as possible to the outside of the seam line. Remove the pins.

3. Machine stitch along the seam line and remove the basting.

B PRESSING AND TRIMMING THE SEAM

4. Open out the garment pieces so that both pieces are wrong side up. Fold both seam allowances over in the direction the finished welt is to lie and press them flat.

5. Trim the underneath seam allowance to 1/4 inch.

6. Finish the topmost seam allowance as in the rest of the garment; hand overcast (page 204) as shown in the drawing, or use machine zigzag stitches.

C COMPLETING THE SINGLE WELT SEAM

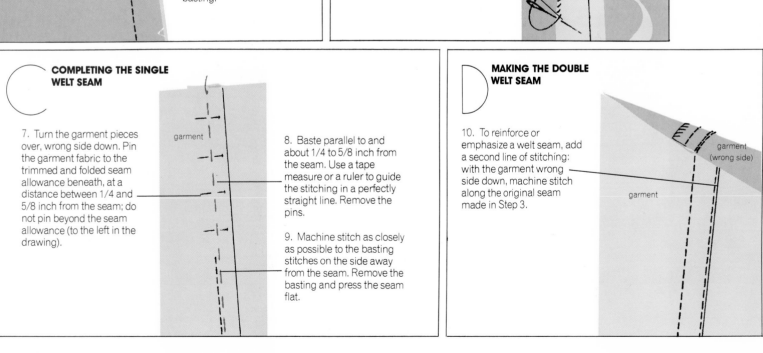

7. Turn the garment pieces over, wrong side down. Pin the garment fabric to the trimmed and folded seam allowance beneath, at a distance between 1/4 and 5/8 inch from the seam; do not pin beyond the seam allowance (to the left in the drawing).

8. Baste parallel to and about 1/4 to 5/8 inch from the seam. Use a tape measure or a ruler to guide the stitching in a perfectly straight line. Remove the pins.

9. Machine stitch as closely as possible to the basting stitches on the side away from the seam. Remove the basting and press the seam flat.

D MAKING THE DOUBLE WELT SEAM

10. To reinforce or emphasize a welt seam, add a second line of stitching: with the garment wrong side down, machine stitch along the original seam made in Step 3.

Fasteners: covered or concealed

The perfection of a custom garment is evidenced in even its tiniest details, such as the covered buttons and faultlessly finished bound buttonholes on the belt at left.

Bound buttonholes, which have edges finished with a patch of fabric—as opposed to "worked" buttonholes, which have edges finished with thread—are among the most intricate fastening elements to sew, involving careful stitching in a very small area. Their handsome looks, however, make the effort worthwhile. The binding for the buttonholes may be made from the same fabric as the garment or—for a dramatic effect—from a contrasting fabric. Before you begin the buttonholes, it is a good idea to practice on spare pieces of all the materials involved—the binding and garment fabric, interfacing and lining or underlining. Then start on the garment itself with the buttonhole that will be least conspicuous.

Equally elegant, though less visible than buttons and buttonholes, are hand-sewn zippers *(pages 142 and 143).* Here the custom touch consists of delicate prick stitches that give the zippers a flexibility that enables them to follow the soft contours of the body.

THE BOUND BUTTONHOLE

A INTERFACING THE BUTTONHOLE AREA

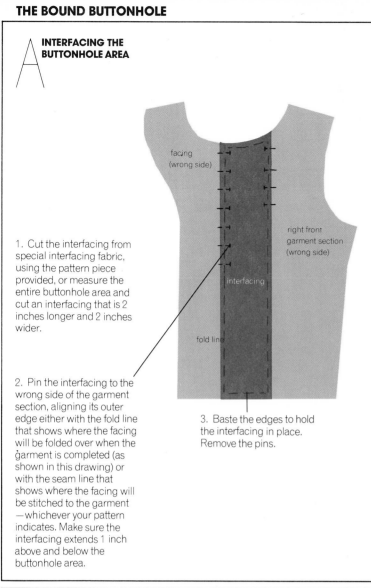

1. Cut the interfacing from special interfacing fabric, using the pattern piece provided, or measure the entire buttonhole area and cut an interfacing that is 2 inches longer and 2 inches wider.

2. Pin the interfacing to the wrong side of the garment section, aligning its outer edge either with the fold line that shows where the facing will be folded over when the garment is completed (as shown in this drawing) or with the seam line that shows where the facing will be stitched to the garment —whichever your pattern indicates. Make sure the interfacing extends 1 inch above and below the buttonhole area.

3. Baste the edges to hold the interfacing in place. Remove the pins.

B MARKING THE BUTTONHOLE PLACEMENT LINES

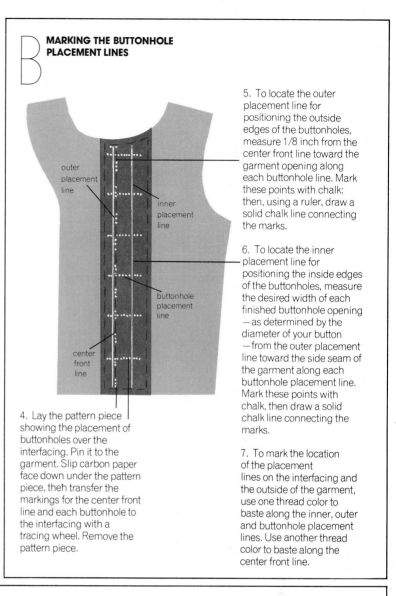

4. Lay the pattern piece showing the placement of buttonholes over the interfacing. Pin it to the garment. Slip carbon paper face down under the pattern piece, then transfer the markings for the center front line and each buttonhole to the interfacing with a tracing wheel. Remove the pattern piece.

5. To locate the outer placement line for positioning the outside edges of the buttonholes, measure 1/8 inch from the center front line toward the garment opening along each buttonhole line. Mark these points with chalk; then, using a ruler, draw a solid chalk line connecting the marks.

6. To locate the inner placement line for positioning the inside edges of the buttonholes, measure the desired width of each finished buttonhole opening —as determined by the diameter of your button —from the outer placement line toward the side seam of the garment along each buttonhole placement line. Mark these points with chalk, then draw a solid chalk line connecting the marks.

7. To mark the location of the placement lines on the interfacing and the outside of the garment, use one thread color to baste along the inner, outer and buttonhole placement lines. Use another thread color to baste along the center front line.

C PREPARING THE PATCH

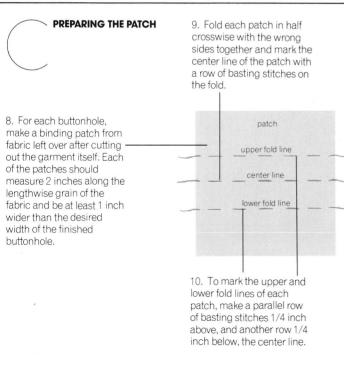

8. For each buttonhole, make a binding patch from fabric left over after cutting out the garment itself. Each of the patches should measure 2 inches along the lengthwise grain of the fabric and be at least 1 inch wider than the desired width of the finished buttonhole.

9. Fold each patch in half crosswise with the wrong sides together and mark the center line of the patch with a row of basting stitches on the fold.

10. To mark the upper and lower fold lines of each patch, make a parallel row of basting stitches 1/4 inch above, and another row 1/4 inch below, the center line.

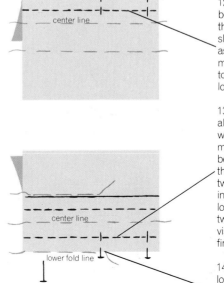

11. Fold the patch along the upper fold line, wrong sides together, and pin it.

12. Machine stitch halfway between the center line and the upper fold line. Stitch slowly, slipping out the pins as you go. The stitching must be straight and even to ensure a professional-looking buttonhole.

13. Fold and pin the patch along the lower fold line, wrong sides together, then machine stitch halfway between the center line and the lower fold line. These two rows of stitching, 1/4 inch apart by the upper and lower fold lines, will create two tucks that will form the visible bound edges of the finished buttonhole.

14. Remove the upper and lower fold line bastings, but leave in the basting stitches along the center line of the patch.

D ▷ ATTACHING THE PATCH TO THE GARMENT

15. Turn the garment wrong side down and place a patch, wrong side up, on one buttonhole. Spread the patch open so that the basted center line is visible, then match the basting to the buttonhole placement line. Let the ends of the patch extend 1/2 inch beyond the inner and outer placement lines.

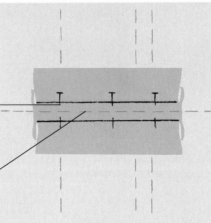

center line

buttonhole placement line

patch (wrong side)

inner placement line

outer placement line

garment

18. Fold the top of the patch down so that the upper row of stitching made in Box C, Step 12, is visible, and place a pin at each end of the patch inside the outer and inner placement lines.

19. Replace the presser foot on your machine with a zipper foot. Insert the machine needle at the inside edge of the pin at the outer placement line. Turn the machine wheel by hand to make one stitch backwards over the pin. Remove the pin and stitch forward until you reach the second pin.

16. Pin the patch to the garment, checking again to be sure that the center line on the patch exactly matches the buttonhole placement line.

17. Baste over the center line of the patch to fasten it to the interfacing and garment fabric. Remove the pins.

20. Turning the wheel again by hand, make one stitch over the second pin, slip it out, and secure the thread with two backstitches.

21. Fold the bottom of the patch up so that the lower row of stitching made in Box C, Step 13, is visible. Pin and stitch as described in Steps 18-20, sewing just outside the visible stitching. Remove the bastings from the patch.

E ☐ OPENING THE BUTTONHOLE

22. Spread the patch open. Using the row of basting stitches on the buttonhole placement line as your guide, cut the patch in half with small, sharp-pointed scissors.

23. Turn the garment wrong side up. To open the buttonhole from the interfacing side, make a 1/4-inch-long cut at the center of the buttonhole, parallel to the visible rows of machine stitching, midway between them. Be sure to cut through the interfacing, lining or underlining, and garment fabric.

24. Make diagonal cuts through all the fabric layers from the center cut to each of the four corners of the buttonhole. Cut up to but not through the ends of the machine stitching. Make sure to keep the edges of the patch on the opposite side of the garment out of the way of the scissors.

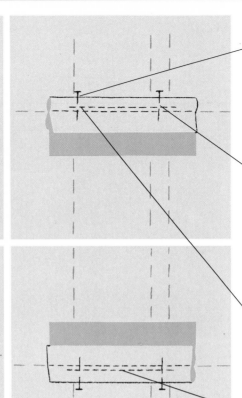

garment

patch (wrong side)

garment

patch

patch

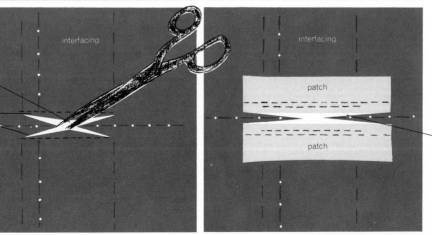

interfacing

interfacing

patch

patch

25. Turn the garment wrong side down and, with your fingers, push the edges of the patch and the triangles of fabric at each end of the buttonhole through the opening to the wrong side of the garment.

26. Turn the garment wrong side up and make sure that the little triangles formed by the diagonal cuts in Step 24 are pushed completely through the buttonhole opening. Press the edges of the patch flat with an iron.

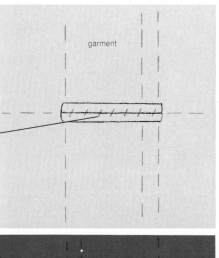

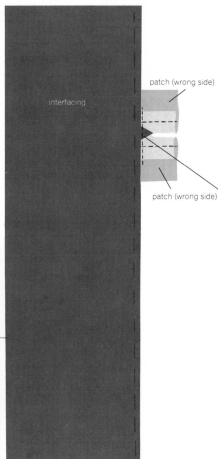

27. To hold the buttonhole in shape while you make the finishing stitches, turn the garment wrong side down and baste the visible bound edges of the buttonhole together with diagonal basting stitches (page 100).

28. Turn the garment wrong side up so that the buttonhole patch is visible.

29. Fold over one side of the patch along the outer placement line.

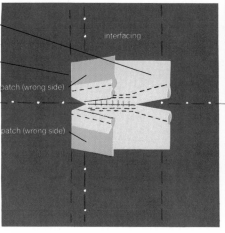

30. Fold the garment and interfacing back along the outer placement line so that the underside of the patch extends away from the folded garment.

31. Machine stitch parallel to the outer placement line from about 1/8 inch above to 1/8 inch below the two visible rows of stitching. Make sure to catch the little triangles.

32. Fold the opposite side of the patch along the inner placement line and repeat Step 31.

33. Complete all the other buttonholes called for by your pattern to this stage. Remove all basting stitches except those marking the center front line of the garment and those holding the lips of the buttonholes together.

FINISHING THE BUTTONHOLES

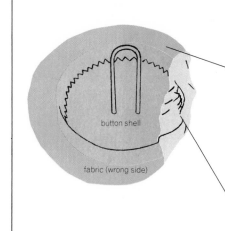

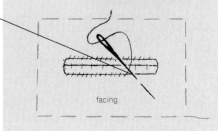

34. Fold the facing wrong side down over the interfacing along the fold line or the seam line and pin it down.

35. Baste the facing to the garment around each buttonhole. Insert pins through the fabric at each corner and at the center of one buttonhole. Turn the garment wrong side up. Follow the pin markings and cut open the facing as in Box E, Steps 23-24. Remove the pins.

36. Tuck under the top and bottom edges of the cut and the triangles at either side. Sew the edges with tiny hemming stitches (page 204).

37. Repeat Steps 35-36 at all other buttonholes and remove all bastings.

MAKING COVERED BUTTONS

1. Cut a circle of fabric big enough to cover and tuck inside the button shell. (Most buttons come with a pattern.) If fabric is loosely woven, cut another circle for lining to go under it.

2. Place the fabric circle wrong side up and center the button shell on it. Tuck the fabric edges inside the shell. If you have trouble getting all the material tucked in, baste a draw thread around the fabric edge and use it to pull the edge together.

3. Place the button back over the shell, making sure all the fabric is tucked in. Press down the button back, using a spool over the shank as a pressing tool, until you feel the back snap firmly into place.

THE LAPPED ZIPPER

A PREPARING THE ZIPPER OPENING

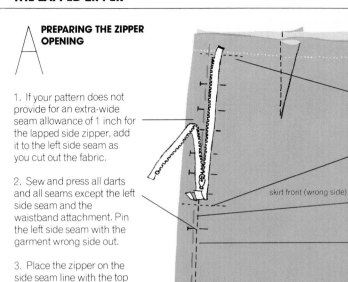

1. If your pattern does not provide for an extra-wide seam allowance of 1 inch for the lapped side zipper, add it to the left side seam as you cut out the fabric.

2. Sew and press all darts and all seams except the left side seam and the waistband attachment. Pin the left side seam with the garment wrong side out.

3. Place the zipper on the side seam line with the top stop 1/4 inch below the waist seam-line markings.

4. Using chalk or a pin, mark the position of the top and bottom zipper stops across both sides of the seam line. Remove the zipper and re-mark the stop positions with a horizontal running stitch.

5. Baste the side seam from the hemline up to the waist. Remove the pins.

6. Machine stitch the side seam from the hemline to the marking for the bottom stop.

7. Press open the side seam.

skirt front (wrong side)

B ATTACHING THE ZIPPER TO THE SKIRT BACK

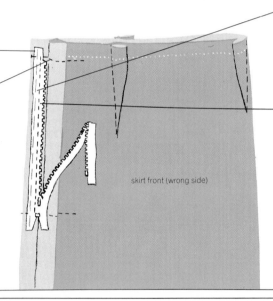

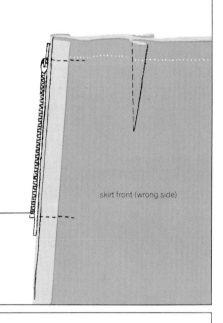

8. Fold over the back seam allowance of the side seam so that it lies flat.

9. With the zipper open, place it face down on the extended back seam allowance, aligning its top and bottom stops at the horizontal markings made in Box A, Step 4. The teeth should be flush against the basted side seam. Pin the left tape to the back seam allowance at the top stop.

10. Baste the zipper tape to the extended back seam allowance, stitching close to the teeth from the bottom of the zipper tape to the top.

11. Using a zipper foot, machine stitch as close to the teeth as possible, but be careful to sew the tape only to the seam allowance, not the garment itself. To stitch past the slider, stop the machine with the needle in the fabric, raise the zipper foot and move the slider out of the way.

12. Close the zipper and turn it face up by folding it to the left. Fold the back seam allowance under the garment and press both seam allowances away from the zipper.

skirt front (wrong side)

skirt front (wrong side)

C ATTACHING THE ZIPPER TO THE SKIRT FRONT

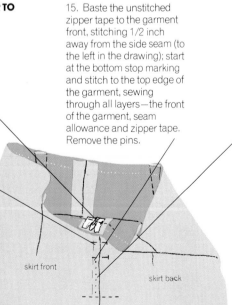

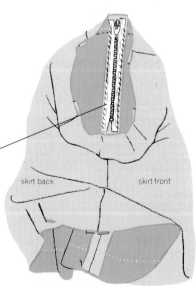

13. Turn the garment right side out and hold the zipper inside the skirt so that it is centered over the seam.

14. Working from the right side—the side that is normally visible—pin the zipper tape to the garment front across both seam allowances.

15. Baste the unstitched zipper tape to the garment front, stitching 1/2 inch away from the side seam (to the left in the drawing); start at the bottom stop marking and stitch to the top edge of the garment, sewing through all layers—the front of the garment, seam allowance and zipper tape. Remove the pins.

16. Using the prick stitch (page 99), fasten the basted zipper tape to the garment front. Start with a fastening stitch (page 204), securing the bottom of the zipper tape at the lapped opening, sew to the left 3/8 inch, then sew up the length of the zipper to the top edge of the garment.

17. Turn the skirt wrong side out and hem stitch each side of the zipper tape to the seam allowance. Remove all bastings and press.

skirt front

skirt back

skirt back

skirt front

THE CENTERED ZIPPER

A PREPARING THE ZIPPER OPENING

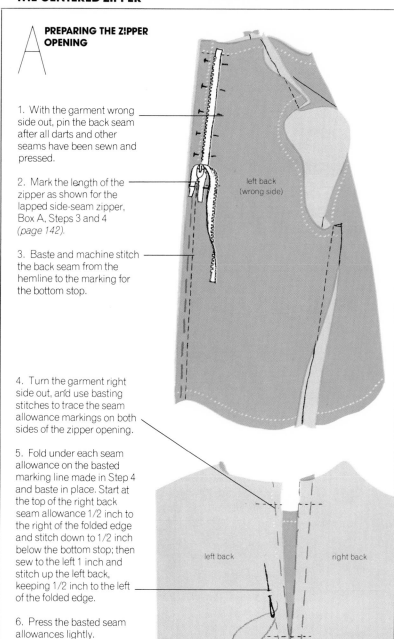

1. With the garment wrong side out, pin the back seam after all darts and other seams have been sewn and pressed.

2. Mark the length of the zipper as shown for the lapped side-seam zipper, Box A, Steps 3 and 4 *(page 142)*.

3. Baste and machine stitch the back seam from the hemline to the marking for the bottom stop.

4. Turn the garment right side out, and use basting stitches to trace the seam allowance markings on both sides of the zipper opening.

5. Fold under each seam allowance on the basted marking line made in Step 4 and baste in place. Start at the top of the right back seam allowance 1/2 inch to the right of the folded edge and stitch down to 1/2 inch below the bottom stop; then sew to the left 1 inch and stitch up the left back, keeping 1/2 inch to the left of the folded edge.

6. Press the basted seam allowances lightly.

B ATTACHING THE ZIPPER

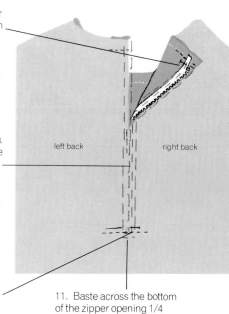

7. Open the zipper and hold it up wrong side facing away from you. Working from inside the garment, align the top stop of the right-hand side of the zipper with the top stop marking on the right-hand side of the garment; then pin the stop to the right back seam allowance 1/16-inch in from the folded edge.

8. With the garment still right side out, hold the zipper inside while you work from the outside to baste the right-hand zipper tape in place, stitching through both the right back seam allowance and the garment. Begin at the top edge of the zipper opening 1/4 inch in from the folded edge and sew to within about 1 inch from the bottom of the opening.

9. Close the zipper and pin the bottom of the zipper to the bottom of the zipper opening. Make sure that the teeth of the zipper are concealed by the folds of the opening.

10. Align the top stop of the left-hand zipper tape with the top stop marking on the left back. Open the zipper and pin the top stop in place about 1/16 inch in from the folded edge as shown for the right top stop in Step 7.

11. Baste across the bottom of the zipper opening 1/4 inch below the horizontal running stitches that mark the bottom stop.

C FINISHING THE ZIPPER

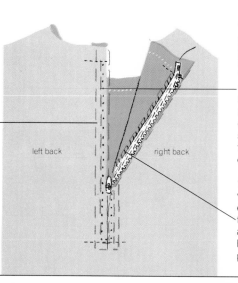

12. Baste the left-hand zipper tape to the left side of the garment 1/4 inch to the left of the opening, stitching from the bottom of the zipper to the top edge of the garment. Close the zipper as you proceed. The folded-in edges should more than just meet in the middle; they should overlap very slightly, concealing the zipper teeth.

13. Open the zipper and prick stitch *(page 99)* the zipper tape just inside the bastings made in Steps 8, 11 and 12. Start at the top right back with a fastening stitch *(page 204)* in the zipper tape, prick stitch down to the bottom running stitches, then 1/4 inch to the left, then up to the top edge of the left back.

14. Turn the garment wrong side out and stitch each side of the zipper tape to the seam allowance with a hem stitch *(page 204)*. Remove all bastings and press lightly.

Sleeves: fitted or flowing

The sleek appearance of the House of Norell sleeve at right, which is set into the fabric of the armhole, is achieved with the help of the simple basting technique shown on the opposite page *(Box A, Steps 1 and 2)*, which ensures that the sleeve will be perfectly centered and balanced.

Looser fitting sleeves like the kimono and raglan require other techniques. In order to provide freedom of movement without excessive billowing in the kimono sleeve, an insert called a gusset is set into the garment at the underarm. This insert —frequently diamond-shaped—will lie flat without puckering at the corners if it is pinned very carefully, then basted and stitched into position in two halves as shown on page 149. The simpler raglan sleeve, which has a curved seam or dart at the shoulder, is easier to construct than the set-in sleeve and the kimono sleeve. But because the seams on the raglan sleeve are so evident, it is a good idea to insert a piece of brown paper between the seam allowances and the sleeve itself when you press the seams open so there will be no trace of a mark from the seam allowances on the outside.

THE FITTED SLEEVE

A PREPARING THE SLEEVE

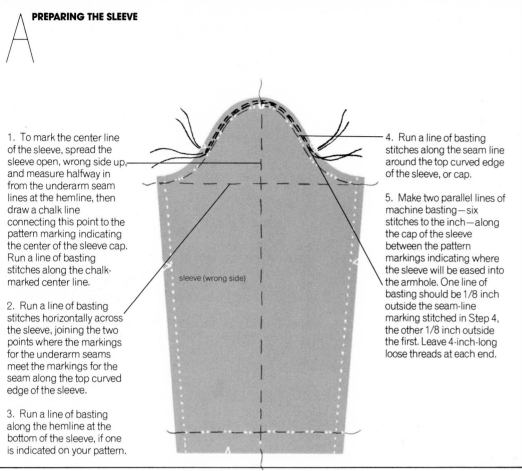

1. To mark the center line of the sleeve, spread the sleeve open, wrong side up, and measure halfway in from the underarm seam lines at the hemline, then draw a chalk line connecting this point to the pattern marking indicating the center of the sleeve cap. Run a line of basting stitches along the chalk-marked center line.

2. Run a line of basting stitches horizontally across the sleeve, joining the two points where the markings for the underarm seams meet the markings for the seam along the top curved edge of the sleeve.

3. Run a line of basting along the hemline at the bottom of the sleeve, if one is indicated on your pattern.

4. Run a line of basting stitches along the seam line around the top curved edge of the sleeve, or cap.

5. Make two parallel lines of machine basting—six stitches to the inch—along the cap of the sleeve between the pattern markings indicating where the sleeve will be eased into the armhole. One line of basting should be 1/8 inch outside the seam-line marking stitched in Step 4, the other 1/8 inch outside the first. Leave 4-inch-long loose threads at each end.

sleeve (wrong side)

B JOINING THE UNDERARM SEAM

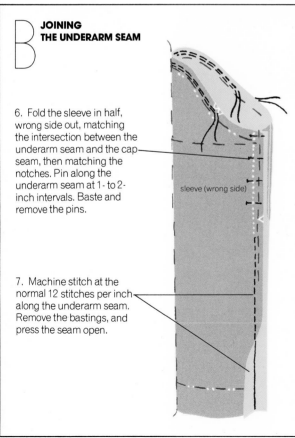

6. Fold the sleeve in half, wrong side out, matching the intersection between the underarm seam and the cap seam, then matching the notches. Pin along the underarm seam at 1- to 2-inch intervals. Baste and remove the pins.

7. Machine stitch at the normal 12 stitches per inch along the underarm seam. Remove the bastings, and press the seam open.

sleeve (wrong side)

C EASING THE SLEEVE CAP

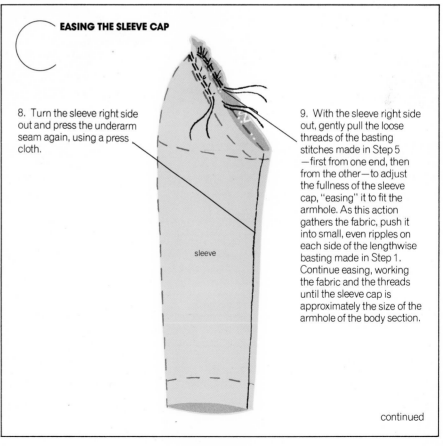

8. Turn the sleeve right side out and press the underarm seam again, using a press cloth.

9. With the sleeve right side out, gently pull the loose threads of the basting stitches made in Step 5 —first from one end, then from the other—to adjust the fullness of the sleeve cap, "easing" it to fit the armhole. As this action gathers the fabric, push it into small, even ripples on each side of the lengthwise basting made in Step 1. Continue easing, working the fabric and the threads until the sleeve cap is approximately the size of the armhole of the body section.

sleeve

continued

145

ALIGNING THE SLEEVE

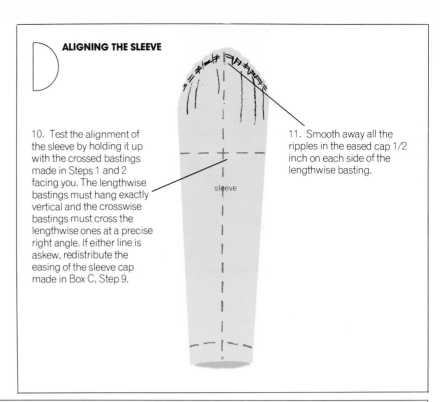

10. Test the alignment of the sleeve by holding it up with the crossed bastings made in Steps 1 and 2 facing you. The lengthwise bastings must hang exactly vertical and the crosswise bastings must cross the lengthwise ones at a precise right angle. If either line is askew, redistribute the easing of the sleeve cap made in Box C, Step 9.

11. Smooth away all the ripples in the eased cap 1/2 inch on each side of the lengthwise basting.

sleeve

ATTACHING THE SLEEVE

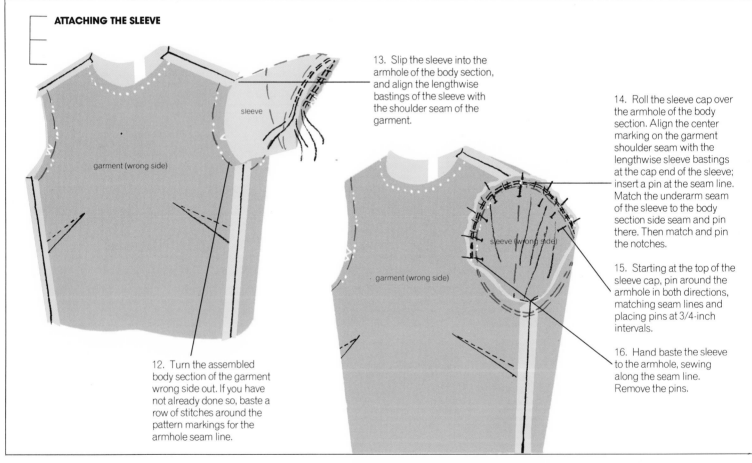

sleeve

garment (wrong side)

13. Slip the sleeve into the armhole of the body section, and align the lengthwise bastings of the sleeve with the shoulder seam of the garment.

14. Roll the sleeve cap over the armhole of the body section. Align the center marking on the garment shoulder seam with the lengthwise sleeve bastings at the cap end of the sleeve; insert a pin at the seam line. Match the underarm seam of the sleeve to the body section side seam and pin there. Then match and pin the notches.

15. Starting at the top of the sleeve cap, pin around the armhole in both directions, matching seam lines and placing pins at 3/4-inch intervals.

16. Hand baste the sleeve to the armhole, sewing along the seam line. Remove the pins.

sleeve (wrong side)

garment (wrong side)

12. Turn the assembled body section of the garment wrong side out. If you have not already done so, baste a row of stitches around the pattern markings for the armhole seam line.

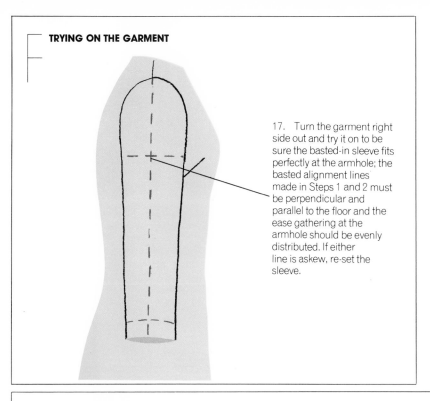

17. Turn the garment right side out and try it on to be sure the basted-in sleeve fits perfectly at the armhole; the basted alignment lines made in Steps 1 and 2 must be perpendicular and parallel to the floor and the ease gathering at the armhole should be evenly distributed. If either line is askew, re-set the sleeve.

G **STITCHING THE SLEEVE TO THE BODY SECTION**

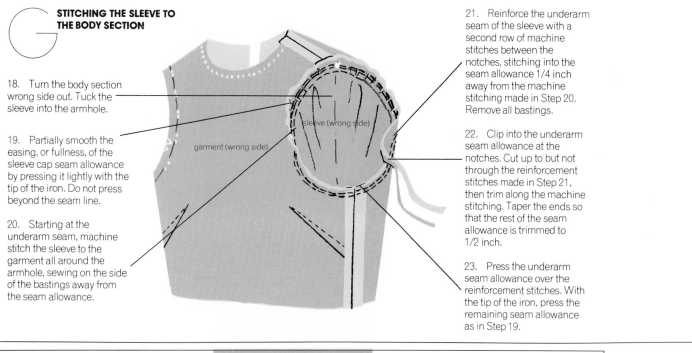

18. Turn the body section wrong side out. Tuck the sleeve into the armhole.

19. Partially smooth the easing, or fullness, of the sleeve cap seam allowance by pressing it lightly with the tip of the iron. Do not press beyond the seam line.

20. Starting at the underarm seam, machine stitch the sleeve to the garment all around the armhole, sewing on the side of the bastings away from the seam allowance.

21. Reinforce the underarm seam of the sleeve with a second row of machine stitches between the notches, stitching into the seam allowance 1/4 inch away from the machine stitching made in Step 20. Remove all bastings.

22. Clip into the underarm seam allowance at the notches. Cut up to but not through the reinforcement stitches made in Step 21, then trim along the machine stitching. Taper the ends so that the rest of the seam allowance is trimmed to 1/2 inch.

23. Press the underarm seam allowance over the reinforcement stitches. With the tip of the iron, press the remaining seam allowance as in Step 19.

H **FINISHING THE SLEEVE HEM**

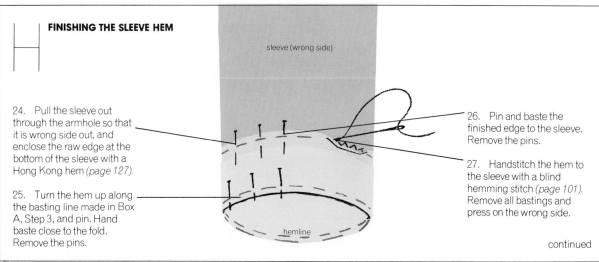

24. Pull the sleeve out through the armhole so that it is wrong side out, and enclose the raw edge at the bottom of the sleeve with a Hong Kong hem *(page 127)*.

25. Turn the hem up along the basting line made in Box A, Step 3, and pin. Hand baste close to the fold. Remove the pins.

26. Pin and baste the finished edge to the sleeve. Remove the pins.

27. Handstitch the hem to the sleeve with a blind hemming stitch *(page 101)*. Remove all bastings and press on the wrong side.

continued

THE KIMONO SLEEVE WITH GUSSET

A — MARKING THE PLACE FOR THE GUSSET

1. With the front section of the garment wrong side up, baste along the underarm seam lines between the pattern markings for insertion of a gusset—an extra piece set between the sleeve underarm seam and the garment side seam to increase freedom of movement.

2. To make the slash-point mark visible on both sides of the fabric, run a line of bastings to mark the slash point—the point to which you will slash the underarm section of the garment to make room for the gusset.

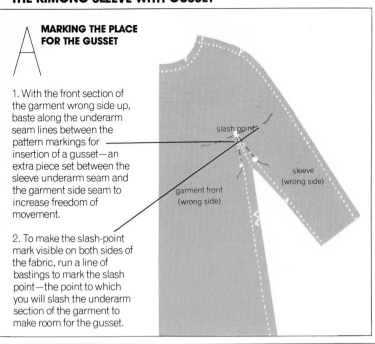

slash point

garment front
(wrong side)

sleeve
(wrong side)

B — MAKING AND ATTACHING THE GUSSET PATCH

3. Make a reinforcement patch for the area to be slashed by cutting a 3-inch square of organza or lining fabric on the bias, that is, diagonally across the weave.

4. Place the garment section wrong side down and center the reinforcement patch over the slash point.

5. Pin the patch to the garment. Baste around the edges and remove the pins.

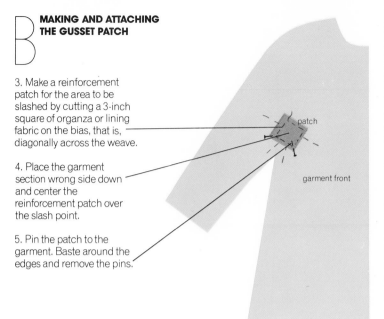

patch

garment front

C — REINFORCING THE SLASH POINT

6. Turn the garment section wrong side up. Machine stitch—at 15 to 20 stitches per inch—into the seam allowance beside the bastings made in Step 1. Stitch from one end of the patch and sew along one side. Take one stitch across the top of the slash point and continue stitching along the seam line to the other end of the patch. Remove the bastings attaching the patch to the garment, but leave in the horizontal bastings and the bastings along the seam line.

7. Slash into the garment along the slash line as indicated by your pattern. Cut up to but not through the horizontal machine stitch at the slash point, cutting through both the garment fabric and the patch.

8. Turn the garment section wrong side down and press the edges of the patch toward the slashed seam allowance.

9. Repeat Steps 1-8 on the back of the body section of the garment.

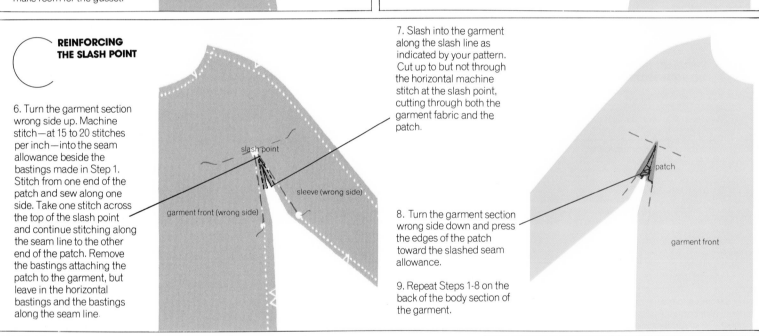

slash point

garment front (wrong side)

sleeve (wrong side)

patch

garment front

D — ASSEMBLING THE BODY SECTION

10. Place the front and back sections of the garment together, wrong sides out.

11. Align pattern markings for the sleeve underarm seam, then pin and baste the seam, starting at the bottom edge of the sleeve and continuing up to the pattern marking that indicates where the gusset will begin. Remove the pins.

12. Machine stitch—at the normal 12 stitches per inch —the basted part of the underarm sleeve seam, starting at the bottom of the sleeve. Remove the bastings.

13. Align pattern markings for the side seam of the garment, then pin and baste the seam from the hem to the pattern marking that indicates where the gusset will begin.

14. Machine stitch the basted garment side seam and remove the bastings.

15. Press open the seams stitched in Steps 12 and 14.

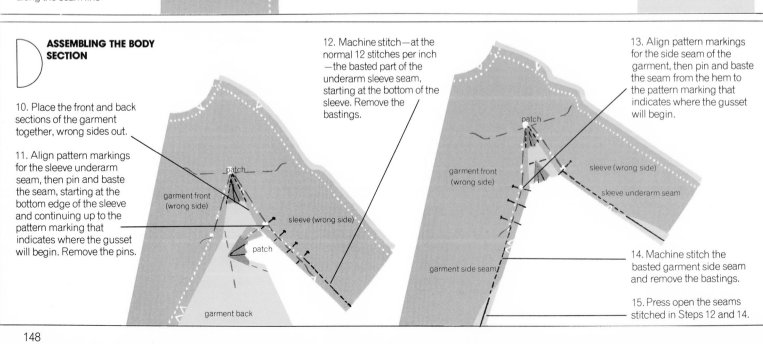

patch

garment front
(wrong side)

sleeve (wrong side)

patch

garment back

patch

garment front
(wrong side)

sleeve (wrong side)

sleeve underarm seam

garment side seam

INSERTING THE GUSSET

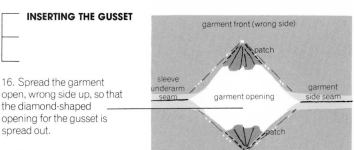

16. Spread the garment open, wrong side up, so that the diamond-shaped opening for the gusset is spread out.

17. Cut the gusset from garment fabric according to pattern instructions and insert it, wrong side up. Match the basted seam lines on one side of the garment back opening to the seam lines of the gusset.

18. Pin the gusset in place. Start at the reinforced slash point on the garment back. Add pins at 1/2-inch intervals until you reach the sleeve underarm seam. Match all pattern markings.

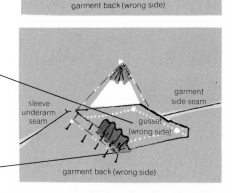

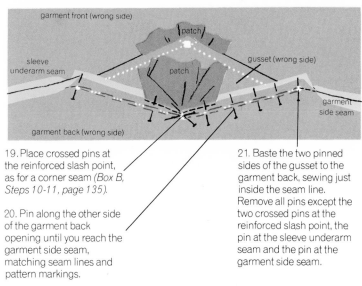

19. Place crossed pins at the reinforced slash point, as for a corner seam (Box B, Steps 10-11, page 135).

20. Pin along the other side of the garment back opening until you reach the garment side seam, matching seam lines and pattern markings.

21. Baste the two pinned sides of the gusset to the garment back, sewing just inside the seam line. Remove all pins except the two crossed pins at the reinforced slash point, the pin at the sleeve underarm seam and the pin at the garment side seam.

STITCHING THE GUSSET TO THE GARMENT

22. Machine stitch the basted sides of the gusset to the garment. Begin at the sleeve underarm seam and make one backstitch over the pin there. Remove the pin, then stitch forward to the reinforced slash point.

24. Stop the machine, leaving the needle in the garment, and raise the presser foot. Push the bunched-up garment fabric out of the way and pivot at the slash point. Lower the presser foot and remove the second crossed pin.

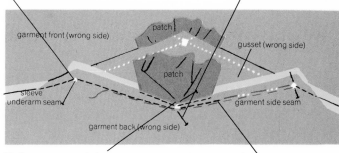

23. As you approach the reinforced slash point, stitch slowly, making sure the edges of the patch are out of the way of the needle. Remove one of the crossed pins at the reinforced slash point.

25. Continue stitching along the basted side of the gusset toward the garment side seam. Take one stitch over the pin there. Remove the pin, then make one backstitch. Remove the bastings.

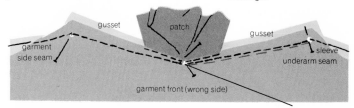

26. Turn the garment over so that the stitched sides of the gusset on the back of the garment face down. Repeat Steps 18-25 on the remaining two sides of the gusset, thus attaching them to the garment front.

FINISHING THE GUSSET

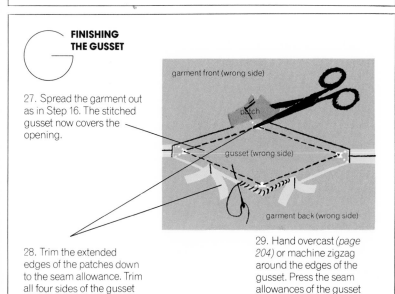

27. Spread the garment out as in Step 16. The stitched gusset now covers the opening.

28. Trim the extended edges of the patches down to the seam allowance. Trim all four sides of the gusset to 1/2 inch.

29. Hand overcast (page 204) or machine zigzag around the edges of the gusset. Press the seam allowances of the gusset flat.

FINISHING THE SLEEVE

30. Pin and baste the shoulder-sleeve seam from neckline to sleeve bottom, matching seam lines and notches. Remove the pins.

31. Machine stitch the shoulder-sleeve seam. Remove the bastings and press the seam open.

32. Finish the hem at the sleeve bottom as shown for The Fitted Sleeve, Box H, Steps 24-27 (page 147).

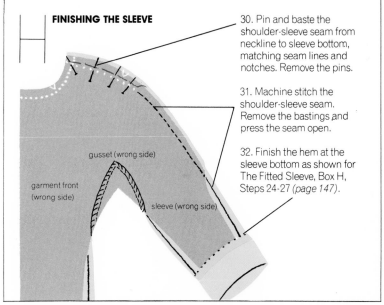

149

THE ONE-PIECE RAGLAN SLEEVE

A MAKING THE SLEEVE UNDERARM SEAM

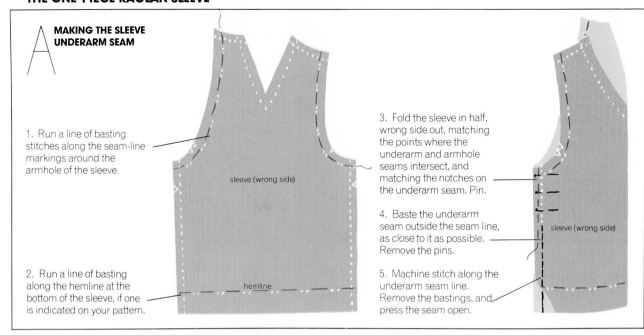

1. Run a line of basting stitches along the seam-line markings around the armhole of the sleeve.

2. Run a line of basting along the hemline at the bottom of the sleeve, if one is indicated on your pattern.

3. Fold the sleeve in half, wrong side out, matching the points where the underarm and armhole seams intersect, and matching the notches on the underarm seam. Pin.

4. Baste the underarm seam outside the seam line, as close to it as possible. Remove the pins.

5. Machine stitch along the underarm seam line. Remove the bastings, and press the seam open.

B ATTACHING THE SLEEVE TO THE BODY SECTION

6. If you have not already done so, turn the assembled garment wrong side out and run a line of basting stitches around the armhole seam line.

7. Turn the sleeve right side out and slip it into the armhole of the body section. Place the sleeve and the body section together and pin, matching the notches, the basting stitches made in Steps 1 and 6, and the intersection between the sleeve underarm seam and the side seam of the body section.

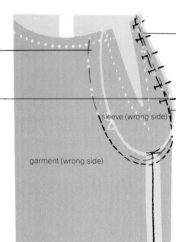

8. Baste all around the armhole just outside the basted line marking the sleeve seam line. Remove the pins.

9. Machine stitch on the sleeve seam line all around the armhole. Start at the point where the top of the sleeve meets the garment back. Remove the bastings.

10. To reinforce the underarm area, make a second row of machine stitching between the notches, stitching 1/4 inch into the seam allowance.

11. Clip into the underarm seam allowance at the notches up to, but not through, the reinforcement stitches and trim close to the stitches.

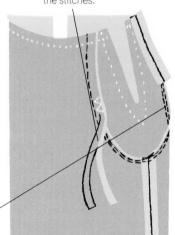

12. Press open the untrimmed seam allowances above the clipping, placing brown wrapping paper between the seam allowances and the garment fabric to prevent marks on the outside of the garment.

13. Press the trimmed seam allowance flat.

C MAKING THE DART SEAM

14. Pin closed the dart seam—which unlike the standard dart is cut open at one end. Match the dart seam lines and the intersection between the dart seam and the neck seam line at the shoulder or upper edge of the sleeve. Baste the dart seam just outside the seam line. Remove the pins.

15. Machine stitch the dart seam, beginning at the neckline and sewing a few stitches off the point of the dart. Tie off the ends of the machine threads at the point. Remove the bastings.

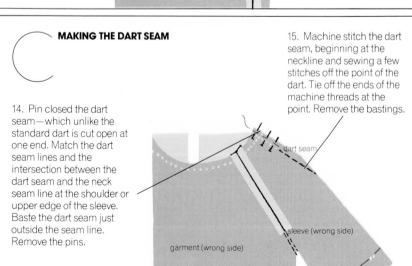

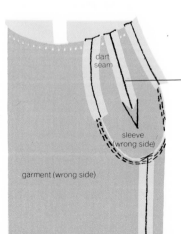

16. Press the dart seam open, placing brown wrapping paper between the seam allowances of the dart seam and the garment fabric to prevent marks that may show on the outside of the garment.

17. Finish the hem at the bottom of the sleeve as shown in the directions for The Fitted Sleeve, Box H, Steps 24-27 *(page 147)*.

THE TWO-PIECE RAGLAN SLEEVE

A MAKING THE UNDERARM AND SHOULDER SEAMS

1. Run a line of basting stitches along the seam-line markings around the armhole of the front and back sleeve sections.

2. Run a line of basting along the hemline at the bottom of the sleeve, if one is indicated on your pattern.

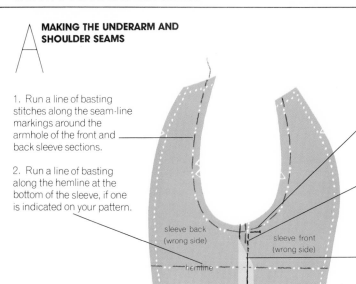

sleeve back (wrong side)

sleeve front (wrong side)

hemline

3. Pin the front and back sections of the sleeve together at the underarm seam. Match the seam intersections and notches.

4. Baste the underarm seam as closely as possible outside the seam line. Remove the pins.

5. Machine stitch along the underarm seam line. Remove the bastings and press the seam open.

6. Fold the sleeve sections along the underarm seam, then pin the sleeve front to the sleeve back along the shoulder seam line, matching the seam intersections and the notches. Baste outside the seam line, as close to it as possible. Remove the pins.

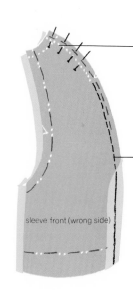

sleeve front (wrong side)

7. Machine stitch along the shoulder seam line the full length of the sleeve. Remove the bastings and press the seam open. Place brown wrapping paper between the seam allowances and the garment fabric to prevent any marks that may show on the outside of the garment.

B ATTACHING THE SLEEVE TO THE BODY SECTION

8. If you have not already done so, turn the garment wrong side out and run a line of basting stitches around the armhole seam line.

9. Turn the sleeve right side out and slip it into the armhole of the body section. Place the sleeve and the body section together and pin, matching the notches, the basting stitches made in Steps 1 and 8, and the intersection between the sleeve underarm seam and the side seam of the body section.

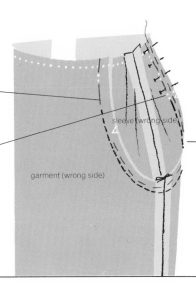

sleeve (wrong side)

garment (wrong side)

10. Baste all around the armhole just outside the basted line marking the sleeve seam line (made in Step 1). Remove the pins.

11. Machine stitch along the sleeve seam line all around the armhole, starting from the point where the top of the sleeve meets the garment back. Remove all the bastings.

C REINFORCING THE UNDERARM SEAM

12. Make a second row of machine stitches between the notches, stitching 1/4 inch into the seam allowance.

13. Clip into the underarm seam allowance at the notches up to, but not through, the reinforcement stitches and trim between the notches close to the stitches.

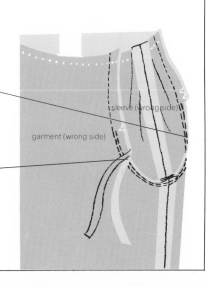

sleeve (wrong side)

garment (wrong side)

D FINISHING THE SLEEVE

14. Press open the untrimmed seam allowances above the clipping, placing brown wrapping paper between the seam allowances and the garment fabric to prevent marks that may show on the outside of the garment. Press the trimmed seam allowance flat.

15. Finish the hem at the bottom of the sleeve as shown in the directions for The Fitted Sleeve, Box H, Steps 24-27 (page 147).

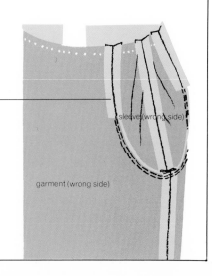

sleeve (wrong side)

garment (wrong side)

151

Flourishes: pleats or godets

It is a time-honored dressmaker's custom to use pleats or godets to give a skirt fullness and flare. The controlled fullness of pleats, overlapping folds that often reach all the way from waist to hem, is flattering to many figures. But to provide special interest and fullness at the hem alone, a designer may employ godets, triangular insets of fabric sewn into seams or slashes as in the House of Norell dress at right.

Pleats are simple to construct, especially if care is taken in choosing the pattern size closest to your hip measurement (it is harder to make adjustments at the hip than at the waist) and in marking the pleat lines accurately *(page 156)*. If the waist of the skirt needs to be adjusted, the total amount of adjustment should be divided among all the pleats and should not be more than 1/4 inch per pleat; if more is needed, use another pattern size.

Godets *(pages 153-156)* are slightly trickier to construct than pleats are, partly because they are cut on the bias, which makes the fabric liable to stretch. But if the godets are stitched in at their top point and then hung up for 24 hours before their sides are sewn down, they will stretch and excess can be trimmed.

THE GODET IN A SLASH

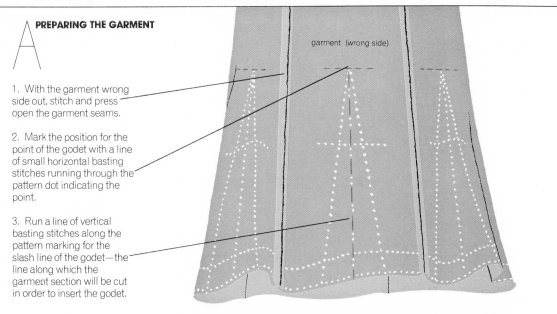

A PREPARING THE GARMENT

1. With the garment wrong side out, stitch and press open the garment seams.

2. Mark the position for the point of the godet with a line of small horizontal basting stitches running through the pattern dot indicating the point.

3. Run a line of vertical basting stitches along the pattern marking for the slash line of the godet—the line along which the garment section will be cut in order to insert the godet.

garment (wrong side)

B REINFORCING THE SLASH POINT

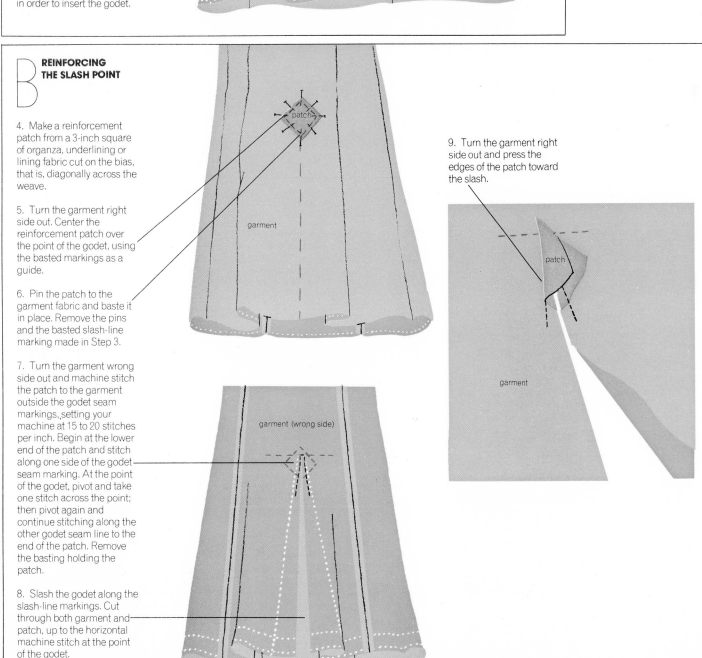

4. Make a reinforcement patch from a 3-inch square of organza, underlining or lining fabric cut on the bias, that is, diagonally across the weave.

5. Turn the garment right side out. Center the reinforcement patch over the point of the godet, using the basted markings as a guide.

6. Pin the patch to the garment fabric and baste it in place. Remove the pins and the basted slash-line marking made in Step 3.

7. Turn the garment wrong side out and machine stitch the patch to the garment outside the godet seam markings, setting your machine at 15 to 20 stitches per inch. Begin at the lower end of the patch and stitch along one side of the godet seam marking. At the point of the godet, pivot and take one stitch across the point; then pivot again and continue stitching along the other godet seam line to the end of the patch. Remove the basting holding the patch.

8. Slash the godet along the slash-line markings. Cut through both garment and patch, up to the horizontal machine stitch at the point of the godet.

9. Turn the garment right side out and press the edges of the patch toward the slash.

patch

garment

garment

patch

garment (wrong side)

continued

C INSERTING THE GODET

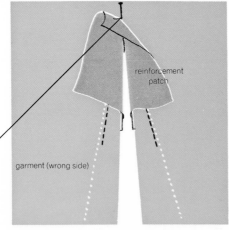

10. Turn the garment wrong side out, spread open the slash and turn the patch to the wrong side of the garment.

11. Push a pin from the wrong side of the garment fabric through the point of the slashed godet opening.

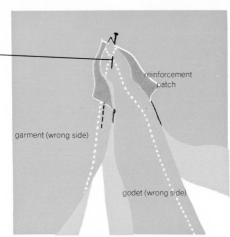

12. Place the godet wrong side up in the slashed godet opening of the garment. Push the pin inserted in Step 11 through the godet at the point where the seam lines marked on the godet intersect.

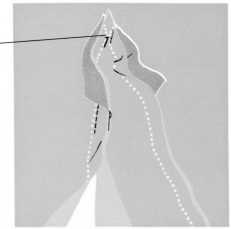

13. Match the seam line markings of the garment and the godet along one side and push the pin inserted in Step 12 through both the godet and the garment fabric parallel to the seam line.

14. Align the other matching seam lines of the garment and the godet and insert a second pin parallel to the seam lines, following the directions for Steps 11-13. The two pins will cross at the point of the godet.

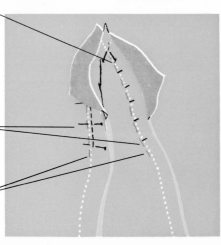

15. Pin the garment to the godet at 1/2-inch intervals along the seam lines to a point about 1 inch below the end of the reinforcement patch. Insert these pins at right angles to the seam lines.

16. Baste the garment to the godet just inside the seam lines. Remove all pins except the two crossed pins at the point of the godet.

D STITCHING THE GODET

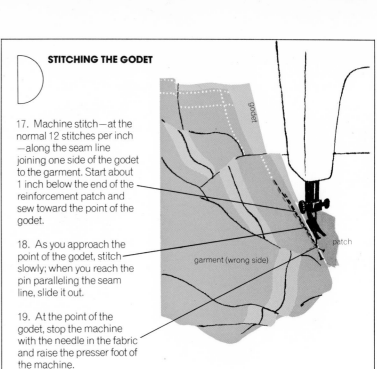

17. Machine stitch—at the normal 12 stitches per inch —along the seam line joining one side of the godet to the garment. Start about 1 inch below the end of the reinforcement patch and sew toward the point of the godet.

18. As you approach the point of the godet, stitch slowly; when you reach the pin paralleling the seam line, slide it out.

19. At the point of the godet, stop the machine with the needle in the fabric and raise the presser foot of the machine.

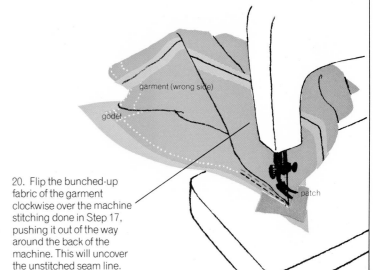

20. Flip the bunched-up fabric of the garment clockwise over the machine stitching done in Step 17, pushing it out of the way around the back of the machine. This will uncover the unstitched seam line.

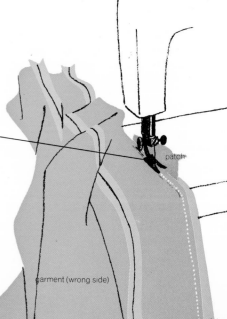

21. Swing the entire garment counterclockwise so the fabric will be to the left of the machine presser foot. Then lower the presser foot, remove the pin from the seam line and continue stitching down the seam line to a point 1 inch below the end of the reinforcement patch.

22. Hang up the garment overnight to set the bias, that is, to allow for any stretching in the godet.

E COMPLETING THE GODET

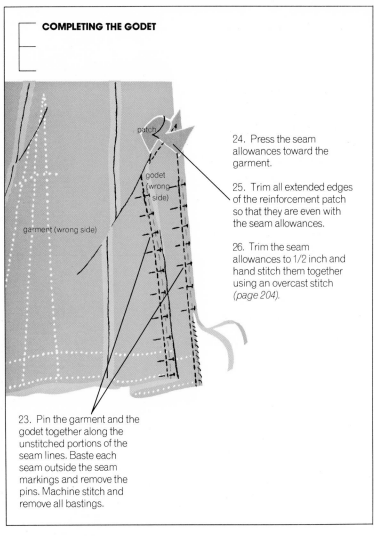

24. Press the seam allowances toward the garment.

25. Trim all extended edges of the reinforcement patch so that they are even with the seam allowances.

26. Trim the seam allowances to 1/2 inch and hand stitch them together using an overcast stitch (*page 204*).

23. Pin the garment and the godet together along the unstitched portions of the seam lines. Baste each seam outside the seam markings and remove the pins. Machine stitch and remove all bastings.

A PREPARING TO INSERT THE GODET

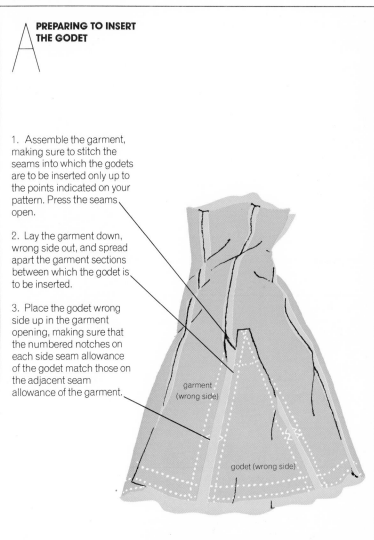

1. Assemble the garment, making sure to stitch the seams into which the godets are to be inserted only up to the points indicated on your pattern. Press the seams open.

2. Lay the garment down, wrong side out, and spread apart the garment sections between which the godet is to be inserted.

3. Place the godet wrong side up in the garment opening, making sure that the numbered notches on each side seam allowance of the godet match those on the adjacent seam allowance of the garment.

B INSERTING THE GODET

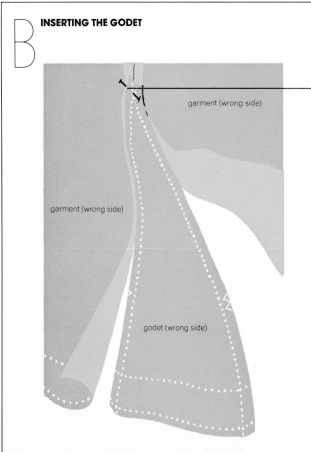

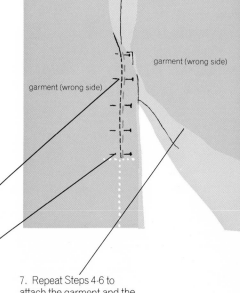

4. With the wrong sides of the fabric facing out, begin to pin the garment and the godet together along one seam line. Insert the first pin into the garment seam line just beyond the end of the stitched portion of the seam. Push the pin through the godet at the point where the two godet seam lines intersect. Finish inserting the pin at right angles to the seam line.

5. Continue to pin the garment and godet together for 3 inches along the seam line, inserting the pins at 1/2-inch intervals.

6. Baste the godet to the garment just outside the seam line. Begin where the stitched portion of the garment seam ends and continue stitching for 3 inches to the godet point. Then remove the pins and machine stitch this 3-inch segment of the godet seam.

7. Repeat Steps 4-6 to attach the garment and the godet along the other seam line.

8. Hang up the garment overnight to set the bias, that is, to allow for any stretching in the godet.

continued

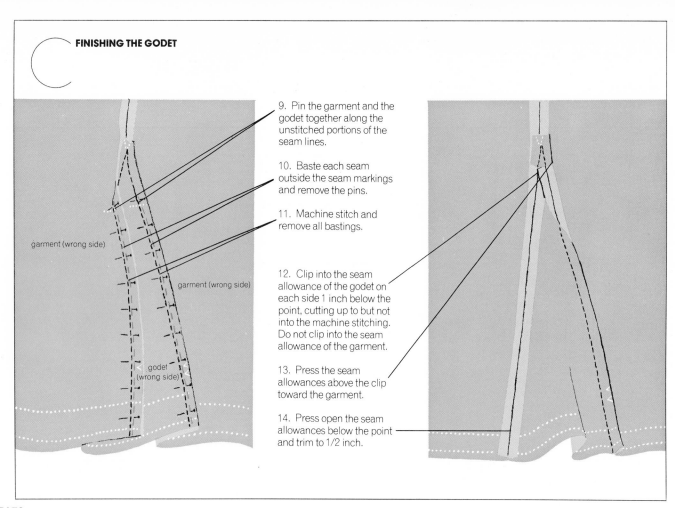

garment (wrong side)

garment (wrong side)

godet (wrong side)

9. Pin the garment and the godet together along the unstitched portions of the seam lines.

10. Baste each seam outside the seam markings and remove the pins.

11. Machine stitch and remove all bastings.

12. Clip into the seam allowance of the godet on each side 1 inch below the point, cutting up to but not into the machine stitching. Do not clip into the seam allowance of the garment.

13. Press the seam allowances above the clip toward the garment.

14. Press open the seam allowances below the point and trim to 1/2 inch.

KNIFE PLEATS

A PREPARING TO MAKE THE PLEATS

1. With each skirt section wrong side up, run a line of basting stitches along the waistline seam markings.

2. Run basting stitches along the pattern markings for each pleat. To differentiate them, use one color thread for the pleat fold lines and another color thread for the pleat placement lines (the lines against which the folded pleats will be placed).

3. If you plan to topstitch the pleats partway closed, use a horizontal running stitch to mark the point on the pleat fold lines where the topstitching should end.

4. Assemble the skirt, stitching and pressing open the seams, except for seams that will fall on either the inner or outer fold of a pleat. In this case, leave the bottom 8 inches of the seam unstitched and do not press the seam open.

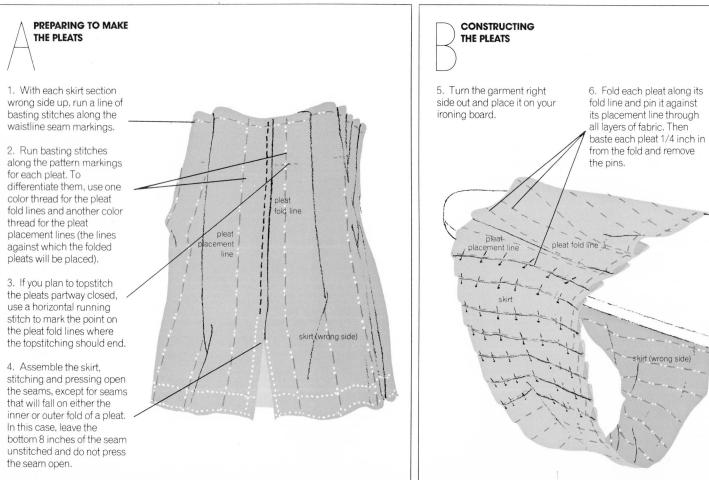

pleat fold line

pleat placement line

skirt (wrong side)

B CONSTRUCTING THE PLEATS

5. Turn the garment right side out and place it on your ironing board.

6. Fold each pleat along its fold line and pin it against its placement line through all layers of fabric. Then baste each pleat 1/4 inch in from the fold and remove the pins.

pleat placement line

pleat fold line

skirt

skirt (wrong side)

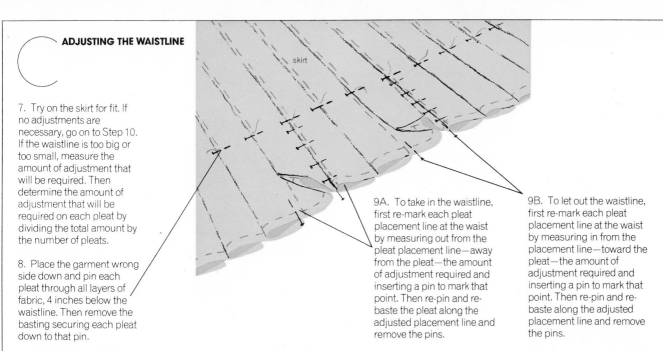

C ADJUSTING THE WAISTLINE

7. Try on the skirt for fit. If no adjustments are necessary, go on to Step 10. If the waistline is too big or too small, measure the amount of adjustment that will be required. Then determine the amount of adjustment that will be required on each pleat by dividing the total amount by the number of pleats.

8. Place the garment wrong side down and pin each pleat through all layers of fabric, 4 inches below the waistline. Then remove the basting securing each pleat down to that pin.

9A. To take in the waistline, first re-mark each pleat placement line at the waist by measuring out from the pleat placement line—away from the pleat—the amount of adjustment required and inserting a pin to mark that point. Then re-pin and re-baste the pleat along the adjusted placement line and remove the pins.

9B. To let out the waistline, first re-mark each pleat placement line at the waist by measuring in from the placement line—toward the pleat—the amount of adjustment required and inserting a pin to mark that point. Then re-pin and re-baste along the adjusted placement line and remove the pins.

D FINISHING THE PLEATS AT THE WAISTLINE

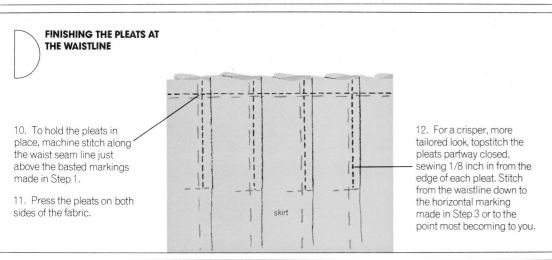

10. To hold the pleats in place, machine stitch along the waist seam line just above the basted markings made in Step 1.

11. Press the pleats on both sides of the fabric.

12. For a crisper, more tailored look, topstitch the pleats partway closed, sewing 1/8 inch in from the edge of each pleat. Stitch from the waistline down to the horizontal marking made in Step 3 or to the point most becoming to you.

E MAKING THE HEM

13. Turn the garment wrong side out and remove the bottom 8 inches of pleat bastings.

15. Finish the raw hem edge of each section between the open vertical seams with a line of zigzag or regular machine stitching.

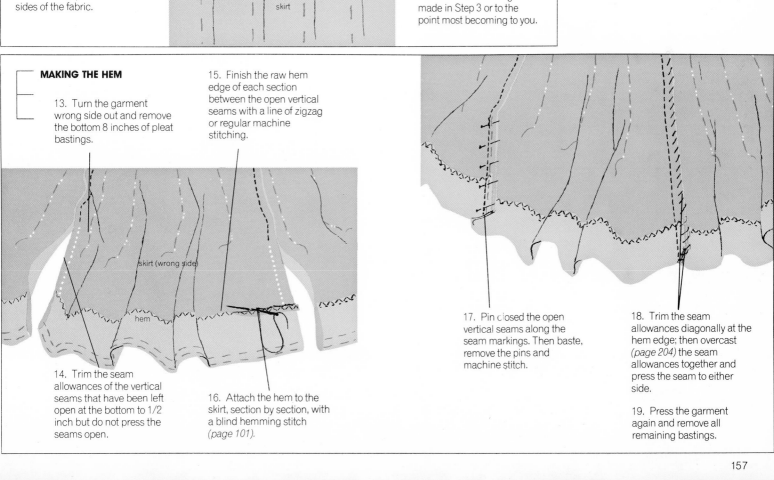

14. Trim the seam allowances of the vertical seams that have been left open at the bottom to 1/2 inch but do not press the seams open.

16. Attach the hem to the skirt, section by section, with a blind hemming stitch (page 101).

17. Pin closed the open vertical seams along the seam markings. Then baste, remove the pins and machine stitch.

18. Trim the seam allowances diagonally at the hem edge; then overcast (page 204) the seam allowances together and press the seam to either side.

19. Press the garment again and remove all remaining bastings.

5

CUSTOM DETAILS FOR THE HOME

Elements of fine dressmaking suitable for the home are the godet, the pleat, the bias panel and the scallop.

Most people when they think of custom decorating for their homes imagine a fantastic living room like the one interior designer Valerian Stux Rybar created for his own New York apartment. It specified a silver-gray mink-tail rug, curved walls covered with red velvet, a stainless-steel floor, a chromium-plated fireplace beneath a crystal bust of a 16th Century Medici duke, a lumpy chaise longue covered in ba-

FURNISHINGS WITH A TOUCH OF INDIVIDUALITY

tik and steel ottomans topped with embroidered silver satin pillows. Slightly less exuberant dreamers imagine an exotic bathroom like the one ordered by author Ben Hecht. As described by Dorothy Rodgers in her book *My Favorite Things,* "He knew exactly what he wanted: flocked velvet walls, a marble washstand, a mural by Henry Varnum Poor, an Aubusson rug cut down to upholster a baroque Italian stool and a mercury-backed French mirror lit by two oil lamps." Mrs. Rodgers added tartly, "For practical reasons (he couldn't see to shave), he later allowed me to substitute a modern clear-faced mirror and electric lights. There were problems involved, but compared to building a room around a personality that doesn't exist, furnishing Ben's bath was childishly easy."

Building a room around a personality is what makes home decoration custom. By definition, custom means made to personal order, to fit the exact physical dimensions of an individual home and to satisfy individual preferences in color, design and materials. If you want stainless-steel floors or walls covered with Harris tweed, then you ought to have them if you can afford them. There are no insuperable technical obstacles and the effects can, with the right touch, be handsome as well as startling. But most people restrain their fancies; they seek a custom look within strictures of the definition—working for perfection of fit and a pleasingly individualistic combination of design elements. And unless they are wealthy enough to summon the services of a talented designer who, in turn, commands platoons of craftsmen and seamstresses, they can express their personalities in interior design with things they create themselves, often in the form of home-sewn draperies, table covers, bedspreads and pillows. Particularly when made using the couturier techniques described in previous chapters of this book, such furnishings provide the individualistic appearance that says they were created for this house and no other.

The first requirement for the custom-made look in clothing your house is the same as that for clothing your person: precise fit. Even though most modern windows, beds and tables are mass-produced in factories, supposedly to standardized dimensions, they are no more identical than human figures (and old house equipment follows no standard at all). To avoid spreads or coverlets that spill heel-catching cascades of fabric over the floor or reveal gaps as embarrassing as a too-tight shirt, you must start by measuring certain key dimensions of your bed (page 170). Similar attention to the actual measurements of tables, window frames and rooms is necessary when cutting fabric to decorate them.

This kind of concern for fit makes even conventional panels of silk or chintz look like very special curtains. But expressing the extra element of personality calls for the addition of something unique in fabric, construction or detail.

Some of the details that characterize couturier dressmaking—godets, scallops, knife pleats and bias panels—are particularly useful. They all provide means of making fabric change direction—turning it over the edge of bed or table, for example—or of introducing fullness. Some couturier details, such as godets and scallops, soften sharp lines; others, such as knife pleats, introduce them.

The real charm of adapting couturier details is that they are rarely employed in home decoration. Interior designers avoid them because they are time-consuming. For the home sewer, however, the effort required is rewarded by the handsome results couturier techniques create.

Pleats for crispness and formality

Many ways of adding elegance to ordinary home furnishings can be found in the custom dressmaker's bag of tricks. The familiar knife pleat, long a standby for skirts, is used here to give a full and formal look to a floor-length tablecloth, a curtain valance, a bedspread and two pillow covers—all of them fashioned from an antique-finished satin of rayon and acetate that effectively holds the pleats' sharp lines.

Pleats can vary in height and width, but since busy patterns tend to mar their linear look they are best attempted only in materials of solid colors. The bedspread is an example of how effectively colors can be combined. Pleats are as masculine as a Scotsman's kilt. They are also severe, and severity can be a virtue in a bedroom that is to be a well-ordered refuge.

Scallops for a natural softness

Scallops, which adorned garment hems as far back as the Middle Ages, have been put to similar uses here on the borders of a round tablecloth, a curtain valance and a coverlet and throw pillows. Since their outlines suggest those of flower petals as much as the seashells after which they were named, scallops are particularly appropriate with floral patterns. The scalloped edge of the pillows shown here, cut from plain materials of contrasting colors, gives them the added appealing look of a flower in bloom.

Slanting stripes for contrast

The wide stripes slashing across the fabrics on these pages create a severe, startling effect. The design was created by sewing together broad strips of cotton velour in emphatically constrasting colors.

The diagonal pattern of the valance and the pillow cover consists of a series of strips cut out on the bias *(pages 38-39)* and sewn together. For the bed throw, the strips were sewn with the lengthwise grain of the fabric into a huge rectangle, and a paper pattern was pinned to it on the bias—like a diamond within the rectangle—and the throw was then cut from the rectangle. The tablecloth was simply cut and sewn from a round pattern over the straight strips of another rectangle; because of its circular shape, its stripes fall from the table top diagonally, matching the angles introduced by diagonal cutting of the other items.

Godets for fullness and flair

The godet, a billowing insert used in dresses for a fuller, less-tailored look than pleats, lends flair to a home as well. Here godets of sateen-finished cotton are closely spaced on a table-cloth and more widely spaced on a bedspread and curtain valance. Although often made of the same fabric, they are even more striking in contrasting material: these godets of white polka dots and squares on a dark background stand out prominently against the same material in a reverse pattern.

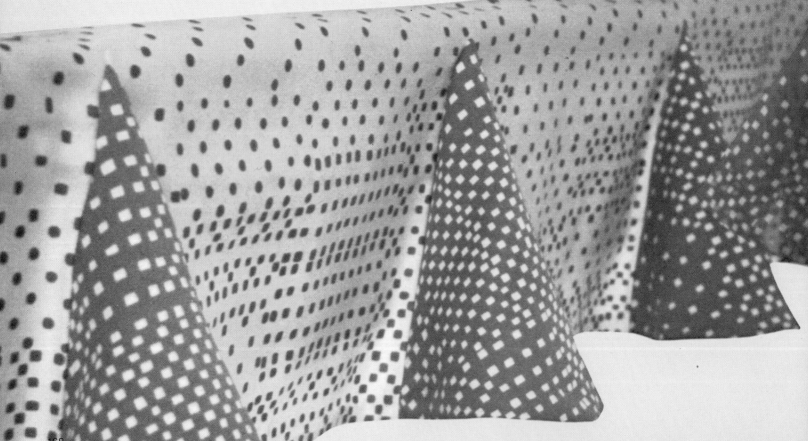

How to make the basic coverings

Plain or fancy, home furnishings gain that costly, made-to-order-by-an-expert look when they are given the attention ordinarily reserved for haute couture gowns. Elementary shapes can be embellished with details borrowed from the couturier's techniques *(pages 184-187)*—or they can be used simply as they are. Either way, they must fit precisely to be properly haute couture.

To guarantee such precision in home furnishings, follow the instructions for measuring the items to be covered by the shapes—pillows, tables, window valances and beds. It is best to make larger shapes like bed covers or table throws in muslin first; a mistake in measuring the intended fabric can be costly. Before measuring any piece of fabric remove the selvages, so that none is included in the measurements. Figure on a seam allowance of 1/2 inch, rather than the 5/8 inch generally used in dressmaking calculations.

FABRIC NEEDED FOR BED COVERS

The tables below indicate the approximate yardage of 36-, 44- or 54-inch-wide material that will be required to make coverlets or bedspreads for beds of the four most common standard sizes.

COVERLETS

BED SIZE	36-INCH MATERIAL	44-INCH MATERIAL	54-INCH MATERIAL
TWIN	5¾ yards	5¾ yards	5¾ yards
DOUBLE	8¾ yards	5¾ yards	5¾ yards
QUEEN	9¼ yards	9¼ yards	6¼ yards
KING	9¼ yards	9¼ yards	9¼ yards

BEDSPREADS

BED SIZE	36-INCH MATERIAL	44-INCH MATERIAL	54-INCH MATERIAL
TWIN	9 yards	9 yards	6¼ yards
DOUBLE	9¼ yards	9¼ yards	7¾ yards
QUEEN	12¾ yards	10 yards	8¼ yards
KING	15¾ yards	13 yards	10¼ yards

HOW TO MEASURE A BED

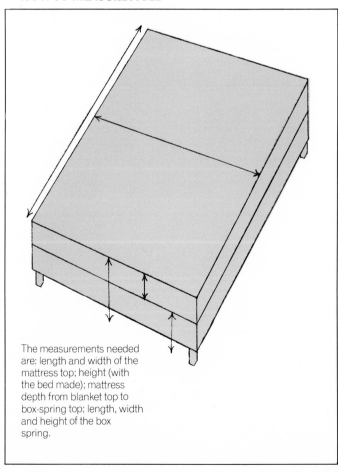

The measurements needed are: length and width of the mattress top; height (with the bed made); mattress depth from blanket top to box-spring top; length, width and height of the box spring.

THE BASIC COVERLET

A MEASURING AND CUTTING THE COVERLET

1. To find the length of each of the three coverlet panels, measure the length of the bed top and add 10 inches. If the coverlet is to tuck under and over pillows, add another 16 inches.

2. To find the width of each side panel, measure the width of the bed top, add 18 inches for the side drops, divide the total by four, and then add 1 inch for seam allowances to each side panel.

3. To find the width of the center panel, double the figure found in Step 2 and subtract 1 inch.

4. Cut the three panels to the dimensions calculated in Steps 1-3.

B CUTTING CURVED CORNERS

5. To curve the bottom corners, cut a square of shelf paper 9 1/2 inches on each side and pin to a bottom corner of the coverlet, aligning the paper edges with the fabric corners.

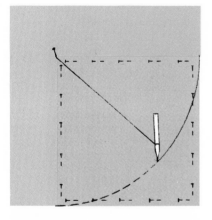

7. Insert the thumbtack at the corner of the paper square that is diagonally opposite the coverlet corner, and holding the string taut, draw an arc on the paper.

8. Cut paper and fabric along the arc drawn in Step 7. Remove the pins and the paper pattern.

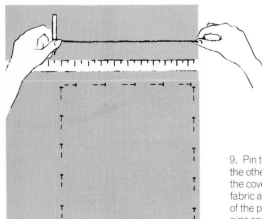

6. Tie one end of a piece of string to a pencil and the other end to a thumbtack so that the separation is 9 1/2 inches.

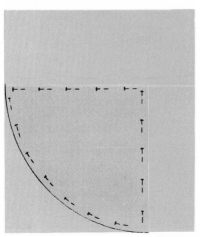

9. Pin the paper pattern to the other bottom corner of the coverlet and cut the fabric along the arced edge of the pattern. Remove the pins and pattern.

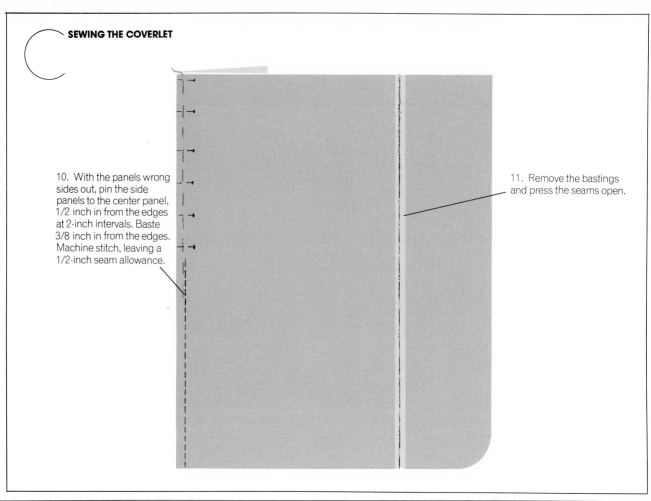

SEWING THE COVERLET

10. With the panels wrong sides out, pin the side panels to the center panel, 1/2 inch in from the edges at 2-inch intervals. Baste 3/8 inch in from the edges. Machine stitch, leaving a 1/2-inch seam allowance.

11. Remove the bastings and press the seams open.

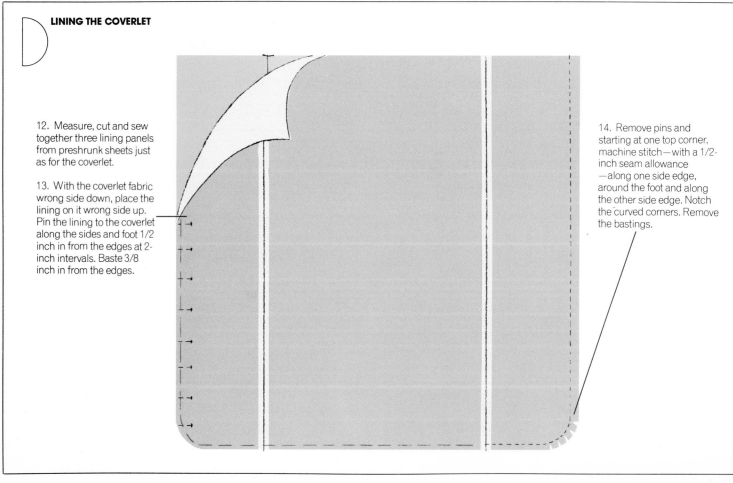

LINING THE COVERLET

12. Measure, cut and sew together three lining panels from preshrunk sheets just as for the coverlet.

13. With the coverlet fabric wrong side down, place the lining on it wrong side up. Pin the lining to the coverlet along the sides and foot 1/2 inch in from the edges at 2-inch intervals. Baste 3/8 inch in from the edges.

14. Remove pins and starting at one top corner, machine stitch—with a 1/2-inch seam allowance—along one side edge, around the foot and along the other side edge. Notch the curved corners. Remove the bastings.

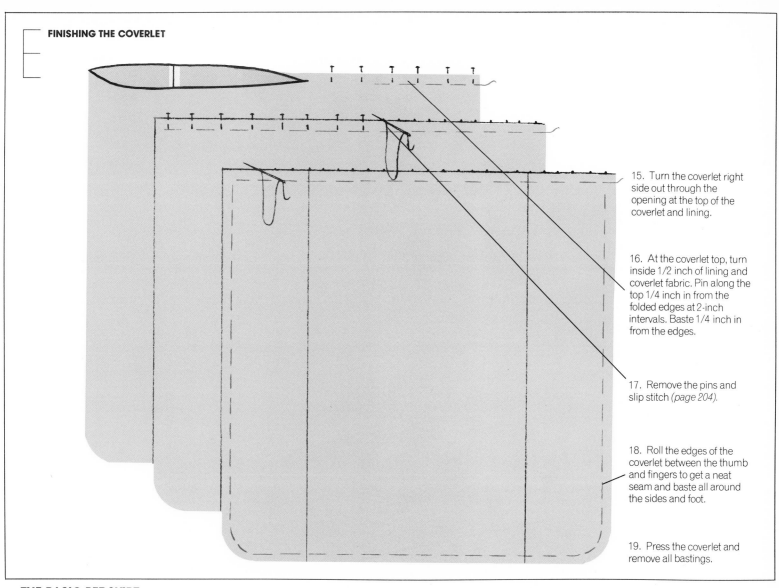

15. Turn the coverlet right side out through the opening at the top of the coverlet and lining.

16. At the coverlet top, turn inside 1/2 inch of lining and coverlet fabric. Pin along the top 1/4 inch in from the folded edges at 2-inch intervals. Baste 1/4 inch in from the edges.

17. Remove the pins and slip stitch *(page 204)*.

18. Roll the edges of the coverlet between the thumb and fingers to get a neat seam and baste all around the sides and foot.

19. Press the coverlet and remove all bastings.

THE BASIC BEDSKIRT

A **MEASURING AND CUTTING THE BEDSKIRT**

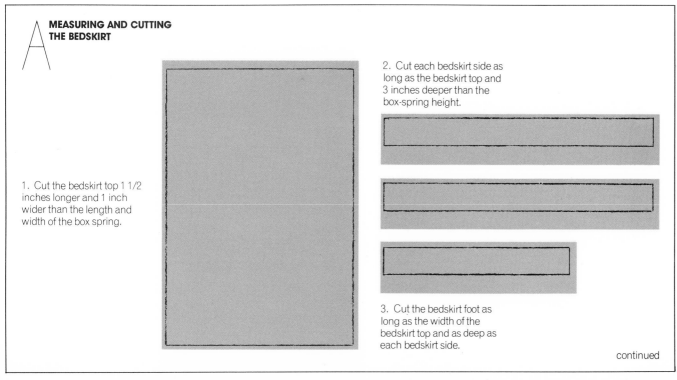

1. Cut the bedskirt top 1 1/2 inches longer and 1 inch wider than the length and width of the box spring.

2. Cut each bedskirt side as long as the bedskirt top and 3 inches deeper than the box-spring height.

3. Cut the bedskirt foot as long as the width of the bedskirt top and as deep as each bedskirt side.

continued

4. With the bedskirt sides and foot wrong side out, pin the foot end of each side to one end of the foot 1/2 inch in from the edges at 2-inch intervals. Baste 3/8 inch in from the edges. Remove the pins.

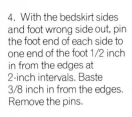
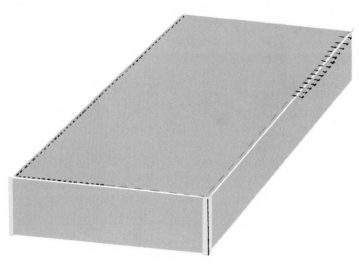

5. Machine stitch with a 1/2-inch seam allowance, leaving 1/2 inch open at the upper part of each seam. Remove the bastings. Press the seams open.

7. Starting from one corner, machine stitch along one side edge, around the foot and along the other side edge with a 1/2-inch seam allowance. Remove the bastings. Press the seam allowances toward the skirt top.

6. Place the bedskirt top wrong side up on the bare box spring and align its foot corners with the seams at the ends of the skirt foot, wrong side out. Pin the skirt foot to the skirt top and the sides of the skirt top to each of the skirt sides 1/2 inch in from the edges at 2-inch intervals. Baste the sides and foot to the top 3/8 inch in from the edges. Remove the pins.

8. With the bedskirt wrong side up, turn the head end up 1/2 inch and press flat; then turn it up another 1/2 inch. Pin at 2-inch intervals. Turn the foot and sides up 1/2 inch and press flat; then turn them up another 2 inches. Pin at 2-inch intervals. Baste all around and remove the pins. Hem with a slip stitch (page 204). Remove bastings and press.

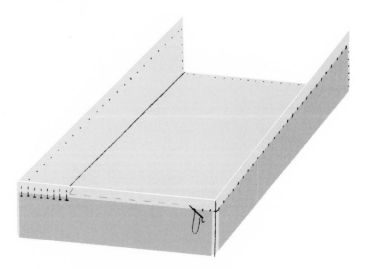

A **MEASURING AND CUTTING THE BEDSPREAD**

1. Cut each of the bedspread top panels 1 1/2 inches longer than the length of the bed. If the bedspread is to go over pillows, add another 16 inches.

2. Decide on the finished width of the bedspread top center panel, subtract that figure from the bed top width, and divide the difference in half to obtain the finished width of each side panel. Add 1 inch for seam allowances to the finished width of each of the three panels to obtain the total widths, and cut.

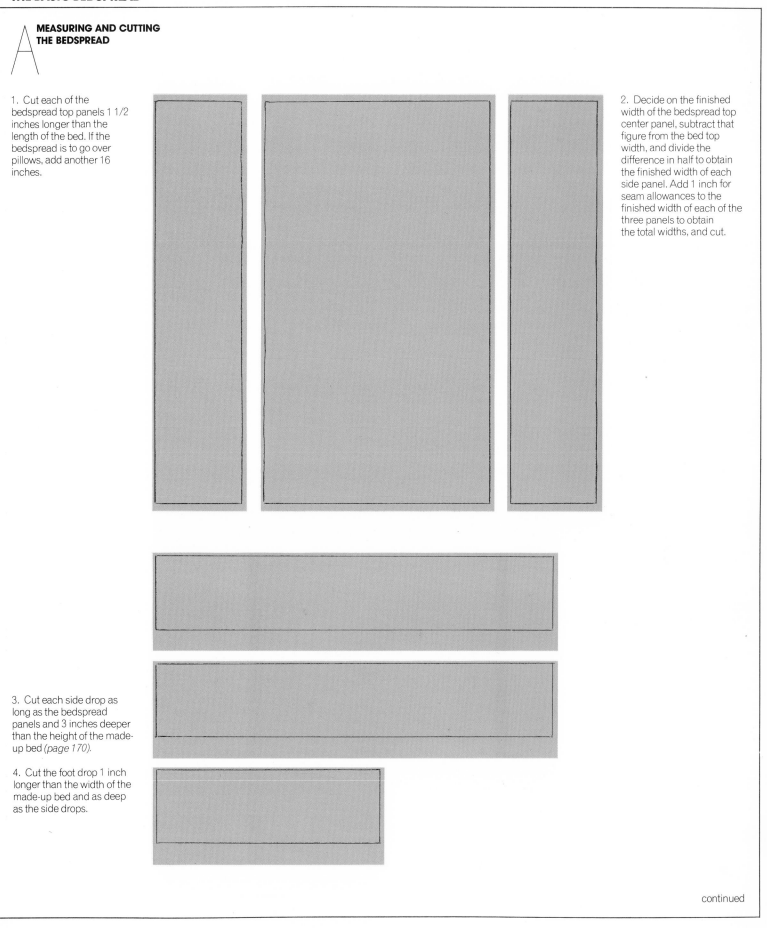

3. Cut each side drop as long as the bedspread panels and 3 inches deeper than the height of the made-up bed *(page 170)*.

4. Cut the foot drop 1 inch longer than the width of the made-up bed and as deep as the side drops.

continued

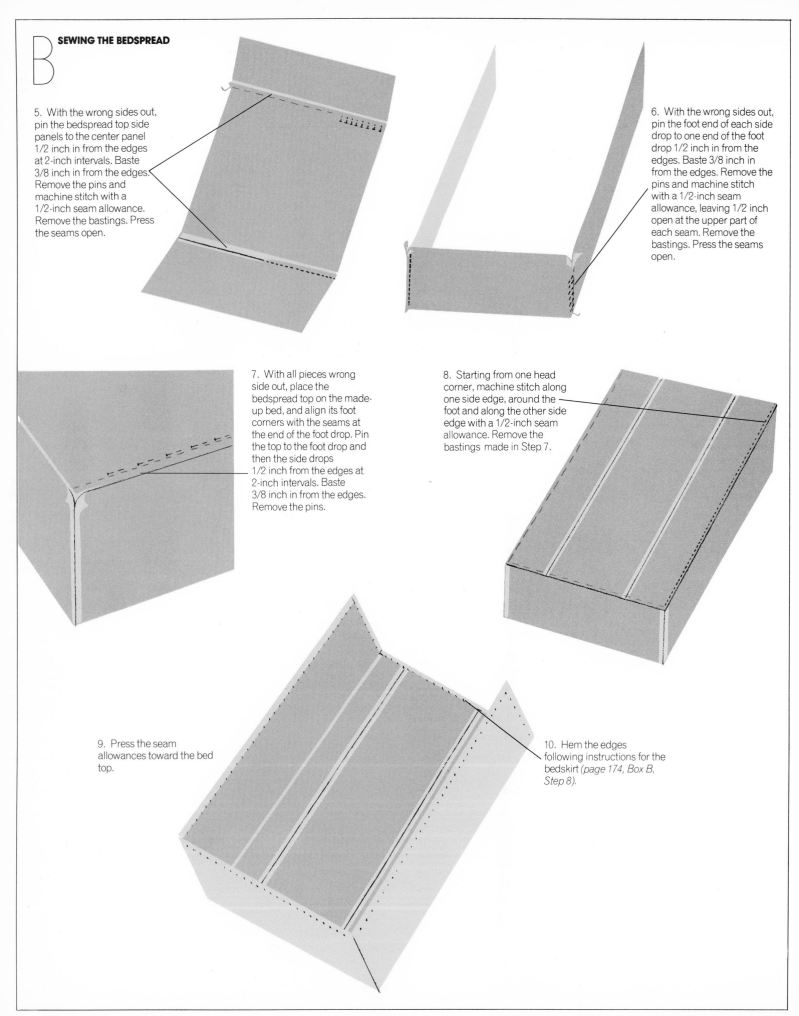

5. With the wrong sides out, pin the bedspread top side panels to the center panel 1/2 inch in from the edges at 2-inch intervals. Baste 3/8 inch in from the edges. Remove the pins and machine stitch with a 1/2-inch seam allowance. Remove the bastings. Press the seams open.

6. With the wrong sides out, pin the foot end of each side drop to one end of the foot drop 1/2 inch in from the edges. Baste 3/8 inch in from the edges. Remove the pins and machine stitch with a 1/2-inch seam allowance, leaving 1/2 inch open at the upper part of each seam. Remove the bastings. Press the seams open.

7. With all pieces wrong side out, place the bedspread top on the made-up bed, and align its foot corners with the seams at the end of the foot drop. Pin the top to the foot drop and then the side drops 1/2 inch from the edges at 2-inch intervals. Baste 3/8 inch in from the edges. Remove the pins.

8. Starting from one head corner, machine stitch along one side edge, around the foot and along the other side edge with a 1/2-inch seam allowance. Remove the bastings made in Step 7.

9. Press the seam allowances toward the bed top.

10. Hem the edges following instructions for the bedskirt *(page 174, Box B, Step 8).*

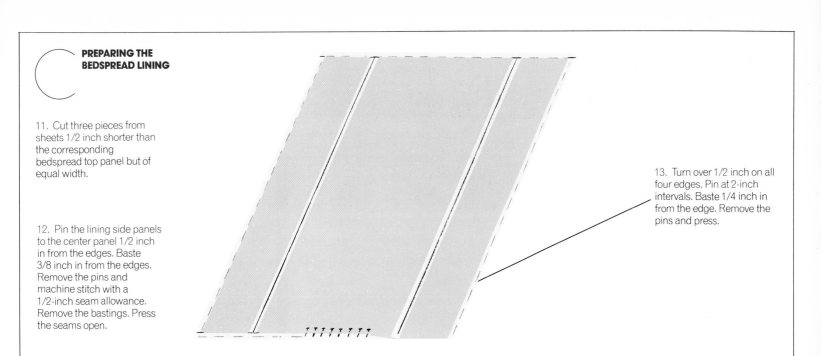

PREPARING THE BEDSPREAD LINING

11. Cut three pieces from sheets 1/2 inch shorter than the corresponding bedspread top panel but of equal width.

12. Pin the lining side panels to the center panel 1/2 inch in from the edges. Baste 3/8 inch in from the edges. Remove the pins and machine stitch with a 1/2-inch seam allowance. Remove the bastings. Press the seams open.

13. Turn over 1/2 inch on all four edges. Pin at 2-inch intervals. Baste 1/4 inch in from the edge. Remove the pins and press.

SEWING THE LINING TO THE BEDSPREAD

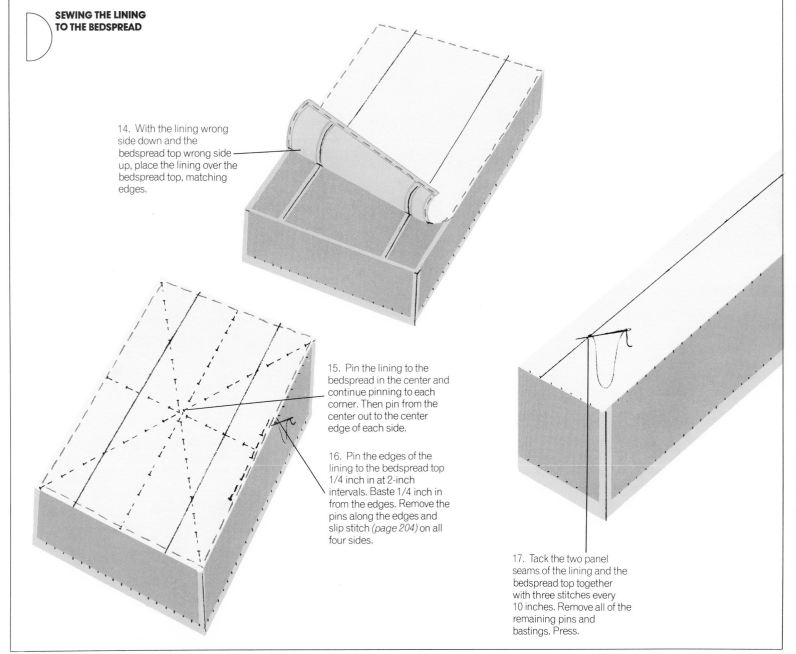

14. With the lining wrong side down and the bedspread top wrong side up, place the lining over the bedspread top, matching edges.

15. Pin the lining to the bedspread in the center and continue pinning to each corner. Then pin from the center out to the center edge of each side.

16. Pin the edges of the lining to the bedspread top 1/4 inch in at 2-inch intervals. Baste 1/4 inch in from the edges. Remove the pins along the edges and slip stitch (page 204) on all four sides.

17. Tack the two panel seams of the lining and the bedspread top together with three stitches every 10 inches. Remove all of the remaining pins and bastings. Press.

THE BASIC UNLINED VALANCE

1. Cut the valance 2 inches wider than the distance around the three sides of the valance board from one wall to the other.

2. Cut the valance 3 inches deeper than the desired finished depth of the valance (10 to 14 inches is a fairly common finished depth).

6. Attach the valance to the board with fabric glue or staples, or by fastening to the board and the wrong side of the valance any of several types of adhesive tapes sold for this purpose.

3. With the valance wrong side up, turn the top edge under 1/2 inch and pin. Baste.

4. Turn each side edge under 1/2 inch, then 1/2 inch again and pin. Baste. Remove pins and slip stitch (page 204). Remove bastings and press.

5. Turn the bottom edge under 1/2 inch, then 2 inches again and pin. Baste. Remove pins and slip stitch. Remove bastings and press.

THE BASIC PILLOW SHAM

 **MEASURING AND CUTTING**

1. With a pillow case on the pillow, measure length and width across the middle, draping the tape measure lightly to avoid flattening the pillow.

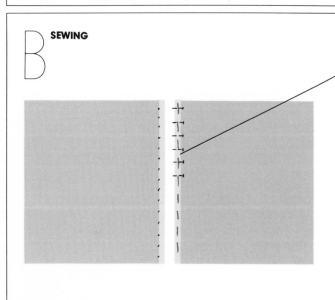

2. Cut the sham front 1 inch longer and wider than the pillow to provide seam allowances.

3. Cut two pieces for the sham back, making each the same width as the sham front and half the length plus 2 1/2 inches to provide overlap and hem allowance.

B SEWING

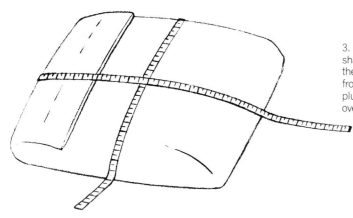

4. Place the sham backs wrong side up and turn the inner width edge of each up 1/2 inch; press. Turn up another 1/2 inch and pin along each side. Baste. Remove pins and hem with a slip stitch (page 204). Remove bastings and press.

5. Pin the sham backs to the sham front, wrong sides out, 1/2 inch in from the edges so that the hemmed edges of the backs overlap each other 1 1/2 inches. Baste 3/8 inch in from the edges. Remove pins; machine stitch with a 1/2-inch seam allowance. Remove the basting.

6. Trim the four corners diagonally and turn the sham right side out and press. Insert the pillow.

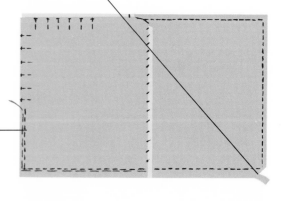

THE BASIC ROUND PILLOW COVER

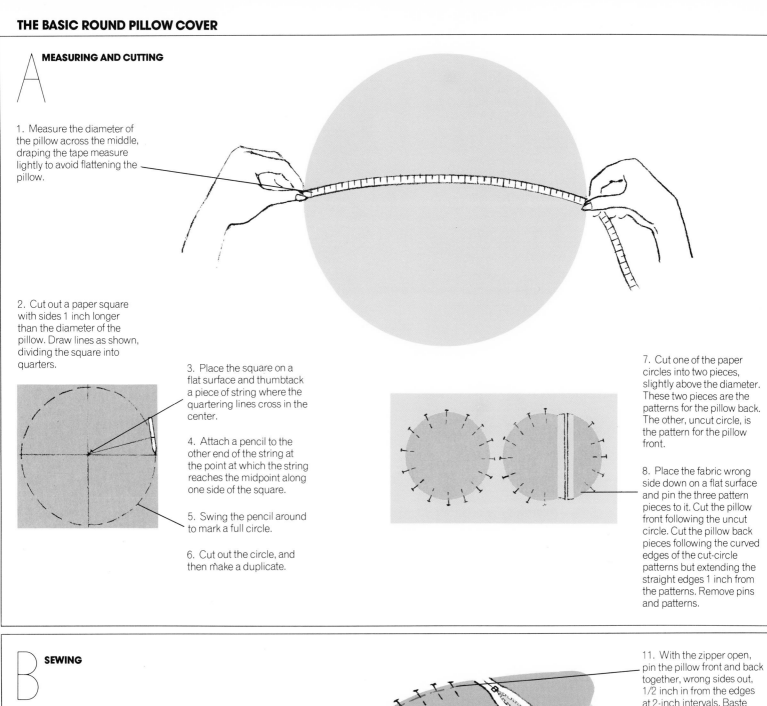

A MEASURING AND CUTTING

1. Measure the diameter of the pillow across the middle, draping the tape measure lightly to avoid flattening the pillow.

2. Cut out a paper square with sides 1 inch longer than the diameter of the pillow. Draw lines as shown, dividing the square into quarters.

3. Place the square on a flat surface and thumbtack a piece of string where the quartering lines cross in the center.

4. Attach a pencil to the other end of the string at the point at which the string reaches the midpoint along one side of the square.

5. Swing the pencil around to mark a full circle.

6. Cut out the circle, and then make a duplicate.

7. Cut one of the paper circles into two pieces, slightly above the diameter. These two pieces are the patterns for the pillow back. The other, uncut circle, is the pattern for the pillow front.

8. Place the fabric wrong side down on a flat surface and pin the three pattern pieces to it. Cut the pillow front following the uncut circle. Cut the pillow back pieces following the curved edges of the cut-circle patterns but extending the straight edges 1 inch from the patterns. Remove pins and patterns.

B SEWING

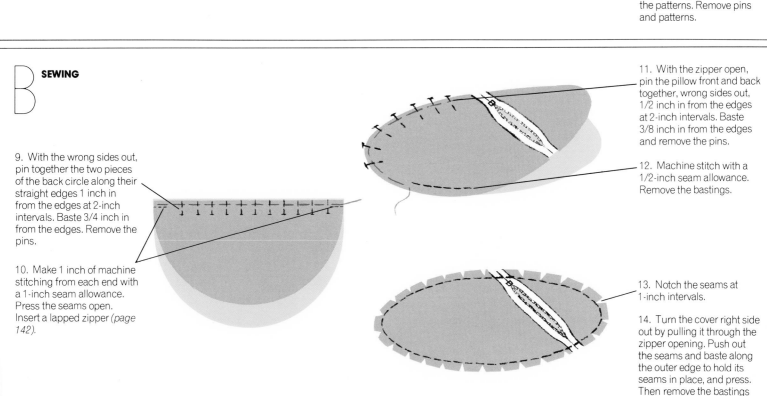

9. With the wrong sides out, pin together the two pieces of the back circle along their straight edges 1 inch in from the edges at 2-inch intervals. Baste 3/4 inch in from the edges. Remove the pins.

10. Make 1 inch of machine stitching from each end with a 1-inch seam allowance. Press the seams open. Insert a lapped zipper (*page 142*).

11. With the zipper open, pin the pillow front and back together, wrong sides out, 1/2 inch in from the edges at 2-inch intervals. Baste 3/8 inch in from the edges and remove the pins.

12. Machine stitch with a 1/2-inch seam allowance. Remove the bastings.

13. Notch the seams at 1-inch intervals.

14. Turn the cover right side out by pulling it through the zipper opening. Push out the seams and baste along the outer edge to hold its seams in place, and press. Then remove the bastings and insert the pillow.

MEASURING THE ROUND TABLE

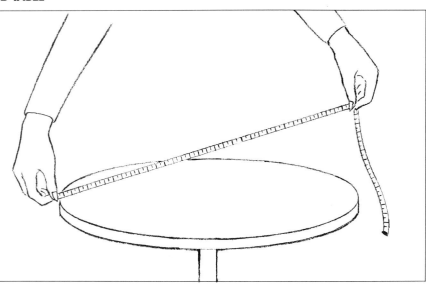

1. To find the diameter of a round table top, hold one end of a tape measure at any point along the edge of a table and swing the other end along the edge opposite until the distance measured is a maximum. For the circumference, simply wrap the tape snugly around the table edge. Be sure to measure height where the table will be used; if it is to stand on a rug, measure from table edge to the top of the rug pile, not to bare floor.

THE FITTED ROUND TABLE COVER

A CUTTING

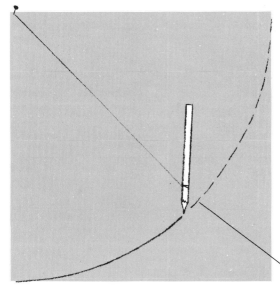

1. Cut a paper square with each side equal to half the diameter of the table top plus 1/2 inch.

2. Tie one end of a piece of string to a pencil and the other end to a thumbtack so that the separation is equal to one side of the paper pattern.

3. Place the paper pattern on a flat surface, and insert the thumbtack at one top corner.

4. Holding the string taut, draw an arc from one corner of the square to the corner diagonally opposite it.

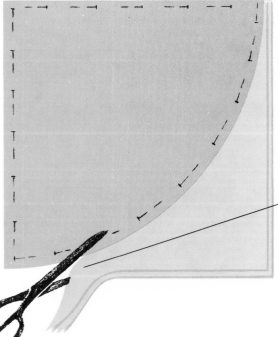

5. Cut along the arc to make a quarter circle pattern.

6. Cut out a square of fabric with sides 1 inch longer than the diameter of the table top.

7. Fold the fabric in half, wrong sides together. Then fold the fabric crosswise.

8. Pin the quarter circle pattern made in Step 5 to the fabric with its right angle at the twice folded corner. Cut through the 4 thicknesses of fabric following the pattern arc. Remove the pins and pattern and unfold the fabric circle.

SEWING

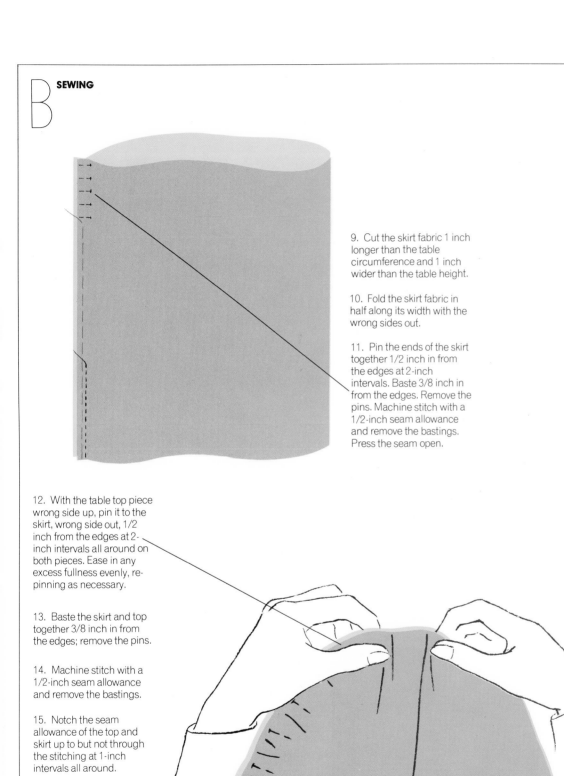

9. Cut the skirt fabric 1 inch longer than the table circumference and 1 inch wider than the table height.

10. Fold the skirt fabric in half along its width with the wrong sides out.

11. Pin the ends of the skirt together 1/2 inch in from the edges at 2-inch intervals. Baste 3/8 inch in from the edges. Remove the pins. Machine stitch with a 1/2-inch seam allowance and remove the bastings. Press the seam open.

12. With the table top piece wrong side up, pin it to the skirt, wrong side out, 1/2 inch from the edges at 2-inch intervals all around on both pieces. Ease in any excess fullness evenly, re-pinning as necessary.

13. Baste the skirt and top together 3/8 inch in from the edges; remove the pins.

14. Machine stitch with a 1/2-inch seam allowance and remove the bastings.

15. Notch the seam allowance of the top and skirt up to but not through the stitching at 1-inch intervals all around.

16. Press the notched seam allowances toward the table top.

17. Finish the skirt with a Hong Kong hem *(page 127)*.

THE LINED ROUND TABLE THROW

A MEASURING AND CUTTING

1. Make a pattern for the throw from a paper rectangle, piecing if necessary, with width equal to the sum of these three figures: the diameter of the table, twice the table height and 3 inches. Make the length equal the sum of the diameter of the table, twice the table height and 1 inch. (For measuring instructions, see page 180.) Divide the pattern with lines marking three panels: one wide center panel and two equal, narrower side panels. Cut out three equal patterns along these lines.

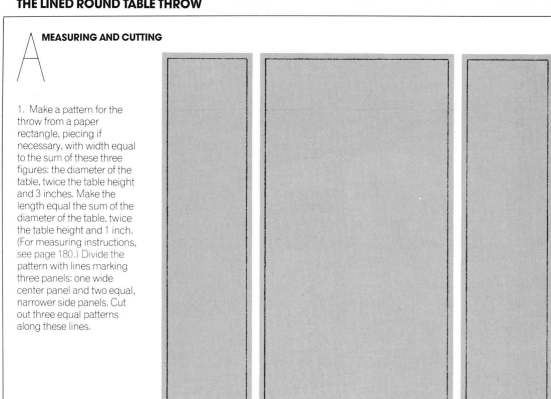

B SEWING

2. Pin the throw fabric to the three pattern pieces and cut out. Remove pins and patterns.

3. With wrong sides up, pin the fabric side panels to the center panel 1/2 inch in from the edges at 2-inch intervals. Baste 3/8 inch in from the edges. Remove pins. Machine stitch with a 1/2-inch seam allowance.

4. Cut out a square paper pattern whose sides are equal to the intended radius of the fabric throw.

5. Tie one end of a piece of string to a pencil and the other end to a thumbtack so that the separation is equal to one side of the paper pattern.

6. Place the pattern on a flat surface and insert the thumbtack at one top corner.

7. Holding the string taut, draw an arc from one corner of the square to the corner diagonally opposite it. Then cut along the arc to make a quarter circle pattern. Fold the throw, as constructed in Step 3, in half one way, keeping the wrong sides together. Then fold it the other way.

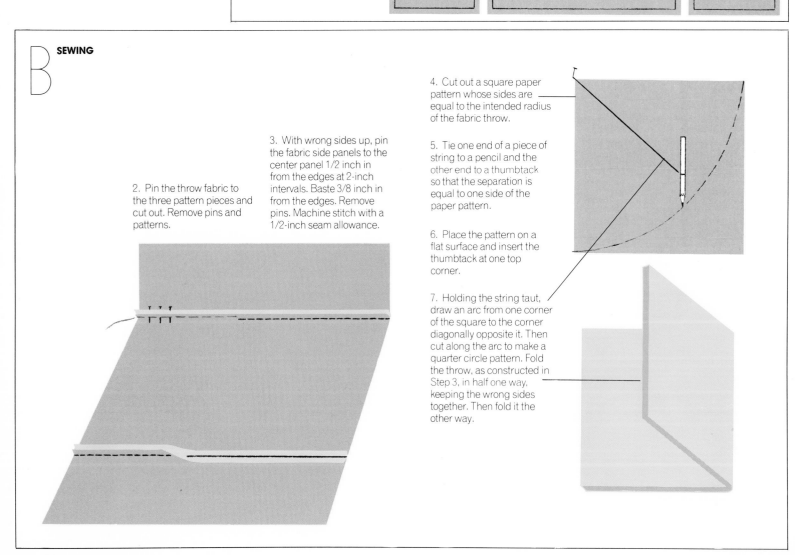

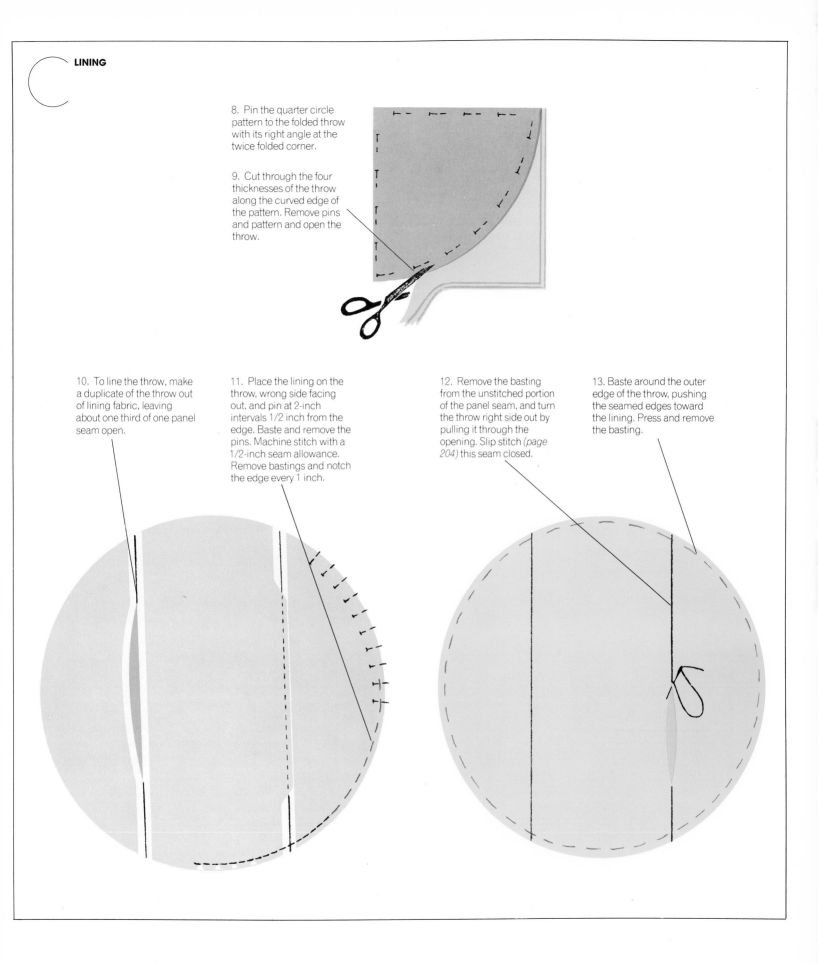

8. Pin the quarter circle pattern to the folded throw with its right angle at the twice folded corner.

9. Cut through the four thicknesses of the throw along the curved edge of the pattern. Remove pins and pattern and open the throw.

10. To line the throw, make a duplicate of the throw out of lining fabric, leaving about one third of one panel seam open.

11. Place the lining on the throw, wrong side facing out, and pin at 2-inch intervals 1/2 inch from the edge. Baste and remove the pins. Machine stitch with a 1/2-inch seam allowance. Remove bastings and notch the edge every 1 inch.

12. Remove the basting from the unstitched portion of the panel seam, and turn the throw right side out by pulling it through the opening. Slip stitch (page 204) this seam closed.

13. Baste around the outer edge of the throw, pushing the seamed edges toward the lining. Press and remove the basting.

How to make patterns for custom details

Some of the techniques couturiers use in making dresses also give home furnishings a distinctive look that reflects personal taste. Godets, for example, inserted in a contrasting color around a bedspread, create a startling three-dimensional effect. Or a rim of scallops transforms the familiar knife edge of a pillow into a flamboyant fancy.

The following pages show how to make patterns for transplanting several high-fashion devices to pillows, bed covers, table covers and valances. Once you have made the patterns, refer to the appropriate sections in the earlier part of this book for instructions on how to insert the various devices.

Custom sewing for home furnishings, like haute couture dressmaking, entails a substantial amount of effort. But the one-and-only quality of the finished items you create makes the effort worthwhile.

 MAKING THE PLEATS

1. To find the length of fabric required for knife pleats, measure the perimeter of the item to be given a pleated drop or skirt —three sides of a bed, the length of a valance, the circumference of a round table—multiply by 3 and add 1 inch for every end hem and 1/2 inch on each adjoining edge for every seam.

2. To find the depth of the knife pleat, measure the depth of the item to be pleated and add 1/2 inch for any top seam and from 1/2 to 2 1/2 inches for any bottom hem, depending on the depth of the item to be pleated.

3. Cut the fabric to the dimensions measured in Steps 1 and 2, piecing it if necessary with 1/2-inch machine-stitched seams.

4. With the fabric wrong side up, turn up along the bottom edge, 1/2 inch and press flat. Turn up again another 1 or 2 inches, depending on the desired hem, and pin at 2-inch intervals. Baste. Remove pins and, using a blind hemming stitch (page 101), sew a finished hem. Remove the bastings and press.

5. Turn the fabric wrong side down. At one end of the fabric, mark with pins 1 inch from and parallel to the side edge for an end hem allowance; at the other end mark off another 1 inch for a hem allowance or 1/2 inch at each end for a seam allowance if the pleated object is to be tubular or if another piece of fabric is to be added there.

6. Beginning at either the end hem or the seam allowance, use an L square to mark with pins a series of vertical parallel lines separated by the desired width of the finished pleat —usually 2 or 3 inches.

7. Fold the fabric along the first pinned pleat line and place the fold against the third pinned pleat line.

8. Pin the two lines together horizontally 1/4 inch in from the edge of the fold. Remove the vertical pins. Repeat this same procedure until all the pleats have been made and pinned.

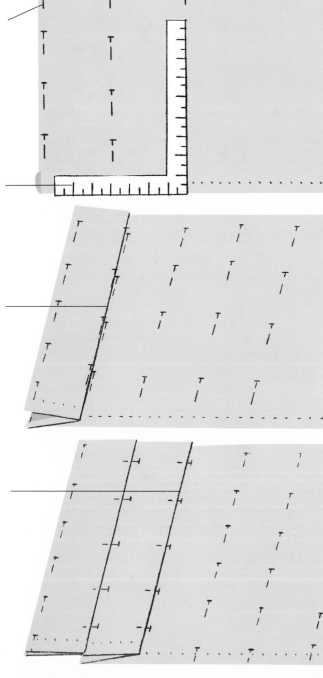

ATTACHING THE PLEATS

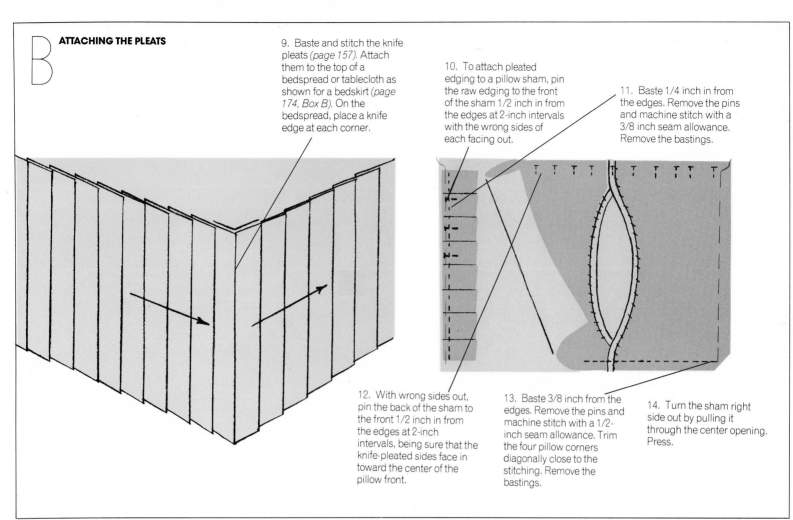

9. Baste and stitch the knife pleats *(page 157)*. Attach them to the top of a bedspread or tablecloth as shown for a bedskirt *(page 174, Box B)*. On the bedspread, place a knife edge at each corner.

10. To attach pleated edging to a pillow sham, pin the raw edging to the front of the sham 1/2 inch in from the edges at 2-inch intervals with the wrong sides of each facing out.

11. Baste 1/4 inch in from the edges. Remove the pins and machine stitch with a 3/8 inch seam allowance. Remove the bastings.

12. With wrong sides out, pin the back of the sham to the front 1/2 inch in from the edges at 2-inch intervals, being sure that the knife-pleated sides face in toward the center of the pillow front.

13. Baste 3/8 inch from the edges. Remove the pins and machine stitch with a 1/2-inch seam allowance. Trim the four pillow corners diagonally close to the stitching. Remove the bastings.

14. Turn the sham right side out by pulling it through the center opening. Press.

HOW TO MAKE SCALLOPS

MAKING A PATTERN

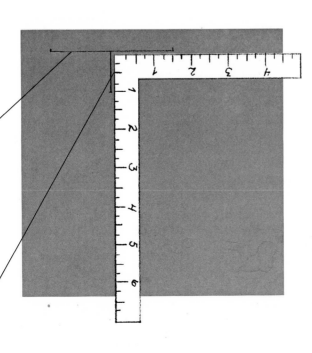

1. Using an L square, draw a straight line on a piece of cardboard the length of the scallop. It should divide evenly into the finished perimeter of the edge to be scalloped. To find this dimension, subtract 3 inches from the unfinished circumference of a table skirt, 1 inch from the unfinished length of a valance and 1 inch from the unfinished length of the foot and each side of a coverlet. For a rectangular tablecloth (or a coverlet visible from all sides), the scallop length must divide evenly into both finished foot and side dimensions.

2. Mark the center of the line drawn in Step 1. There, put an L square at a right angle to the line and draw a new line one third as long as the first line.

3. Choose a small round plate, glass or ashtray that makes a pleasing arc when its edge touches the tips of the "T" drawn in Steps 1 and 2. Trace around the edge to make an arc connecting the tips of the T.

4. Cut the scallop pattern along the lines drawn in Steps 1 and 3.

continued

TRACING A SCALLOP ON A STRAIGHT-EDGED OBJECT

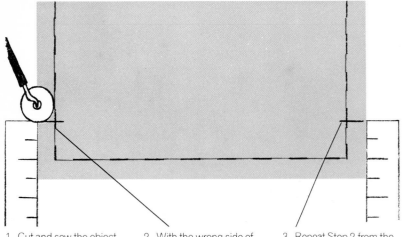

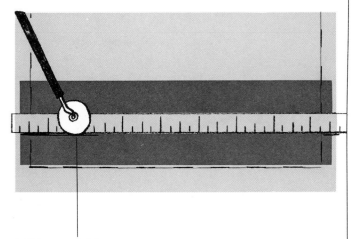

1. Cut and sew the object and its lining. With the object wrong side down and the lining wrong side up, pin the lining to the fabric 1/2 inch from the edges. Mark and baste 1/2 inch in from the edges. Remove the pins.

2. With the wrong side of the lining up, place the object on a flat surface. Measure from one corner up the side a distance equal to the scallop depth plus 1/2 inch. Mark the lining with a smooth-edged tracing wheel and carbon paper.

3. Repeat Step 2 from the other corner on the same edge.

4. Using a yardstick as a guide, draw a line with tracing wheel and carbon paper, connecting the points marked in Steps 2 and 3.

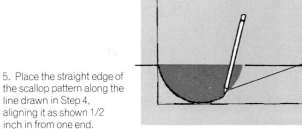

5. Place the straight edge of the scallop pattern along the line drawn in Step 4, aligning it as shown 1/2 inch in from one end.

6. Using a sharp pencil, trace the scallop curve onto the lining. Move the pattern and continue tracing across the edge. The last scallop should fall 1/2 inch in from the corner.

7. Repeat Steps 2-6 on the other edges to be scalloped.

8. Finish, following the instructions on page 126.

TRACING A SCALLOP ON A ROUND OBJECT

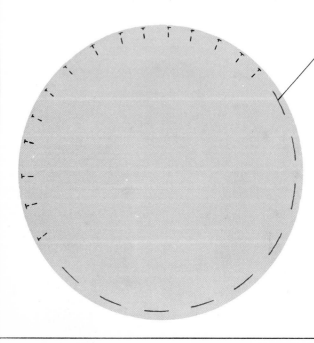

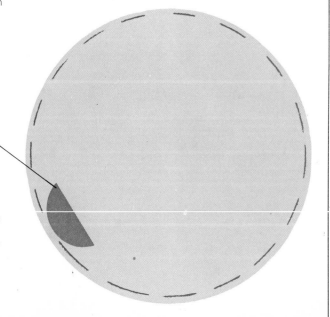

1. Cut and sew the object and its lining. With the object wrong side down and the lining wrong side up, pin the lining to the fabric 1/2 inch from the edges. Baste 1/2 inch in from the edges. Remove the pins.

2. With the lining wrong side up, place the object on a flat surface and position the scallop pattern so that the deepest point on its curved edge is 1/2 inch from the edge of the lining.

3. Using a sharp pencil, trace the scallop curve onto the lining. Move the pattern, keeping the deepest point on the curved edge 1/2 inch from the lining edge, and continue tracing around the circumference.

4. Finish, following the instructions on page 126, and turn right side out.

HOW TO MAKE PATTERNS FOR GODETS

PREPARING CUT-OUT PATTERNS

1. Make a triangular paper pattern for the cut-out in which the godet will fit, adjusting its size to suit the object and godet placement. The two sloping sides must be of equal length. The base should be about one third to one half the height from it to the apex. For valances and bedspreads, triangles 7 1/2 inches and 17 1/2 inches high are suitable. For a table cover, the height might be 4 inches less than the table height.

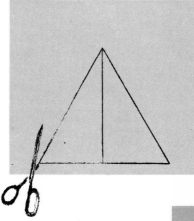

2. With the fabric wrong side up, place the pattern with its base along the bottom edge of the fabric at points where godets are desired. (They are generally placed at regular intervals and, if the object turns a corner—as a bedspread does—in each corner seam.)

3. With a sharp pencil, trace the sloping sides of the triangle. Move the pattern and trace again at other points where godets are desired.

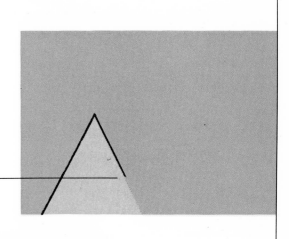

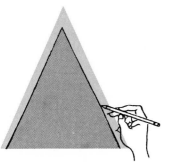

4. Mark and cut out another triangular paper pattern whose base is 1 inch shorter and whose height is 1/2 inch shorter than the one made in Step 1.

5. Place the smaller triangle inside the first triangle traced on the fabric, aligning it so that its bottom edge falls along the edge of the fabric and its left corner is 1/2 inch from the corner traced earlier. Trace its sloping sides. Make a line connecting the two apexes.

6. Repeat Step 5 at each point where godets are desired.

7. Cut along the inner triangle sides at the location of each godet.

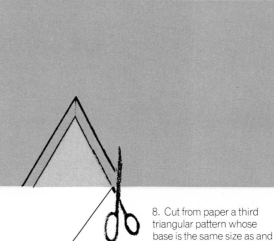

8. Cut from paper a third triangular pattern whose base is the same size as and whose height is 1/2 inch more than the one made in Step 1.

9. Cut the pattern in half along its height—from the center of its base to the apex.

10. Place the halves on a piece of paper. Keeping the apexes of the halves just touching each other, spread the halves apart until their base lines are separated by a distance equal to at least two or three times the original base line, depending on the fullness desired in the finished godet. Pin the halves to the paper.

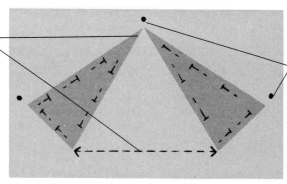

11. Measure outward from each base line 1/2 inch and mark with a dot. Measure up from the apex point 1/2 inch and mark with a dot.

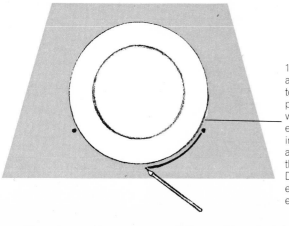

12. Find a plate or round ashtray whose edge will touch the extended base points made in Step 11 when its center is near the extended apex point made in Step 11. Trace an arc around the edge connecting the extended base points. Draw lines from the extended base points to the extended apex point.

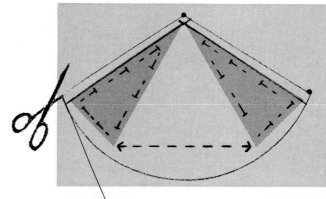

13. Mark along the outer legs of the triangles from the apexes to the arc. Cut along the lines made in Step 12.

14. Using the godet pattern made in Steps 12 and 13, mark and cut godets from the desired fabric. Insert them in the cut-outs made in Step 7, as shown on pages 153-155.

6
NEEDLEPOINT

When Mary Martin was starring on Broadway in *South Pacific* some years ago, her husband, Richard Halliday, presented her with a 5 1/2- by 7 1/2-foot roll of perforated canvas and a basketful of colored wool yarns. The actress had hardly used needle and thread before in her life except to sew on buttons, but she started stitching away with characteristic determination. Two and a half years

A PRIVATE ART FROM YARN AND CANVAS

later, after working on her canvas at odd moments in dressing rooms and vacation cottages from New York to Sicily, she finished what had become known backstage as "The Rug"—a pleasant pastiche of flowers, animals, domestic scenes and a Chinese proverb—which she eventually placed in front of her fireplace. In the process she discovered that needlepoint was indeed relaxing; more than that, it was fun. Happily launched upon her new avocation, Mary followed The Rug with a prodigious and varied string of other projects, including pillows, handbags, a number of chair seats and a large "theater sampler" on which she depicted props and scenes from all of her most celebrated roles.

Mary Martin is only one example, if an admittedly talented one, of the people who have sparked the spectacular revival of interest in the ancient art of needlepoint. Among the thousands of other women who are enthusiasts of the craft are former actress Grace Kelly, whose favorite projects include a flower-decked vest for her husband, Prince Rainier of Monaco; Betty Furness, television personality and consumer affairs expert, who designed her whole living room around a large needlepoint rug she had made; and actress Joan Fontaine, who once stitched up a canvas on which her friend Salvador Dali had obligingly painted a picture of his pet ocelot.

Stitching for relaxation has also appealed to a number of men in recent years; many a busy surgeon, in fact, has found that he can keep his fingers nimble while turning out a needlepoint pillow as a gift for his wife or a friend. And Roosevelt Grier, the 6-foot 5-inch, 300-pound former professional football star, not only finds needlepoint soothing himself, but has converted several of his old football colleagues to it as well.

Needlepoint's popularity is understandable, for it is not difficult to learn, yet it calls for the patience and esthetic sense that make a craft into an art form. Technically, needlepoint is the working of yarn through the meshes of a piece of stiff canvas to create a complete pattern. It differs from other kinds of needlework in that it always requires the meshed canvas ground and covers it completely; if the finished work is intended to be used as an element of some other project, the design is executed on the canvas and the completed work is then combined with the other elements to finish the project (unlike embroidery, for example, which might be done directly on a piece of clothing). But the principal distinction of needlepoint is the sense of high quality and understated elegance it generates. Like many of the custom-sewing techniques, needlepoint takes time. And like them, it repays this effort with beauty that expresses the maker's personal artistry.

Needlepoint as an art is firmly rooted in history. Apparently all ancient societies sufficiently advanced to accumulate wealth and leisure practiced it in some form. It was in the 17th Century, however, that it entered its golden age. In this era the Gobelin stitch was developed in France to produce canvases that resembled the great Gobelin tapestries, which were woven on looms. English needlepoint, which flourished under the Tudors, focused mainly on a revival of Biblical themes, often in contemporary guise (in the famous "Finding of Moses" the Pharaoh's daughter and her handmaidens are all dressed in 17th Century English finery). Both French and English enthusiasts often ornamented their work with beads, bits of bas-relief stitchery and gold and silver thread. Needlepoint was used to decorate everything from pillows and the backs and seats of chairs to *objets d'art* like the English boudoir box pictured opposite, which was made to contain a well-born lady's jewels, ribbons or snuff. With the invention of aniline dyes in Queen Victoria's time, woolen yarns became available in dazzling new colors, and today a wide array of yarns, both synthetic and natural, makes possible either brilliant or subtle effects. Professional painters have become so intrigued with the way the hues and tones of their designs can be rendered in wool that they have experimented with original designs in the medium.

Today's dedicated amateurs are also discovering more and more uses for the craft. Mary Martin has fashioned entire garments out of needlepoint, including a flowered white jacket that her daughter Heller wore over her wedding gown. Less ambitious designs can be used with equal effectiveness to give a custom look to personal accessories such as the belt pictured on page 199 or the carrying case on pages 200-201. Other projects popular among amateurs include wall hangings, rugs, seat and pillow covers, and summer fireplace screens.

Needlepoint is long lasting, because its foundation—the canvas—is practically indestructible. Top-grade canvas has evenly spaced mesh of smooth cotton, linen or sometimes acrylic threads that have been chemically treated, or sized, to give them a polished, stiff finish. There are several basic types of canvas, but the single-threaded monocanvas, described on page 194, is the most versatile. Good canvas becomes pliable as it is worked; the final blocking restores the original rigidity. No matter how good the canvas, however, it should not show through the finished design. A light beige or white canvas is commonly used because it blends inconspicuously with most colors of yarn. Canvas can also be colored with an indelible marking pen of the same color as the yarn you plan to use to be certain it does not show through.

Correctly transposing the outlines of the design to the canvas is an essential step. The design can be either drawn on by hand first, or the outlines stitched on directly, by carefully following the spacings of a master plan traced on graph paper (page 195). After the outlines have been stitched, the dark areas are filled in first and the light ones last to prevent the light ones from being soiled as the work is handled.

Needlepoint can be executed with a variety of materials, ranging from coarse rug wool for projects such as throw rugs, which require heavy yarn for durability and best effect, to fine silk thread, generally used only as an embellishment to create contrast in texture for special details. The most versatile yarn is three-strand Persian; it can be used as is for many common needlepoint designs, separated into individual strands or double strands for finer work or combined with single or double strands for heavier work. For an even-looking design, use short strands of yarn, about 16 inches long; larger strands—aside from being unwieldy to work with—require the yarn to pass through the mesh so often that the yarn frays. Keep extra yarn available to replace strands that have been misstitched; ripping such misstitched strands out of a canvas invariably damages their fibers so they cannot be reused.

Needles for needlepoint have long eyes

for easy threading and blunt points that will not harm the mesh of the canvas. To properly "seat" the yarn, stitching should be done with firm and consistent pressure on the yarn. If the stitches are too loose, the needlepoint takes on a lumpy look. If too tight, they wrench the canvas out of shape.

There are several hundred kinds of needlepoint stitches, but most projects can be done with one of the two "tent" stitches described on pages 196-197, which produce the smooth, tapestry-like results that most people associate with needlepoint. As a matter of fact, quite a few people who are accomplished in needlepoint work employ only the tent stitch. As Mary Martin says:

"For me the limitation of making just one stitch do everything is the challenge."

After the canvas is completed, it is held up to a strong light to locate any missing stitches. Next it is blocked to restore the canvas to its original shape, as shown on page 197: it is mounted with carpet tacks, pattern side down, to an old table or a board, then the underside is soaked with cold water and rubbed with a cloth to flatten and smooth the work. Once dried, the needlepoint will hold its shape permanently.

For a lover of the art, this is a blissful moment. When Mary Martin finished The Rug, she celebrated her labor of love by opening a well-deserved bottle of champagne.

An exquisite English boudoir case, shown above with some details magnified, is 17th Century "raised," or "stump," work, an intricate mélange of needlepoint and appliqué. Stump work called for fastidious stitching techniques. To embellish the raised needlepoint design, mica was used for castle windows, coral beads for necklaces and real lace for cuffs and collars. Stump boxes usually held jewelry but sometimes milady's snuff.

Adapting designs and equipment

The most important piece of equipment for needlepoint is the canvas. Its perforations determine the size of the needle, the weight of the yarn to be used and the texture of the finished work. The first step in needlepoint is transferring a design onto the canvas, as shown opposite.

Except for very delicate or very large heavy projects, most needlepoint is done on a canvas known as mono, which is available with a range of perforation sizes classified by the number of canvas strands to the inch. The finest mono has 24 strands per inch; the coarsest, three. Blunt tapestry needles are used for needlepoint; the larger the needle number, the smaller the needle. The most practical yarn is Persian wool because it is made of three strands that are easily separated, permitting the use of all three strands, two strands or only a single strand of the yarn. However, other yarns such as knitting worsted or embroidery floss may also be used.

For fine needlepoint, use No. 14 canvas with two strands of Persian wool *(left)* or one strand of cotton embroidery floss in a Size 20 blunt tapestry needle.

For relatively coarse needlepoint, use No. 10 canvas with three strands of Persian wool or acrylic knitting worsted, in a Size 18 blunt tapestry needle.

For medium-weight needlepoint, use No. 12 canvas with two strands of Persian wool (left) or acrylic sports yarn in a Size 18 blunt tapestry needle.

TRANSFERRING A DESIGN TO CANVAS

A TRACING A DESIGN

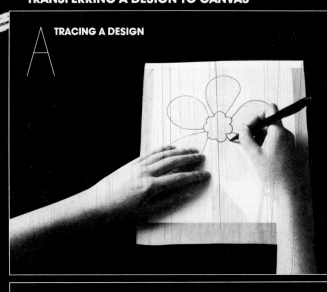

1. Tape a piece of tracing paper over the drawing, print or photograph to be traced.

2. Trace the major forms of the design with a black fine-tipped pen: leave minor details and shadings to be "painted in" by eye as you do the needlepoint.

3. Remove the tracing.

B ENLARGING OR REDUCING A DESIGN

4. Fold the tracing across its width, then across its length. Unfold and fold in quarters and eighths across its width and length. With a ruler, draw pencil lines along the folds to make a grid eight blocks on each side.

5. Cut a piece of drawing paper approximately the size you want your needlepoint to be. Make the length and width the same ratio as the length and width at the tracing. Then fold and mark the drawing paper as you did the tracing in Step 2.

6. Identify horizontal and vertical coordinates, on both tracing and drawing paper, as on a map, by marking each grid block along the top with a letter and each grid along the side with a number.

7. Using the coordinates to locate matching blocks in tracing paper and drawing paper, copy the design freehand, block by block.

C TRACING THE DESIGN ONTO THE CANVAS

9. Align the intersection marking the center of the design with the intersection of the lines marked on the canvas in Step 8. Tape the canvas in place.

8. Cut a piece of canvas 2 or 3 inches larger than your enlarged or reduced design. Fold it in quarters; then unfold it and mark the fold lines with a pencil.

10. Trace the design directly onto the canvas with a fine-tipped pen and indelible ink. Draw a border limiting the area to be worked.

11. Remove the canvas from the design and attach masking tape to the edges of the canvas to prevent it from unraveling as you work.

Stitching and blocking needlepoint

The oldest and most popular needle-point stitch is the tent stitch. Two variations are demonstrated at right: the horizontal tent stitch, sometimes called the Continental stitch, and the diagonal tent stitch, also known as the basket weave stitch.

The horizontal tent stitch, the easier of the two, is best used for shading colors in design backgrounds. Its disadvantages are that the canvas must be rotated at the end of each row, and that the stitch tends to pull the canvas out of shape. The diagonal tent stitch produces a smoother surface that holds its shape well. It is especially good for solid-color backgrounds in a design.

In order to determine how many ounces of yarn will be needed for a project, double the square-inch area to be worked, then divide by 70.

The canvas is stretched out of shape to some degree as it is worked. To return it to rectangular proportions and eliminate distortions in the design, the completed needlepoint must be blocked as illustrated on the opposite page.

THE HORIZONTAL TENT STITCH

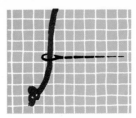

1. Knot the end of the yarn and insert the needle, away from you through the canvas three or four holes to the left of the hole in which you wish to begin.

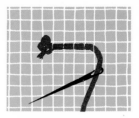

2. Bring the needle up from underneath through the beginning hole and pull the yarn through, leaving the knot on the side of the canvas facing you.

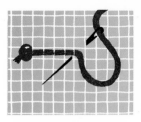

3. Insert the needle into the canvas one row above and one hole to the right of the beginning hole. Slant the needle and pull it through on the row below, through the hole to the left of the hole through which the yarn emerged.

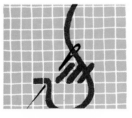

4. Continue to work from right to left, inserting the needle diagonally and bringing it out on a slant. After you have made several stitches, cut off the knot made in Step 1.

5. At the end of the row, insert the needle diagonally one row above and one hole to the right and pull the needle through to the back of the canvas without beginning a new stitch.

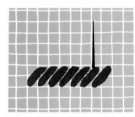

6. With the needle still on the back of the canvas, rotate the canvas 180 degrees so that the last stitch made is now on the right and bring up the needle from the back one hole above the hole through which the yarn entered the canvas in Step 5.

7. Insert the needle one row above and one hole to the right of the hole through which the yarn last emerged, continuing the same sequence of stitching as before. Continue across the row.

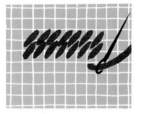

8. At the end of the row, leave the needle on the back instead of beginning a new stitch, and rotate the canvas 180 degrees again so that the last stitch made is on the right. Then bring the needle up from the back one hole below the hole through which the yarn entered the canvas.

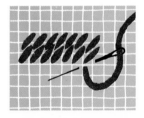

9. Continue the pattern, always working from right to left, and rotating the canvas at the end of every row.

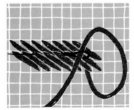

10. When you reach the end of each piece of yarn, run the last 1 1/2 inches through the finished stitches on the back of the canvas.

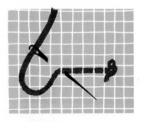

IF YOU ARE LEFT-HANDED...
Start to the left of the canvas area to be worked and insert the needle from left to right as shown.

THE DIAGONAL TENT STITCH

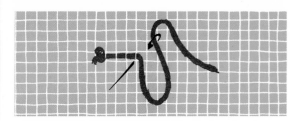 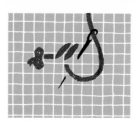 

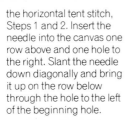 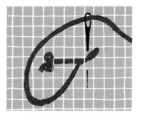

1. Knot the end of the yarn and insert the needle away from you three or four holes to the left of the hole in which you wish to begin. Bring the needle up from underneath the canvas, leaving the knot on the top of the canvas as shown for the horizontal tent stitch, Steps 1 and 2. Insert the needle into the canvas one row above and one hole to the right. Slant the needle down diagonally and bring it up on the row below through the hole to the left of the beginning hole.

2. Insert the needle into the canvas diagonally as for the horizontal tent stitch but bring it out vertically two holes below.

3. Insert the needle diagonally and bring it out at a slant two holes down and one to the left, in the hole below the one from which the yarn emerged in the previous step.

4. Insert the needle diagonally and bring it out horizontally two holes to the left.

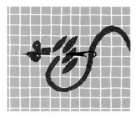 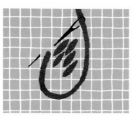 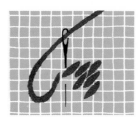 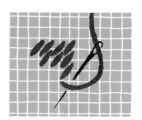 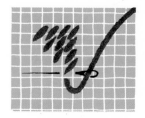

5. Insert the needle diagonally and bring it out horizontally two holes to the left as in the previous step.

6. Insert the needle diagonally and bring it out diagonally on the row below, in the hole to the left of the hole from which the yarn last emerged, as in Step 1. Cut off the knot.

7. Repeat Step 2 three times, inserting the needle diagonally and bringing it out vertically.

8. At the bottom of the diagonal, repeat Step 3 —insert the needle diagonally and bring it up at a slant two holes down and one to the left.

9. Repeat Step 4 four times —insert the needle diagonally and bring it up horizontally two holes to the left.

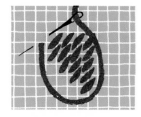 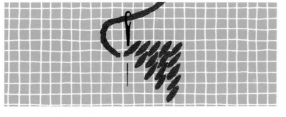 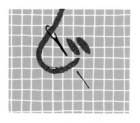

10. At the top of the diagonal, repeat Step 6.

11. Continue to follow the shape of the diagonal. Repeat Step 2, working vertically as many times as it takes to get to the bottom of the diagonal. Repeat Step 3 once at the bottom. Repeat Step 4, working horizontally back up the diagonal and then repeat Step 6 once at the top to complete the pattern.

IF YOU ARE LEFT-HANDED... Begin at the top left-hand corner and work from left to right as shown.

BLOCKING NEEDLEPOINT

1. Pad a board with a folded piece of muslin.

2. Place the needlepoint face down on the board. Align one edge of the needlepoint with one side of the board, pulling the canvas with pliers if necessary, and pin it down with rustproof carpet tacks at the corners.

3. Work around the canvas to align the edges with the edges of the board, pulling the canvas with pliers if necessary, and tack the edges in place as you go.

4. Take a sponge and cold water and thoroughly wet the back of the needlepoint, rubbing it hard.

5. Leave the canvas on the board to dry for at least 24 hours. If the canvas is still askew when you remove it, repeat the process.

A fancy belt to cinch a simple costume

The exuberant needlepoint design on the belt at right sets off the lines of a restrained white sheath. Much the same effect could be achieved by using the design to decorate the hem or the cuffs.

Make a transfer of the design from the drawing at right. Use a piece of No. 10 monocanvas cut 6 inches longer and 3 inches wider than the final belt size. The quantity of Persian wool yarn needed depends on the size of the design. Use the diagonal tent stitch, instructions for which are given on page 197.

After completing the needlepoint, block it *(page 197),* and make the belt by folding the edges of the canvas over buckram stiffening that has been cut to the exact size of the belt so that none of the canvas shows. Pin the needlepoint and buckram to a backing of grosgrain ribbon, suede, canvas or felt, then sew the canvas to the backing with a slip stitch *(page 204).* Finally, attach a hook and eye to the ends for fastening. If you are using the design to decorate a hemline or cuffs, the canvas can be trimmed and the embroidery sewn directly to the garment without any backing.

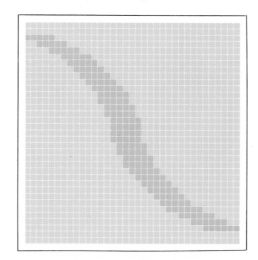

The design, sketched on the grid above, can be enlarged and transferred to canvas as shown on page 195. Add stripes as needed to obtain the desired length by moving the tracing paper so that the design on the paper fits into the last stripe made on the canvas.

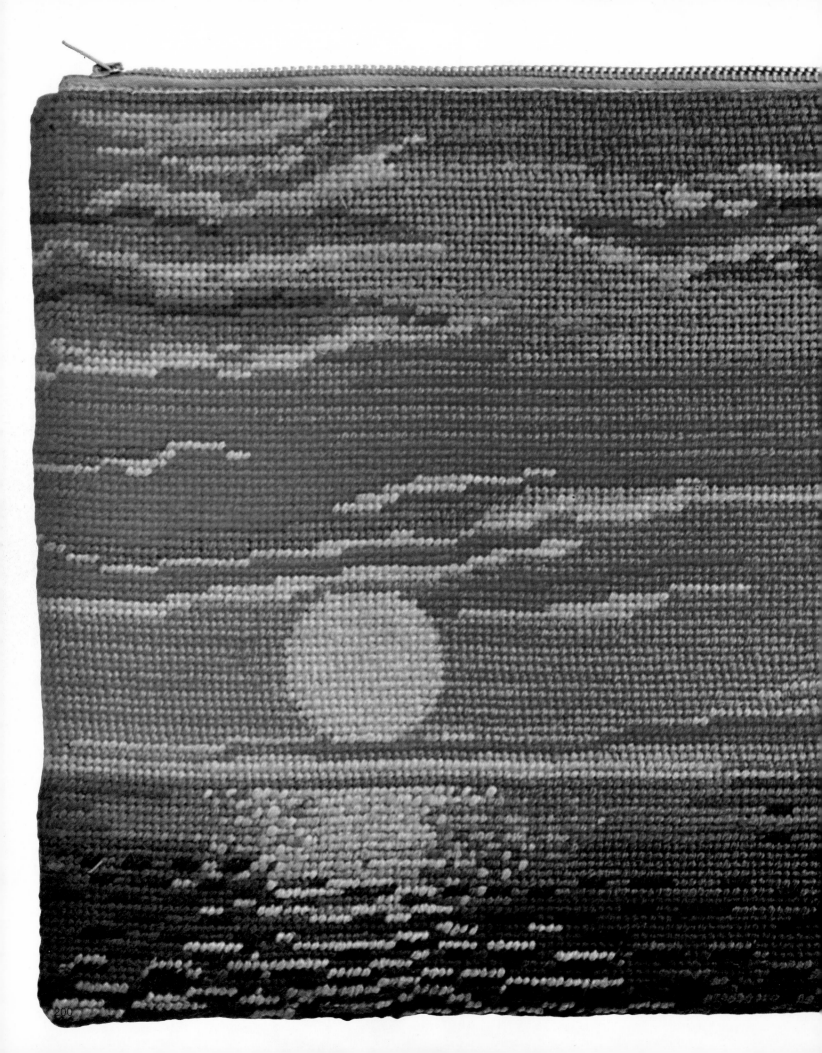

A colorful scene for a lady's case

A colorful pictorial design, like this one of a sunset on the sea, gives a zippered carrying case an arresting, extravagant look. The first step in making the design is to trace its outlines on a No. 10 monocanvas, using the method shown on page 195; the picture is then "painted" in horizontal tent stitches made with three-strand Persian wool yarn. Begin with the sun, to get its circular shape. When you start filling in the other areas, keep several needles threaded, with different colors, to avoid having to stop and rethread.

To make the case, block the needlepoint (*page 197*), and place the design face down on the finished side of a piece of stiff fabric, such as canvas. Stitch a centered zipper (*page 143*) to the top of the needlepoint and the fabric. Then turn the fabric and needlepoint wrong side out, and machine stitch around the bottom and both sides.

GLOSSARY

BACKSTITCH: A hand stitch used for strong seams in awkward places and for decoration (*page 98*).

BAR TACK: A hand-worked trim for reinforcing the ends of buttonholes and other points of strain.

BASTE: To stitch pieces together temporarily, or to indicate pattern markings on both sides of the fabric. Basting stitches can be made by hand or by machine, generally at six stitches per inch, and are removed when permanent stitching is completed.

BIAS: A direction diagonal to the threads forming woven fabric—the warp and the woof, or "grains." The true bias is at a 45° angle to the grains. Fabric is cut on a bias to make it drape in folds, as in a skirt, or to make it stretch slightly, as in a belt.

BIAS TAPE: A strip of cotton, cut diagonally to the fabric threads—on the bias—so that it will stretch to cover curved edges of a garment piece.

BLANKET STITCH: A hand stitch used for decoration and for protecting the raw edges of fabric (*page 101*).

BLIND HEMMING STITCH: A hand stitch used to create an almost invisible hem and to attach facings (*page 101*).

BLOCK: To shape finished needlepoint by mounting it on a firm surface, soaking the underside with cold water, and rubbing it to flatten and smooth the work. When dry it will hold its shape permanently.

CATCH STITCH: A hand stitch used for hemming and attaching interfacings (*page 204*).

CLIP: A short cut into the fabric outside a seam to help it lie flat around curves and corners.

CLOSURE: The part of a garment on which fasteners—such as buttons or zippers—are placed to open and close the garment; also, the fasteners themselves.

CROSSWISE GRAIN: See GRAIN.

DART: A stitched fabric fold, tapering to a point at one or both ends, that shapes fabric around curves.

DESIGN MUSLIN: See MUSLIN.

DIAGONAL BASTING STITCH: A hand stitch used to hold together layers of fabric such as underlinings and garment fabric during construction of the garment (*page 100*).

DRESS MUSLIN: See MUSLIN.

EASE: The even distribution of fullness, without forming gathers or tucks, that enables one section of a garment to be smoothly joined to a slightly smaller section, as in the seam attaching a sleeve to its armhole or in the hem of a flared skirt.

EDGE STITCH: Machine stitching that is made on the visible side of the garment, very close to the finished edges.

FACING: A piece of fabric, frequently the same as that used in the garment, that covers the raw fabric edge at openings such as necklines and armholes. It is first sewn to the visible side of the opening, then turned to the inside so that the seam between it and the garment is enclosed.

FASTENER: Any device that opens and closes a garment—button, hook and eye, snap or zipper.

FASTENING STITCH: A stitch used at the beginning or end of a row of hand sewing to hold the stitching securely (*page 204*).

FITTING MUSLIN: See MUSLIN.

FOOT: See PRESSER FOOT.

FRENCH TACK: A 1-inch-long chain of thread used to connect the hem of a lining to the hem of the garment.

GODET: A triangular piece sewn into a seam or into a slash cut up from a hemline to provide a flaring section.

GRADING: Trimming each seam allowance within a multilayer seam—the fabric, facing, interfacing, etc.—to a different width in order to reduce bulk and make the finished seam lie flat.

GRAIN: The direction of threads in woven fabrics. The warp—the threads running from one cut end of the material to the other—forms the lengthwise grain. The woof

—the threads running across the lengthwise grain from one finished edge of the fabric to the other—forms the crosswise grain. Only if the two grains are at right angles to each other is the fabric aligned on the "true grain."

GUSSET: A diamond-shaped piece sewn between a sleeve underarm seam and a garment side seam to increase freedom of movement for the arm without causing the fabric to billow.

HALF BACKSTITCH: A hand stitch for strong seams in awkward places and for topstitching (*page 99*).

HEMMING STITCH: A hand stitch for hemming bound or raw edges (*page 204*).

HONG KONG FINISH: A method of hemming in which a hem edge is covered with a bias strip and the finished hem edge is then hand stitched to the garment.

INTERFACING: A special fabric sewn between two layers of garment fabric to stiffen, strengthen and support parts of the garment. It is usually used around necklines, in collars, cuffs, pockets, waistbands or bound buttonholes.

INTERLINING: A special fabric, sewn and shaped exactly like the garment and lining to add warmth.

LENGTHWISE GRAIN: See GRAIN.

LINING: A fabric, usually lightweight, constructed in the shape of a garment to cover the inside of part or all of the garment. It can also stiffen and strengthen the garment. A set-in lining is one that is fully attached at the bottom of the garment.

MACHINE BASTE: See BASTE.

MUSLIN: An inexpensive cotton fabric used for making prototypes of garments—also called muslins—as an aid to styling and fitting a design. A fitting muslin is a special snug, straight-skirted muslin "shell" used only to make accurate and detailed body measurements for cutting and fitting other garments. A design muslin is a preliminary muslin version of a garment made by a couturier as an aid to visualizing the garment while designing it. A dress muslin is a preliminary muslin version of an actual garment that is used to perfect the fit of the design to the wearer before the garment fabric is cut and assembled.

NAP: The short fibers on the surface of the fabric that have been drawn out and brushed in one direction, such as on velvet or corduroy.

NOTCH: A V- or diamond-shaped marking made on the edge of a garment piece as an alignment guide. It is meant to be matched with a similar notch or group of notches on another piece when the two pieces are joined. Also a triangular cut into a curved seam to help it lie flat.

OVERCAST STITCH: A hand stitch used to finish raw seam edges (*page 204*).

PATCH: A small piece of bias-cut fabric used to reinforce a seam at a corner in making a gusset or a godet.

PILE: A surface of upright yarns found on fabrics such as corduroy, velvet and terry cloth. The pile tends to lie in a preferred direction, so that the fabric's orientation affects its appearance. To determine the direction of the pile, brush the fabric lightly with your fingers; if the surface looks and feels smooth, you are brushing with the pile.

PLACKET: A garment opening with an overlapping edge covered by a visible strip of fabric running the length of the opening. It is used with openings that are equipped with fasteners.

PLEATS: Folds of fabric that are used in controlling fullness.

PRESSER FOOT: The part of a sewing machine that holds fabric steady at the point it is being advanced and the needle is stitching it. The "all-purpose," or general purpose, foot has two prongs, or "toes," of equal length, and is used for most stitching. The "straight-stitch" foot has one long and one short toe, and can be used for straight stitching and stitching over fabrics of varying thicknesses. The "zipper" foot has only one toe and is used to stitch zippers and cording.

PRICK STITCH: A hand-sewing stitch used as topstitching for decorative purposes and also used for sewing zippers into position (*page 99*).

REINFORCE: To strengthen an area that will be subjected to strain, such as a waistline with seam ribbon, an underarm seam with extra stitches, or a corner seam or a pocket with a small patch of fabric.

ROLL: To manipulate fabric between the fingers, usually along a seam line, in order to bring the line of seam stitching out to the edge or to turn the stitching to the invisible side; also, to establish a softly curved shape, as on a collar.

RUNNING STITCH: A basic hand stitch that is made by weaving the needle and thread in and out of the fabric (*page 204*).

SADDLE STITCH: A hand stitch used for bold decorative topstitching, using buttonhole twist thread or embroidery floss (*page 100*).

SEAM ALLOWANCE: The extra width of fabric—usually 5/8 inch—that extends outside the seam line.

SEAM BINDING: Ribbon, 1/2 inch or 1 inch wide, of rayon, silk or nylon, that is sewn over fabric edges to cover them, concealing their raw appearance and preventing raveling. Seam binding is also available cut diagonally to the fabric threads—that is, on the bias—for the purpose of sewing around curved edges. See also BIAS TAPE.

SELVAGE: The lengthwise finished edges on woven fabric.

SLASH: A long, straight cut to make a garment opening, to insert a godet, or to open a fold of fabric so that it will lie flat, reducing bulkiness.

SLIDE FASTENER: See ZIPPER.

SLIP BASTING: A hand stitch used to match fabric and designs at seams (*page 100*).

SLIP STITCH: An invisible hand-sewing stitch (*page 204*).

SLOT SEAM: A decorative seam used as accent on a garment, made by sewing a strip of fabric of matching or contrasting color under a basted-together seam and then removing the basting.

STAY STITCH: A line of machine stitches sewn at 12 stitches per inch on the seam line of a garment piece before the seam is stitched. Stay stitching is used as a reinforcement to prevent curved edges from stretching, and as a guide for folding an edge accurately.

STIFFENING FABRIC: See INTERFACING.

TOPSTITCH: A line of machine or hand stitching on the visible side of the garment parallel to a seam.

TRIM: To cut away excess fabric in the seam allowance after the seam has been stitched. Also, a strip of fabric—such as braid or ribbon—used to decorate a garment.

UNDERLINING: A tightly woven fabric cut in the shapes of the main pieces of a garment and attached to these pieces before they are sewn together; the two layers are treated as one when the garment is constructed. Underlining is used to stabilize the shape of a garment and conceal construction details.

UNDERSTITCHING: Sewing into the seam allowance just outside a line of machine stitching, to prevent a facing from rolling out.

WARP: See GRAIN.

WELT POCKET: A pocket constructed in such a way that only the top edge, or welt (a horizontal strip of garment fabric), is visible on the outside part of the garment and the rest of the pocket is entirely hidden inside.

WELT SEAM: A seam that is finished by stitching fabric and seam allowances together parallel to the original seam. Welt seams are used to accent the structure of a dress. A double welt seam is made with two parallel rows of stitching.

WOOF: See GRAIN.

ZIGZAG STITCH: A serrated line of machine stitching used as decoration or to prevent raveling of raw edges, particularly on knits.

ZIPPER, sometimes called slide fastener: A mechanical fastener consisting of two tapes on the edges of which are parallel lines of teeth or coils that can be interlocked by a sliding bracket, or slider.

ZIPPER FOOT: See PRESSER FOOT.

HAND STITCHES

The diagrams below indicate how to make the elementary hand stitches referred to in this volume.

THE FASTENING STITCH

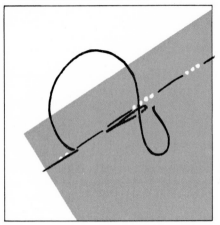

After the last stitch, insert the needle back 1/4 inch and bring it out at the point at which the thread last emerged. Make another stitch through these same points for extra firmness. To begin a row with a fastening stitch, leave a 4-inch loose end and make the initial stitch the same way as an ending stitch.

THE RUNNING STITCH

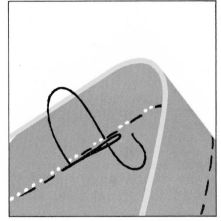

Insert the needle, with knotted thread, from the wrong side of the fabric and weave the needle in and out of the fabric several times in 1/8-inch, evenly spaced stitches. Pull the thread through. Continue across, making several stitches at a time, and end with a fastening stitch. When basting, make longer stitches, evenly spaced.

THE CATCH STITCH

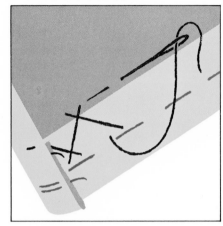

Working from left to right, anchor the first stitch with a knot inside the hem 1/4 inch down from the edge. Point the needle to the left and pick up one or two threads on the garment directly above the hem, then pull the thread through. Take a small stitch in the hem only (not in the garment), 1/4 inch down from the edge and 1/4 inch to the right of the previous stitch. End with a fastening stitch.

THE SLIP STITCH

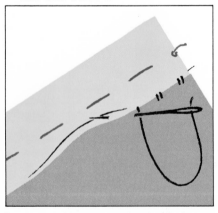

Fold under the hem edge and anchor the first stitch with a knot inside the fold. Point the needle to the left. Pick up one or two threads of the garment fabric close to the hem edge, directly below the first stitch, and slide the needle horizontally through the folded edge of the hem 1/8 inch to the left of the previous stitch. End with a fastening stitch.

THE HEMMING STITCH

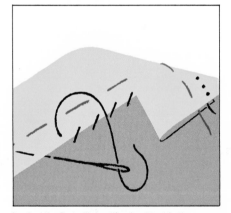

Anchor the first stitch with a knot inside the hem; then pointing the needle up and to the left, pick up one or two threads of the garment fabric close to the hem. Push the needle up through the hem 1/8 inch above the edge; pull the thread through. Continue picking up one or two threads and making 1/8-inch stitches in the hem at intervals of 1/4 inch. End with a fastening stitch.

THE OVERCAST STITCH

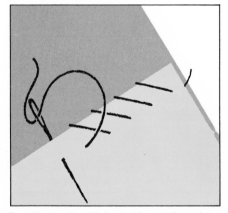

Draw the needle, with knotted thread, through from the wrong side of the fabric 1/8 to 1/4 inch down from the top edge. With the thread to the right, insert the needle under the fabric from the wrong side 1/8 to 1/4 inch to the left of the first stitch. Continue to make evenly spaced stitches over the fabric edge and end with a fastening stitch.

 CREDITS *Sources for the illustrations in this book are shown below. Credits from left to right are separated by semicolons, from top to bottom by dashes.*

Cover—Fabric design by Staron-Lafitte. 6,7—Tasso Vendikos. 11—From *The Unfashionable Human Body* by Bernard Rudofsky. The four figures were designed by the author and modeled by Constantino Nivola for the 1944 exhibition "Are Clothes Modern?" at the Museum of Modern Art in New York. 16 through 21—Drawings by Antonio. 22,23—Alberto dell'Orto. 27—Katrina Thomas courtesy Metropolitan Museum of Art Costume Institute. 28 through 35—Ryszard Horowitz. 36,37—Tasso Vendikos. 38,39—Drawings by Raymond Skibinski. 41—The Brooklyn Museum, gift of Mrs. Paul Pennoyer. 42 through 45—Ryszard Horowitz. 46 through 51—Drawings by Nicholas Fasciano. 52,53—Alberto dell'Orto. 57—Courtesy Centre d'Enseignement et de Documentation du Costume, Paris; *Paris Match*-Rizzo. 58-59—Alberto dell'Orto. 60,61—Tasso Vendikos. 62,63—Drawings by John Sagan. 64,65—Drawings by Dale Gustafson. 66—Drawings by Gene Brod except top by John Sagan. 67—Drawings by Dale Gustafson except top by Gene Brod. 68—Drawings by Dale Gustafson. 69—Drawings by Gene Brod except upper left by John Sagan. 70—Drawings by John Sagan except top by Gene Brod. 71 through 73—Drawings by John Sagan. 74,75—Drawings by Dale Gustafson. 76—Drawings by Gene Brod. 77,78—Drawings by Dale Gustafson. 79—Drawings by Gene Brod. 80—Drawings by John Sagan. 81—Drawings by Gene Brod except upper right by John Sagan. 82—Drawings by Gene Brod except middle right by John Sagan. 83,84—Drawings by Gene Brod. 85 through 87—Drawings by John Sagan. 88,89—Tasso Vendikos. 93—Drawings by Nicholas Fasciano. 94 through 97—Tasso Vendikos, from the exhibit "The World of Balenciaga," presented by The Metropolitan Museum of Art Costume Institute. 94,95—Background: Courtesy Mrs. Harvey Firestone Jr., except middle, courtesy Inge Morath and far right, courtesy The Metropolitan Museum of Art Costume Institute. Foreground: Courtesy Señora de Osborne. 96,97—Background: Courtesy Chicago Historical Society, gift of Mrs. William McCormick Blair Jr.; courtesy Baronne Philippe de Rothschild; courtesy The Metropolitan Museum of Art Costume Institute; courtesy Lola Flores; courtesy Union Française des Arts des Costumes, Paris. Foreground: Courtesy Baronne Philippe de Rothschild. 98,99—Drawings by Frank Pagnato. 100, 101—Drawings by John Sagan. 102—Tasso Vendikos. 103 through 111—Drawings by Mulvey/Crump Associates, Inc. 112—Tasso Vendikos. 113 through 117—Drawings by Raymond Skibinski. 118—Tasso Vendikos. 119 through 121—Drawings by John Sagan. 122—Tasso Vendikos. 123 through 127—Drawings by Mulvey/Crump Associates, Inc. 128—Tasso Vendikos. 129,130—Drawings by Dale Gustafson. 131—Drawings by Dale Gustafson—John Sagan. 132,133—Drawings by John Sagan. 134—Tasso Vendikos. 135 through 137—Drawings by John Sagan. 138—Tasso Vendikos. 139 through 143—Drawings by Mulvey/Crump Associates, Inc. except bottom right 141 by Carolyn Mazzello. 144—Tasso Vendikos. 145 through 151—Drawings by Raymond Skibinski. 152—Tasso Vendikos. 153 through 157—Drawings by Raymond Skibinski. 158, 159—Tasso Vendikos. Sewlage by Virginia Gianakos. 162 through 169—Tasso Vendikos. 170 through 177—Drawings by Angela Alleyne. 178 through 183—Drawings by Carmen Mercadal. 184 through 187—Drawings by Jane Poliotti. 188, 189—Needlepoint by Erica Wilson. 193—Robert Colton courtesy The Metropolitan Museum of Art. 194—Herbert Orth. 195—Al Freni. 196,197—Drawings by Mulvey/Crump Associates, Inc. except bottom 197 by Raymond Skibinski. 198,199—Drawing by Angela Alleyne; Tasso Vendikos. Needlepoint by Erica Wilson. 200,201—Tasso Vendikos. Needlepoint by Erica Wilson. 204—Drawings by John Sagan.

ACKNOWLEDGMENTS

For their help in the preparation of this book the editors would like to thank the following: Abraham Silks; Auburn Fabrics; Bergdorf Goodman; Bonwit Teller; Marie Bottone, Christian Dior-New York; Brauchbar Fabrics; Gabrielle Buchaert, House of Saint Laurent; Regine Cardin, House of Cardin; Centre d'Enseignement et de Documentation du Costume; The Chicago Historical Society; Amos Ciabattoni, Director, Ente Italiano Della Moda; Joyce Clark, Emilio Pucci Fashion House; Marie-Louise de Clermont-Tonnerre, House of Chanel; Elizabeth Ann Coleman, Curator of Costumes and Textiles, The Brooklyn Museum; Milton Dash, Staron-Lafitte; David & Dash, Inc.; Mademoiselle Dubois, Chambre Syndicale de la Haute Couture; William Dugan, Halston Ltd.; The Embroiderer's Guild of America; Fasac Fabrics; Mrs. Harvey S. Firestone Jr.; Pinuccia Fontanesi, Valentino Fashion House; Jacqueline Gault, Staron-Lafitte; Daniela Giardina, Valentino Fashion House; Pia Giustozzi, Valentino Fashion House; Gourdon, Inc.; Hamilton Adams Imports; Held Fabrics; Arno Jakobson, The Brooklyn Museum; Jasco Fabrics; Jax Manhattan; Jeri Silks; Tracy Kendall; Vivian Landsman; Elizabeth Lawrence, Restorer, The Metropolitan Museum of Art Costume Institute; Astrid Lehaire, House of Balmain; Dominique Le Romain, House of Courrèges; Adriana Levi; Jean Mailey, Associate Curator of Textiles, The Metropolitan Museum of Art; Hermine Mariaux, Valentino Fashion House; Maxine Fabrics Co.; Meyer Woolens; Marjorie Miller, Fashion Institute of Technology; Violet Mock; Cristina Morris, Irene Galitzine Fashion House; House of Norell in memory of Mr. Norman Norell for the clothes on pages 89, 102, 112, 118, 122, 128, 134, 138, 144, 152; Onondaga Silk Co.; Madame Paule, Directrice des Ventes, House of Chanel; Catherine Peters, Galanos; Francesco Piccoli, Antonelli Sport; Marie-Claude Poirier, House of Ungaro; Poli Fabrics; William Rose Inc.; Harold Rudin; Bernard Rudofsky; Giovanna Sioli, Missoni Fashions, Sumirago, Varese; Elaine Sobel; E. H. Sormoni; Staron-Lafitte; Pat Sukhaprayura; Edna Sullivan, House of Norell; Taroni Fabrics; Gustave Tassell, House of Norell; Arlette Thébault, House of Givenchy; Nadine Vandermarck, House of Dior; Mrs. Diana Vreeland; Webco Mills Division of Dan River; Weller Fabrics.